W9-BXF-183

BOWLING, BEATNIKS, AND BELL-BOTTOMS

Pop Culture of 20th- and 21st-Century America

Contents

Sports and Games

TV and Radio

Entries by Alphabetical Order

D

Entries by Topic Category

Fashion

Film and Theater

Food and Drink

Music

Print Culture

Sports and Games

TV and Radio

The Way We Lived

First-edition Contributors

Timothy Berg. Visiting assistant professor, Western Michigan University. Ph.D., History, Purdue University, 1999.

Charles Coletta, Ph.D. Instructor, Department of Popular Culture, Bowling Green State University. Contributing writer, *St. James Encyclopedia of Popular Culture* (2000).

Rob Edelman. Instructor, State University of New York at Albany. Author, *Baseball on the Web* (1997) and *The Great Baseball Films* (1994). Co-author, *Matthau: A Life* (2002); *Meet the Mertzes* (1999); and *Angela Lansbury: A Life on Stage and Screen* (1996). Contributing editor, *Leonard Maltin's Movie & Video Guide, Leonard Maltin's Movie Encyclopedia,* and *Leonard Maltin's Family Viewing Guide.* Contributing writer, *International Dictionary of Films and Filmmakers* (2000); *St. James Encyclopedia of Popular Culture* (2000); *Women Film-makers & Their Films* (1998); *The Political Companion to American Film* (1994); and *Total Baseball* (1989). Film commentator, WAMC (Northeast) Public Radio.

Tina Gianoulis. Freelance writer. Contributing writer, *World War I Reference Library* (2001–2); *Constitutional Amendments: From Freedom of Speech to Flag Burning* (2001); *International Dictionary of Films and Filmmakers* (2000); *St. James Encyclopedia of Popular Culture* (2000); and mystories.com, a daytime drama Web site (1997–98).

Sheldon Goldfarb. Archivist, Alma Mater Society of the University of British Columbia. Ph.D., English, University of British Columbia. Author, *William Makepeace Thackeray: An Annotated Bibliography, 1976–1987* (1989). Editor, *Catherine,* by William Makepeace Thackeray (1999).

Jill Gregg Clever, A.A., B.A., M.L.I.S. Graduate of Michigan State University, Thomas Edison State College, and Wayne State University. Business-technology specialist, Toledo–Lucas County Public Library.

Justin Gustainis. Professor of communication, State University of New York at Plattsburgh. Author, *American Rhetoric and the Vietnam War* (1993).

Audrey Kupferberg. Film consultant and archivist. Instructor, State University of New York at Albany. Co-author, *Matthau: A Life* (2002); *Meet the Mertzes* (1999); and *Angela Lansbury: A Life on Stage and Screen* (1996). Contributing editor, *Leonard Maltin's Family Viewing Guide.* Contributing writer, *St. James Encyclopedia of Popular Culture* (2000); *Women Filmmakers & Their Films* (1998); and *The American Film Institute Catalog of Feature Films.*

Edward Moran. Writer of American culture, music, and literature. Associate editor, *World Musicians* (1999); *World Authors* (1996); and *Random House Dictionary of the English Language* (1987; 1991). Contributing writer, *St. James Encyclopedia of Popular Culture* (2000). Editor, *Rhythm,* a magazine of world music and global culture (2001).

Sara Pendergast. President, Full Circle Editorial. Vice president, Group 3 Editorial. Co-editor, *St. James Encyclopedia of Popular Culture* (2000). Co-author, *World War I Reference Library* (2001), among other publications.

Tom Pendergast. Editorial director, Full Circle Editorial. Ph.D., American studies, Purdue University. Author, *Creating the Modern Man: American Magazines and Consumer Culture* (2000). Co-editor, *St. James Encyclopedia of Popular Culture* (2000).

Karl Rahder. M.A., University of Chicago Committee on International Relations. Author, several articles on international history and politics.

Chris Routledge. Freelance writer and editor. Ph.D., American literature, University of Newcastle upon Tyne (UK). Author, "The Chevalier and the Priest: Deductive Method in Poe, Chesterton, and Borges," in *Clues: A Journal of Detection* (2001). Editor, *Mystery in Children's Literature: From the Rational to the Supernatural* (2001).

Robert E. Schnakenberg. Senior writer, History Book Club. Author, *The Encyclopedia Shatnerica* (1998).

Steven Schneider. Ph.D. candidate, philosophy, Harvard University; Ph.D. candidate, cinema studies, New York University. Author, *An Auteur on Elm Street: The Cinema of Wes Craven* (forthcoming). Co-editor, *Horror International* (forthcoming) and *Dark Thoughts: Philosophic Reflections on Cinematic Horror* (forthcoming). Contributing writer, *British Horror Cinema* (2002); *Car Crash Culture* (2001); and numerous film journals.

Robert C. Sickels. Assistant professor of American film and popular culture, Whitman College. Ph.D., English, University of Nevada. Author, "A Politically Correct Ethan Edwards: Clint Eastwood's The Outlaw Josey Wales" in *Journal of Popular Film & Television* (forthcoming); "'70s Disco Daze: Paul Thomas Anderson's Boogie Nights and the Last Golden Age of Irresponsibility" in *Journal of Popular Culture* (forthcoming). Contributor, *St. James Encyclopedia of Popular Culture* (2000).

Reader's Guide

Popular culture—as we know it—was born in America, though historians disagree as to exactly when. Was it in 1893, when magazine publishers used new technologies to cut the costs of their magazines to a dime and sell hundreds of thousands of copies? Or was it in 1905, when the invention of the nickelodeon brought low-cost films to people all across the nation? Or was it back in 1886, when Richard Sears and Alvah Roebuck sent out their first catalog, which allowed people from all over to choose from among hundreds and then thousands of the same goods?

No matter the exact date, by the turn of the twentieth century, American magazine publishers, retailers, moviemakers, and other entertainers were bringing their goods before larger numbers of Americans than ever before. These magazines, movies, advertisements, shopping experiences, sports teams, and more were what we know as "popular culture," because they could be enjoyed firsthand by masses of Americans.

The story of America as revealed by its popular culture is complex and fascinating. Readers of *Bowling, Beatniks, and Bell-Bottoms: Pop Culture of 20th- and 21st-Century America* will discover, for example, that the comedic forms first developed by vaudeville comedians at the turn of the twentieth century lived on in film, radio, and finally television. They will learn that black musicians created the musical forms that are most distinctly American: blues and jazz. And they will realize that popular culture reacted to things like war and economic depressions in ways that were surprising and unexpected. The study of popular culture has a great deal to teach the student who is interested in how people use entertainment and consumption to make sense of their lives and shape their experience.

Bowling, Beatniks, and Bell-Bottoms gathers together essays that reflect the variety, diversity, and excitement of American popular culture of the twentieth and twenty-first centuries. This collection focuses more on events, fads, programs, performances, and products than on biographies of people, which are well documented in other sources. Even so, brief biographies of notables are sprinkled throughout. With approximately 850 essays on individual topics and dozens of overviews of pop culture trends, *Bowling, Beatniks, and Bell-Bottoms* covers a great deal of American popular culture, though not nearly enough. There are hundreds more people, bands, TV programs, films, and products that were worthy of mention but were left out due to space consideration. Our advisory board of media specialists, however, helped assure that the most prominent and studied subjects were included.

Have you ever wondered how the Slinky was invented, what Velveeta cheese is made of, or what people danced to before rock and roll? Those answers are in *Bowling, Beatniks, and Bell-Bottoms,* along with many others. It is our hope that this collection will bring both information and pleasure to all students of American culture.

Organization

Bowling, Beatniks, and Bell-Bottoms is arranged chronologically by decade over six volumes (two decades per volume for the twentieth century, and one volume covering the first decade of the twenty-first century). The approximately 850 entries are grouped into nine topic sections: Commerce, Fashion, Film and Theater, Food and Drink, Music, Print Culture, Sports and Games, TV and Radio, and The Way We Lived (though not all topics appear in every decade). Many subjects can easily appear in several different decades, so those essays are placed in either the decade in which the product was invented or the fad initiated, or in the decade in which the subject was most prominent or popular. In addition, several of the essays could have appeared under different topics (such as a book that was made into a movie), so those essays appear under the topic where it was best known. Users should make frequent use of the index or the two additional tables of contents (arranged alphabetically by entry name and by topic category) to locate an entry.

Essays range in length from 150 to 1000 words, with the majority averaging less than 500 words. Every essay aims to describe the topic and analyze the topic's contribution to popular culture. Each essay lists additional sources on the topic, including books, magazine or journal articles, and Web sites. Whenever possible, references to books are geared to younger readers. The editor and writers have personally visited every Web site mentioned and believe that these sites contain content that will assist the reader in understanding the subject. Due to the nature of the World Wide Web, it is possible that not all Web links will still function at the time of publication.

Bowling, Beatniks, and Bell-Bottoms also provides these features:

- A timeline that highlights key historic and pop culture events of the twentieth and twenty-first centuries
- A general overview of each decade
- A multipaged "At a Glance" box that breaks down "What We Said," "What We Read," "What We Watched," "What We Listened To," and "Who We Knew"
- An overview of each topic section in each decade
- Approximately 450 photos and illustrations
- Extensive use of cross references (pointing to decade, topic, and volume)

Acknowledgments

A thank-you encore goes to the advisors of this publication (their professional affiliation at the time of the publication of the first edition is noted): Catherine Bond, Department Chair, Library and Media Services, Conestoga High School, Berwyn, Pennsylvania; Cathy Chauvette, Assistant Regional Branch Manager, Fairfax County Public Library, Fairfax County, Virginia; Nancy Schlosser Garabed, Library Media Specialist, Council Rock High School, Newtown, Pennsylvania; Ann West LaPrise, Junior High/Elementary Media Specialist, Huron School District, New Boston, Michigan; and Nina Levine, Library Media Specialist, Blue Mountain Middle School, Cortlandt Manor, New York. Their input during the preparation of the first edition remains valuable.

The contributions of the writers from the first edition are noted on the contributors page (which reprints their background at the time of the first edition). For this second edition, much gratitude is given to writers David Larkins, Annette Petrusso, Maureen Reed, Patrick Walsh, and Greg Wilson.

Much appreciation goes to copyeditor Maxwell Valentine, proofreader Rebecca Valentine, indexer Theresa Murray, and typesetter

PreMediaGlobal. Additional thanks to Scott Rosen at the Bill Smith Group for permissions and imaging selection and Barry Puckett for image processing assistance.

Comments and Suggestions

We welcome your comments on *Bowling, Beatniks, and Bell-Bottoms.* Please send correspondence to: Editors, *Bowling, Beatniks, and Bell-Bottoms,* U•X•L, 27500 Drake Rd., Farmington Hills, MI 48331-3535; call toll-free: 800-877-4253; fax to 248-414-5043; or send e-mail via www.cengage.com.

Cynthia Johnson, Editor

Timeline

1900 On January 29, Ban Johnson forms the American League to compete against baseball's National League.

1900 In February, Eastman Kodak introduces the Brownie Camera.

1900 In March, the Good Roads Campaign tries to build support for better roads. At the time, there are only ten miles of paved roads in the nation.

1900 On March 31, the first ad for an automobile appears in the *Saturday Evening Post.*

1900 On April 23, Buffalo Bill Cody's *Wild West Show* opens at Madison Square Garden in New York City.

1900 On November 6, Republican William McKinley is reelected U.S. president, with New York governor Theodore Roosevelt as his vice president.

1900 On November 12, *Floradora,* one of the most popular theatrical musicals of the decade, premieres in New York. It runs for more than five hundred performances.

1901 On February 25, U.S. Steel is formed out of ten companies and becomes the world's largest industrial corporation.

1901 On March 13, steel tycoon Andrew Carnegie donates $2.2 million to fund a New York public library system.

1901 On September 6, President William McKinley is shot by an assassin in Buffalo, New York, and dies eight days later from complications from gangrene due to improperly dressed wounds. Theodore Roosevelt becomes president.

1901 On October 16, President Theodore Roosevelt starts a national controversy when he dines with black leader Booker T. Washington in the White House.

1902 The Teddy Bear is introduced, named after President Theodore Roosevelt.

1902 On January 1, in the first Rose Bowl football game, the University of Michigan defeats Stanford 49–0.

1902 On March 18, Italian opera singer Enrico Caruso produces his first phonographic recording.

1902 On April 16, Tally's Electric Theater, the first theater solely devoted to presenting motion pictures, opens in Los Angeles, California.

1902 On December 21, Guglielmo Marconi transmits the first wireless signals across the Atlantic Ocean.

1903 *Redbook* magazine is founded.

1903 The Portage Lakers of Houghton, Michigan—the first professional hockey team from the United States—win the International Hockey League championship.

1903 On January 22, the United States signs a 99-year lease on what will become the Panama Canal Zone, where it will build a canal that connects the Caribbean Sea to the Pacific Ocean.

1903 In February, the *Ladies' Home Journal* becomes the first American magazine to reach one million paid subscriptions.

1903 On May 23, two men make the first transcontinental automobile trip from San Francisco to New York in sixty-four days. Upon returning home, one driver is ticketed for exceeding the speed limit of six miles per hour.

1903 On August 14, Jim Jeffries defeats James J. "Gentleman Jim" Corbett to retain the world heavyweight boxing title.

1903 On September 12, Scott Joplin's ragtime opera *A Guest of Honor* begins a midwest tour.

1903 In October, the Boston Pilgrims defeat the Pittsburgh Pirates in the first World Series to pit an American League team against a National League team.

1903 On December 1, Edwin S. Porter's film *The Great Train Robbery* is considered the first Western and the first American film with a plot.

1903 On December 17, Wilbur and Orville Wright make the first sustained flight at Kitty Hawk, North Carolina.

1904 The Ford Motor Company sells fourteen hundred of its Model A cars.

1904 On April 20, the World's Fair opens in St. Louis, Missouri.

1904 On May 5, Cy Young pitches baseball's first perfect game.

1904 On November 8, Theodore Roosevelt is reelected president.

1905 The German navy launches the first submarine.

1905 African American leader W. E. B. Du Bois helps found the Niagara Movement, an organization to advance African American issues.

1905 On May 5, the *Chicago Defender,* the first major black newspaper, begins publication.

1905 In June, the era of the nickelodeon begins when Harry Davis's Pittsburgh, Pennsylvania, movie theater offers continuous movie showings. By the end of the decade, more than eight thousand nickel-admission movie theaters are in operation.

1905 On June 18, the Twentieth Century Limited begins train service between Chicago, Illinois, and New York City and boasts a travel time of only eighteen hours.

1906 Kellogg's Corn Flakes breakfast cereal is introduced.

1906 In February, Upton Sinclair publishes *The Jungle,* a novel depicting the horrible conditions in the meat-packing industry. The work prompts the passage of the Meat Inspection Act.

1906 On April 14, President Theodore Roosevelt coins the term "muckraking" when he criticizes journalists who expose abuses and corruption and miss the larger social picture.

1906 On April 18, a major earthquake and fire destroy much of San Francisco, California.

1906 On May 3, the First Annual Advertising Show in New York City heralds the beginning of an important American industry.

1906 On November 21, the first voice radio transmission travels eleven miles from Plymouth to Brant Rock, Massachusetts.

1907 Work begins on the Panama Canal.

1907 On January 23, in what newspapers call the "trial of the century," millionaire Harry K. Thaw is tried for the murder of world-famous architect Stanford White over the honor of Thaw's wife, showgirl Evelyn Nesbit.

1907 On June 10, French motion picture pioneers Auguste and Louis Lumière announce they have developed a method for producing color film.

1907 On July 8, Florenz Ziegfeld's musical revue, the *Ziegfeld Follies,* opens in New York.

1907 On December 3, actress Mary Pickford makes her stage debut in *The Warrens of Virginia.*

1908 The world's first skyscraper, the forty-seven-story Singer Building, is completed in New York City.

1908 The General Motors Corporation is formed and soon becomes the biggest competitor of the Ford Motor Company.

1908 In March, the Original Independent Show, organized in New York, includes works by American painters Edward Hopper, George Bellows, and Rockwell Kent.

1908 On September 6, Israel Zangwill's play *The Melting Pot* opens in New York City; the title becomes an internationally recognized description of the United States.

1908 On October 1, the Ford Motor Company unveils its Model T with a price tag of $825. It soon becomes the best-selling automobile of its time.

1908 On November 3, former U.S. secretary of war William Howard Taft is elected president.

1908 On December 26, Jack Johnson defeats Tommy Burns to become the first black world heavyweight boxing champion. His victory is considered an outrage by white racists.

1909 The fifty-story Metropolitan Life Insurance Tower in New York City becomes the world's tallest building.

1909 The Ford Motor Company manufactures nineteen thousand Model T cars.

1909 On March 16, the Federal Bureau of Investigation is created as a federal law enforcement agency.

1909 On March 23, former president Theodore Roosevelt leaves for a safari in Africa. He is paid $50,000 by *Scribner's Magazine* for his account of the trip.

1909 On April 6, U.S. Navy commander Robert Peary reaches the North Pole.

1909 On May 3, the first wireless press message is sent from New York City to Chicago, Illinois.

1909 On July 12, the U.S. Congress asks the states to authorize a national income tax.

1910 Western novelist Zane Grey's book *Heritage of the Desert* becomes a huge commercial success, starting his career of bringing the American West to the reading world.

1910 Levi Strauss and Company begins making casual play clothes for children.

1910 The Boy Scouts of America are founded in Chicago, Illinois.

1910 On February 28, Russian ballerina Anna Pavlova makes her American debut at the Metropolitan Opera House in New York City.

1910 On March 28, the first one-man show by artist Pablo Picasso opens at photographer and editor Alfred Stieglitz's 291 Gallery in New York City.

1910 In November, the National Association for the Advancement of Colored People (NAACP) publishes the first issue of the *Crisis* magazine, edited by W. E. B. Du Bois.

1910 On November 3, the Chicago Grand Opera opens with a production of *Aida,* by Giuseppe Verdi.

1911 Irving Berlin composes "Alexander's Ragtime Band," the song that popularized ragtime music.

1911 Air conditioning is invented.

1911 *Photoplay,* the first movie fan magazine, is published.

1911 On March 25, in New York City, 146 female workers are killed in the Triangle Shirtwaist Factory fire, alerting Americans to the dangers women face in industrial labor.

1911 On May 23, President William Howard Taft dedicates the New York Public Library.

1911 On May 30, the first Indianapolis 500 auto race is won by Ray Harroun with an average speed of 74.59 mph.

1911 On August 8, *Pathe's Weekly,* the first regular newsreel to be produced in the United States, is released to motion picture theaters.

1911 On December 19, the Association of American Painters and Sculptors is founded.

1912 New Mexico and Arizona become the forty-seventh and forty-eighth states.

1912 The Little Theater in Chicago, Illinois, and the Toy Theater in Boston, Massachusetts, the first influential little theaters in the United States, are founded.

1912 Dancers Irene and Vernon Castle start a craze for ballroom dancing.

1912 On April 15, the *Titanic* sinks on its maiden voyage from Ireland to the United States, killing 1,517.

1912 In August, photographer and editor Alfred Stieglitz devotes an entire issue of his periodical *Camera Work* to the modern art movement.

1912 On August 5, former president Theodore Roosevelt is nominated as the presidential candidate of the newly formed Progressive Party.

1912 On October 31, *The Musketeers of Pig Alley,* a film by D. W. Griffith that points out the social evils of poverty and crime on the streets of New York, is released.

1912 On November 5, New Jersey governor Woodrow Wilson is elected president.

1912 On December 10, the Famous Players Film Company registers for copyright of the five-reel feature film *The Count of Monte Cristo,* directed by Edwin S. Porter.

1913 The 792-foot-high Woolworth Building in New York City becomes the world's tallest building, a record it holds until 1930.

1913 The first crossword puzzle is published.

1913 The Jesse Lasky Feature Play Co., which later would become Paramount Pictures, is established in Hollywood, California.

1913 The Panama Canal is completed, and officially opens on August 15, 1914.

1913 On February 17, the International Exhibition of Modern Art, known as the Armory Show, opens in New York City. It is the first opportunity for many Americans to view modern art.

1913 On February 25, the Sixteenth Amendment to the Constitution is approved, authorizing a federal income tax.

1913 On March 24, the million dollar, eighteen-hundred-seat Palace Theatre opens in New York City.

1913 On May 31, the Seventeenth Amendment to the Constitution is approved, providing for the direct election of U.S. senators by citizens, rather than by state legislatures.

1914 On February 13, the American Society of Composers, Authors, and Publishers (ASCAP), an organization that seeks royalty payments for public performances of music, is founded in New York City.

1914 In March, comedian Charles Chaplin begins to evolve the legendary character of the Little Tramp in the film *Mabel's Strange Predicament.*

1914 On July 3, the first telephone line connects New York City and San Francisco, California.

1914 On August 3, World War I starts in Europe when Germany invades Belgium. Soon all of Europe is drawn into the conflict, though the United States remains neutral.

1914 On September 5, a German submarine scores its first kill, sinking the British cruiser *Pathfinder,* as World War I intensifies.

1914 In September, in the World War I Battle of the Marne, Germany's advance into France is halted.

1914 On November 3, the first American exhibition of African sculpture opens at the 291 Gallery in New York City.

1914 On December 3, the Isadorables, six European dancers trained by American dancer Isadora Duncan, perform at Carnegie Hall in New York City after escaping with Duncan from her war-torn Europe.

1915 The first taxicab appears on the streets of New York City.

1915 The first professional football league is formed in Ohio and is called simply the Ohio League.

1915 Modern dancers Ruth St. Denis and Ted Shawn found the Denishawn School of Dancing in Los Angeles, California.

1915 Five hundred U.S. correspondents cover World War I in Europe.

1915 On March 10, the Russian Symphony Orchestra plays the American debut performance of the symphony *Prometheus* by Aleksandr Scriabin at Carnegie Hall in New York City. Color images are projected onto a screen as part of the show.

1915 On December 10, the Ford Motor Company manufactures its one millionth Model T automobile.

1916 The Boeing Aircraft Company produces its first biplane.

1916 Newspaper publisher William Randolph Hearst inaugurates the *City Life* arts section as a supplement to his Sunday newspapers.

1916 In November, inventor and radio pioneer Lee De Forest begins to transmit daily music broadcasts from his home in New York City.

1916 On November 7, Woodrow Wilson is reelected president after campaigning on the pledge to keep the United States out of the war in Europe.

1917 The Russian Revolution brings communism to Russia, setting the stage for nearly a century of intermittent conflict with the United States.

1917 Showman George M. Cohan composes the song that was a musical call-to-arms during World War I: "Over There."

1917 Motion picture pioneer Cecil B. DeMille directs *The Little American,* a patriotic melodrama starring Mary Pickford.

1917 On April 6, the United States declares war on Germany after German submarines continue to attack U.S. merchant ships.

1917 On May 28, Benny Leonard wins the lightweight boxing championship, which he holds until his retirement in 1924 while building a record of 209–5; he makes a comeback in 1931.

1917 On August 19, the managers of the New York Giants and Cincinnati Reds are arrested for playing baseball on Sunday.

1917 On October 27, sixteen-year-old Russian-born violinist Jascha Heifetz makes his debut American performance at Carnegie Hall in New York City.

1918 The annual O. Henry Awards for short fiction are inaugurated in honor of short story writer O. Henry (a pseudonym for William Sydney Porter).

1918 On January 8, President Woodrow Wilson delivers his "Fourteen Points" address before Congress, outlining his plans for the shape of the postwar world.

1918 In March, *The Little Review* begins to serialize the novel *Ulysses,* by James Joyce, which features stream of consciousness techniques and a kind of private language.

1918 On November 11, Germany signs an armistice with the Allies, ending the fighting in World War I.

1918 In December, the Theatre Guild is founded in New York City.

1919 *Maid of Harlem,* an all-black-cast musical starring "Fats" Waller, Mamie Smith, Johnny Dunn, and Perry Bradford, draws enthusiastic crowds at the Lincoln Theatre in New York City.

1919 On January 29, Prohibition begins with the adoption of the Eighteenth Amendment to the Constitution, which bans the manufacture, sale, and transportation of intoxicating liquors.

1919 On February 5, United Artists, an independent film distribution company, is founded by Charles Chaplin, Douglas Fairbanks, D. W. Griffith, and Mary Pickford.

1919 On June 28, the Treaty of Versailles is signed by the Allied powers, officially ending World War I. Germany is forced to pay costly reparations for the damage it caused during the war.

1919 On July 4, Jack Dempsey defeats Jess Willard to win the world heavyweight boxing championship.

1919 On October 31, the Provincetown Players stage *The Dreamy Kid,* by Eugene O'Neill, with an all-black cast.

1919 On December 22, Attorney General A. Mitchell Palmer authorizes government raids on communists, anarchists, and other political radicals. These "Palmer raids" are part of a nationwide "red scare."

1920 Sinclair Lewis publishes the novel *Main Street.*

1920 Douglas Fairbanks stars in the film *The Mark of Zorro.*

1920 On January 5, the Radio Corporation of America (RCA) is founded and becomes a leading radio broadcaster.

1920 On February 12, the National Negro Baseball League is founded.

1920 On August 20, the first radio news bulletins are broadcast by station 8MK in Detroit, Michigan.

1920 On August 26, the Nineteenth Amendment to the Constitution gives women the right to vote.

1920 On September 28, eight Chicago White Sox players are charged with throwing the 1919 World Series in what becomes known as the "Black Sox Scandal." They are eventually banned from the game for life.

1920 On September 29, New York Yankee Babe Ruth breaks his own single-season home run record with 54 home runs.

1920 On November 1, Eugene O'Neill's play *The Emperor Jones* opens in New York City.

1920 On November 6, U.S. senator Warren G. Harding of Ohio is elected president.

1921 The Ford Motor Company announces a plan to produce one million automobiles a year.

1921 The Phillips Gallery in Washington, D.C., becomes the first American museum of modern art.

1921 In this year, 13 percent of Americans own telephones.

1921 On March 10, the first White Castle hamburger chain opens in Wichita, Kansas.

1921 On April 11, radio station KDKA in Pittsburgh, Pennsylvania, broadcasts the first sports event on radio, a boxing match between Johnny Ray and Johnny Dundee. Later that year, the World Series is broadcast.

1921 On May 23, *Shuffle Along* is the first black Broadway musical written and directed by African Americans.

1921 On July 29, Adolf Hitler is elected dictator of the Nazi Party in Munich, Germany.

1921 On September 8, the first Miss America pageant is held in Washington, D.C.

1921 On November 2, Margaret Sanger founds the American Birth Control League in New York City, raising the anger of many religious groups, especially Catholic groups.

1922 Robert Flaherty releases the documentary film *Nanook of the North.*

1922 Irish author James Joyce publishes *Ulysses,* which is banned in some countries for its alleged obscenity.

1922 F. Scott Fitzgerald publishes *Tales of the Jazz Age.*

1922 The American Professional Football Association changes its name to the National Football League (NFL).

1922 *Reader's Digest* magazine is founded.

1922 Al Jolson pens the popular song "Toot Toot Tootsie."

1922 On May 5, Coco Chanel introduces Chanel No. 5, which becomes the world's best-known perfume.

1922 On August 28, the first advertisement is aired on radio station WEAF in New York City.

1922 On December 30, the Union of Soviet Socialist Republics (USSR) is established with Russia at its head.

1923 Cecil B. DeMille directs the epic film *The Ten Commandments.*

1923 Charles Kettering develops a method for bringing colored paint to mass-produced cars.

1923 Bessie Smith's "Down Hearted Blues" is one of the first blues songs to be recorded.

1923 *Time* magazine begins publication.

1923 On April 6, trumpet player Louis Armstrong records his first solo on "Chimes Blues" with King Oliver's Creole Jazz Band.

1923 On August 3, President Warren G. Harding dies and Vice President Calvin Coolidge takes office.

1924 John Ford directs the Western film *The Iron Horse.*

1924 The Metro-Goldwyn-Mayer (MGM) film studio is formed in Hollywood, California.

1924 Evangelist Aimee Semple McPherson begins broadcasting from the first religious radio station, KFSG in Los Angeles, California.

1924 The stock market begins a boom that will last until 1929.

1924 On January 1, there are 2.5 million radios in American homes, up from 2,000 in 1920.

1924 On February 12, the tomb of King Tutankhamen, or King Tut, is opened in Egypt after having been sealed for four thousand years.

1924 On February 24, George Gershwin's *Rhapsody in Blue* is performed by an orchestra in New York City.

1924 On March 10, J. Edgar Hoover is appointed director of the Federal Bureau of Investigation.

1924 In June, the Chrysler Corporation is founded and competes with General Motors and Ford.

1924 On November 4, incumbent Calvin Coolidge is elected president.

1925 In one of the most famous years in American literature, F. Scott Fitzgerald publishes *The Great Gatsby,* Ernest Hemingway publishes *In Our Time,* and Theodore Dreiser publishes *An American Tragedy.*

1925 Lon Chaney stars in the film *The Phantom of the Opera.*

1925 The *WSM Barn Dance* radio program begins broadcasting from Nashville, Tennessee; the name is later changed to *Grand Ole Opry* and it becomes the leading country music program.

1925 The *New Yorker* magazine begins publication and features the prices paid for bootleg liquor.

1925 In February, the Boeing aircraft company builds a plane capable of flying over the Rocky Mountains with a full load of mail.

1925 On May 8, the Brotherhood of Sleeping Car Porters, founded by A. Philip Randolph, is one of the first black labor unions.

1925 In July, in the Scopes "Monkey" trial, a Tennessee teacher is tried and found guilty of teaching evolution in a trial that attracts national attention.

1925 On August 8, forty thousand Ku Klux Klan members march in Washington, D.C., to broaden support for their racist organization.

1926 Latin idol Rudolph Valentino stars in the film *The Son of the Sheik.*

1926 Ernest Hemingway publishes *The Sun Also Rises.*

1926 The Book-of-the-Month Club is launched to offer quality books to subscribers.

1926 On March 7, the first transatlantic radio-telephone conversation links New York City and London, England.

1926 On March 17, *The Girl Friend,* a musical with songs by Richard Rodgers and Lorenz Hart, opens on Broadway.

1926 On April 18, dancer Martha Graham makes her first professional appearance in New York City.

1927 Al Jolson stars in the film *The Jazz Singer,* the first film to have sound. Clara Bow—the "It" girl—stars in *It.*

1927 On January 1, the Rose Bowl football game is broadcast coast-to-coast on the radio.

1927 On April 7, television is first introduced in America, but investors are skeptical.

1927 On May 21, Charles Lindbergh completes his nonstop flight from New York City to Paris, France, and is given a hero's welcome.

1927 On May 25, the Ford Motor Company announces that production of the Model T will be stopped in favor of the modern Model A.

1927 On September 22, the heavyweight championship fight between Jack Dempsey and Gene Tunney becomes the first sports gate to top $2 million.

1927 On December 4, Duke Ellington's orchestra begins a long run at the Cotton Club nightclub in Harlem, New York.

1927 On December 27, the Jerome Kern and Oscar Hammerstein musical *Show Boat* opens on Broadway in New York City.

1928 On April 15, the New York Rangers become the first American team to win the National Hockey League Stanley Cup.

1928 On May 11, WGY in Schenectady, New York, offers the first scheduled television service, though the high price of televisions keeps most people from owning them.

1928 On July 30, the Eastman Kodak company introduces color motion pictures.

1928 On November 6, former U.S. secretary of commerce Herbert Hoover is elected president.

1928 On December 13, George Gershwin's *An American in Paris* opens at Carnegie Hall in New York City.

1928 On December 26, swimmer Johnny Weissmuller retires from competition after setting sixty-seven world records.

1929 Mickey Mouse makes his first appearance in *Steamboat Willie,* an animated film made by Walt Disney.

1929 Commercial airlines carry 180,000 passengers during the year.

1929 Ernest Hemingway publishes *A Farewell to Arms,* a novel set during World War I.

1929 Nick Lucas's "Tiptoe through the Tulips with Me" and Louis Armstrong's "Ain't Misbehavin'" are two of the year's most popular songs.

1929 On February 14, in the Saint Valentine's Day Massacre, gunmen working for Chicago, Illinois, mobster Al Capone gun down seven members of a rival gang.

1929 On October 29, the stock market collapses on a day known as "Black Tuesday," marking the start of what will become the Great Depression.

1930 Grant Wood paints *American Gothic.*

1930 The Continental Baking company introduces Wonder Bread to the nation, the first commercially produced sliced bread.

1930 Unemployment reaches four million as the economy worsens.

1930 On January 14, jazz greats Benny Goodman, Glenn Miller, Jimmy Dorsey, and Jack Teagarden play George and Ira Gershwin's songs, including "I've Got a Crush on You," in the musical *Strike Up the Band* at the Mansfield Theater in New York City.

1930 On March 6, General Foods introduces the nation's first frozen foods.

1930 On May 3, Ogden Nash, a poet who will become famous for his funny, light verse, publishes "Spring Comes to Murray Hill" in the *New Yorker* magazine and soon begins work at the magazine.

1930 On September 8, the comic strip *Blondie* begins.

1930 On October 14, *Girl Crazy,* starring Ethel Merman, opens at New York's Guild Theater. The musical features songs by George Gershwin, Walter Donaldson, and Ira Gershwin, including "I Got Rhythm" and "Embraceable You."

1931 The horror films *Dracula* and *Frankenstein* are both released.

1931 Nevada legalizes gambling in order to bring revenue to the state.

1931 On March 3, "The Star Spangled Banner" becomes the national anthem by congressional vote.

1931 On April 30, the Empire State Building, the tallest building in the world, opens in New York City.

1931 On June 3, brother-and-sister dancers Fred and Adele Astaire perform for the last time together on the first revolving stage.

1931 On July 27, *Earl Carroll's Vanities,* featuring naked chorus girls, opens at the three-thousand-seat Earl Carroll Theater in New York City.

1931 On October 12, the comic strip *Dick Tracy* begins.

1932 Edwin Herbert Land, a Harvard College dropout, invents Polaroid film.

1932 On May 2, *The Jack Benny Show* premieres as a variety show on radio and runs for twenty-three years and then another ten years on television.

1932 On July 30, the Summer Olympic Games open in Los Angeles, California, and feature record-breaking performances by Americans Babe Didrikson and Eddie Tolan.

1932 On July 31, in German parliamentary elections, the Nazi Party receives the most seats but is unable to form a government.

1932 On November 7, the radio adventure *Buck Rogers in the Twenty-Fifth Century* premieres on CBS and runs until 1947.

1932 On November 8, New York governor Franklin D. Roosevelt is elected president, promising to take steps to improve the economy. In his first one hundred days in office, Roosevelt introduces much legislation to use the government to aid those harmed by the Great Depression.

1932 On December 27, Radio City Music Hall opens at the Rockefeller Center in New York City.

1933 President Franklin D. Roosevelt presents the nation with his first radio address, known as a "fireside chat."

1933 Walt Disney releases the feature film *The Three Little Pigs.*

1933 On January 3, *The Lone Ranger* radio drama premieres on WXYZ radio in Detroit, Michigan.

1933 On January 30, Nazi leader Adolf Hitler becomes chancellor of Germany. Hitler soon seizes all power and sets out to attack his party's political enemies.

1933 On May 27, fan dancer Sally Rand attracts thousands with her performance at the Chicago World's Fair that celebrated the Century of Progress.

1933 On September 30, *Ah, Wilderness,* acclaimed American playwright Eugene O'Neill's only comedy, opens at the Guild Theater in New York City.

1933 On December 5, the Twenty-first Amendment to the Constitution puts an end to Prohibition.

1934 The first pipeless organ is patented by Laurens Hammond. The Hammond organ starts a trend toward more electrically amplified instruments.

1934 Dashiell Hammett publishes *The Thin Man,* one of the first hard-boiled detective novels.

1934 The Apollo Theater opens in Harlem, New York, as a showcase for black performers.

1934 German director Fritz Lang flees Nazi Germany to make movies in the United States.

1934 On May 5, bank robbers and murderers Bonnie Parker and Clyde Barrow are killed by lawmen in Louisiana.

1934 On July 1, the Motion Picture Producers and Distributors of America (MPPDA) association creates the Hay's Office to enforce codes that limit the amount and types of sexuality and other immoral behavior in films.

1934 On July 22, "Public Enemy No. 1" John Dillinger is shot and killed outside a Chicago, Illinois, theater by FBI agents and local police.

1934 On August 13, Al Capp's *Li'l Abner* comic strip debuts in eight newspapers.

1934 On August 19, Adolf Hitler is declared president of Germany, though he prefers the title Führer (leader).

1935 One out of four American households receives government relief as the Depression deepens.

1935 Twenty million Monopoly board games are sold in one week.

1935 The first Howard Johnson roadside restaurant opens in Boston, Massachusetts.

1935 The Works Progress Administration Federal Arts Projects, some of President Franklin D. Roosevelt's many New Deal programs, give work to artists painting post offices and other federal buildings.

1935 In April, *Your Hit Parade* is first heard on radio and offers a selection of hit songs.

1935 On April 16, the radio comedy-drama *Fibber McGee and Molly* debuts on NBC and runs until 1952.

1935 On May 24, the first nighttime major league baseball game is played in Cincinnati, Ohio.

1935 On October 10, *Porgy and Bess,* known as the "most American opera of the decade," opens in New York City at the Alvin Theater. The music George Gershwin wrote for the opera combined blues, jazz, and southern folk.

1936 American Airlines introduces transcontinental airline service.

1936 Ten African American athletes, including Jesse Owens, win gold medals in the Summer Olympics held in Berlin, Germany, embarrassing Nazi leader Adolf Hitler, who had declared the inferiority of black athletes.

1936 Dust storms in the Plains states force thousands to flee the region, many to California.

1936 Popular public-speaking teacher Dale Carnegie publishes his book *How to Win Friends and Influence People.*

1936 To increase feelings of nationalism, the Department of the Interior hires folksinger Woody Guthrie to travel throughout the U.S. Southwest performing his patriotic songs such as "Those Oklahoma Hills."

1936 In the Soviet Union, the Communist Party begins its Great Purge, executing anyone who resists the party's social and economic policies. By 1938, it is estimated that ten million people have been killed.

1936 Throughout Europe, countries scramble to form alliances with other countries for what seems to be a likely war. Germany and Italy join together to support the military government of Francisco Franco in Spain, while Great Britain and France sign nonaggression pacts with the Soviet Union.

1936 On July 18, the Spanish Civil War begins when Spanish military officers rise up against the Republican government of Spain.

1936 In October, the New York Yankees win the first of four World Series in a row.

1936 On November 3, Franklin D. Roosevelt is reelected as president of the United States.

1936 On November 23, the first issue of *Life* magazine is published.

1937 Dr. Seuss becomes a popular children's book author with the publication of *And to Think That I Saw It on Mulberry Street.*

1937 The Hormel company introduces Spam, a canned meat.

1937 A poll shows that the average American listens to the radio for 4.5 hours a day.

1937 *Porky's Hare Hunt,* a short animated cartoon by Warner Bros., introduces audiences to the Bugs Bunny character and the talents of Mel Blanc, the voice of both Bugs Bunny and Porky Pig.

1937 The first soap opera, *Guiding Light,* is broadcast. It continues as a radio program until 1956 and moves to television.

1937 British writer J. R. R. Tolkien publishes *The Hobbit.*

1937 On June 22, black boxer Joe Louis knocks out Jim Braddock to win the world heavyweight boxing championship.

1937 On December 21, *Snow White and the Seven Dwarfs,* the first feature-length animated film, is presented by Walt Disney.

1938 Glenn Miller forms his own big band and begins to tour extensively.

1938 On January 17, the first jazz performance at Carnegie Hall in New York City is performed by Benny Goodman and His Orchestra, with Duke Ellington, Count Basie, and others.

1938 In June, the character Superman is introduced in *Action Comics #1.* By 1939, he appears in his own comic book series.

1938 On August 17, Henry Armstrong becomes the first boxer to hold three boxing titles at one time when he defeats Lou Ambers at New York City's Madison Square Garden.

1938 On October 31, Orson Welles's radio broadcast of H. G. Wells's science fiction novel *The War of the Worlds* is believed by many listeners to be a serious announcement of a Martian invasion, resulting in panic spreading throughout the country.

1938 On November 11, singer Kate Smith's performance of "God Bless America" is broadcast over the radio on Armistice Day.

1939 Singer Frank Sinatra joins the Tommy Dorsey band, where he will soon find great success.

1939 Federal spending on the military begins to revive the economy.

1939 Pocket Books, the nation's first modern paperback book company, is founded.

1939 The National Collegiate Athletic Association (NCAA) holds it first Final Four championship basketball series, which is won by the University of Oregon.

1939 *Gone with the Wind,* David O. Selznick's epic film about the Civil War, stars Vivien Leigh and Clark Gable.

1939 *The Wizard of Oz* whisks movie audiences into a fantasyland of magic and wonder. The film stars Judy Garland and includes such popular songs as "Somewhere Over the Rainbow," "Follow the Yellow Brick Road," and "We're Off to See the Wizard."

1939 On May 2, baseball great Lou "The Iron Man" Gehrig ends his consecutive game streak at 2,130 when he removes himself from the lineup.

1939 On September 1, German troops invade Poland, causing Great Britain and France to declare war on Germany and starting World War II. Days later, the Soviet Union invades Poland as well, and soon Germany and the Soviet Union divide Poland.

1940 The radio program *Superman* debuts, introducing the phrases "Up, up, and away!" and "This looks like a job for Superman!"

1940 On February 22, German troops begin construction of a concentration camp in Auschwitz, Poland.

1940 The first issue of the comic book *Batman* is published.

1940 On May 10, German forces invade Belgium and Holland, and later march into France.

1940 On June 10, Italy declares war on Britain and France.

1940 On June 14, the German army enters Paris, France.

1940 On August 24, Germany begins bombing London, England.

1940 On November 5, President Franklin D. Roosevelt is reelected for his third term.

1940 On November 13, the Disney film *Fantasia* opens in New York City.

1941 "Rosie the Riveter" becomes the symbol for the many women who are employed in various defense industries.

1941 *Citizen Kane,* which many consider the greatest movie of all time, is released, directed by and starring Orson Welles.

1941 On January 15, A. Philip Randolph leads the March on Washington to call for an end to racial discrimination in defense-industry employment. President Franklin D. Roosevelt eventually signs an executive order barring such discrimination.

1941 On March 17, the National Gallery of Art opens in Washington, D.C.

1941 On July 1, CBS and NBC begin offering about fifteen hours of commercial television programming each week—but few consumers have enough money to purchase television sets.

1941 On October 19, German troops lay siege to the Russian city of Moscow.

1941 On December 7, Japanese planes launch a surprise attack on the U.S. naval and air bases in Pearl Harbor, Hawaii, and declare war against the United States.

1941 On December 11, the United States declares war on Germany and Italy in response to those countries' declarations of war.

1942 On January 1, the annual Rose Bowl football game is played in Durham, North Carolina, rather than the usual Pasadena, California, location, to avoid the chance of a Japanese bombing attack.

1942 Humphrey Bogart and Ingrid Bergman star in *Casablanca,* set in war-torn Europe.

1942 On February 19, President Franklin D. Roosevelt signs an executive order placing all Japanese Americans on the West Coast in internment camps for the rest of the war.

1942 On May 5, sugar rationing starts in the United States, followed by the rationing of other products.

1942 In June, American troops defeat the Japanese at the Battle of Midway.

1942 On December 25, the comedy team of Abbott and Costello is voted the leading box-office attraction of 1942.

1943 Gary Cooper and Ingrid Bergman star in *For Whom the Bell Tolls,* the film version of the novel by Ernest Hemingway.

1943 On January 25, the Pentagon, the world's largest office complex and the home to the U.S. military, is completed in Arlington, Virginia.

1943 On March 14, composer Aaron Copland's *Fanfare for the Common Man* premieres in Cincinnati, Ohio.

1943 On March 30, the musical *Oklahoma!* opens on Broadway in New York City.

1943 During the summer, race riots break out in Detroit, Michigan, and Harlem, New York.

1943 On September 8, Italy surrenders to the Allies.

1943 On November 9, artist Jackson Pollock has his first solo show in New York City.

1943 On December 30, *Esquire* magazine loses its second-class mailing privileges after it is charged with being "lewd" and "lascivious" by the U.S. Post Office.

1944 *Seventeen* magazine debuts.

1944 *Double Indemnity,* directed by Billy Wilder, becomes one of the first of a new genre of movies known as *film noir.*

1944 On March 4, American planes bomb Berlin, Germany.

1944 On June 6, on "D-Day," Allied forces land in Normandy, France, and begin the liberation of western Europe.

1944 On June 22, the Serviceman's Readjustment Act, signed by President Franklin D. Roosevelt, provides funding for a variety of programs for returning soldiers, including education programs under the G.I. Bill.

1944 On August 25, Allied troops liberate Paris, France.

1944 On November 7, Franklin D. Roosevelt is reelected for an unprecedented fourth term as president.

1945 Chicago publisher John H. Johnson launches *Ebony* magazine.

1945 The radio program *The Adventures of Ozzie and Harriet* debuts.

1945 On January 27, the Soviet Red Army liberates Auschwitz, Poland, revealing the seriousness of German efforts to exterminate Jews.

1945 On April 12, President Franklin D. Roosevelt dies of a cerebral hemorrhage and Vice President Harry S. Truman takes over as president.

1945 On April 21, Soviet troops reach the outskirts of Berlin, the capital of Germany.

1945 On April 30, German leader Adolf Hitler commits suicide in Berlin, Germany, as Allied troops approach the city.

1945 On May 5, American poet Ezra Pound is arrested in Italy on charges of treason.

1945 On May 8, Germany surrenders to the Allies, bringing an end to World War II in Europe.

1945 On August 6, the United States drops the first atomic bomb on the Japanese city of Hiroshima, killing more than fifty thousand people.

1945 On August 9, the United States drops a second atomic bomb on Nagasaki, Japan.

1945 On September 2, Japan offers its unconditional surrender onboard the U.S.S. *Missouri* in Tokyo Bay, bringing an end to World War II.

1946 The Baby Boom begins as the birthrate rises 20 percent over the previous year.

1946 *It's a Wonderful Life,* starring Jimmy Stewart and directed by Frank Capra, becomes one of the most popular Christmas movies of all time.

1946 On January 10, the first General Assembly of the United Nations meets in London, England.

1946 On June 19, Joe Louis retains his title by knocking out Billy Conn in the first heavyweight boxing match ever shown on television.

1946 On December 11, country singer Hank Williams cuts his first single, "Calling You."

1947 On January 29, Arthur Miller's play *All My Sons* opens in New York City.

1947 On March 12, President Harry S. Truman announces his "containment" policy aimed at stopping the spread of communism. It will later become known as the Truman Doctrine.

1947 On March 21, Congress approves the Twenty-second Amendment, which limits the president to two four-year terms in office. The amendment is ratified in 1951.

1947 On April 10, Jackie Robinson breaks the "color barrier" when he signs a contract to play for professional baseball's Brooklyn Dodgers. He is later named Rookie of the Year by the *Sporting News.*

1947 Beginning September 30, the World Series is televised for the first time as fans watch the New York Yankees defeat the Brooklyn Dodgers in seven games.

1947 On October 13, the Hollywood Ten, a group of film directors and writers, appears before the House Un-American Activities Committee (HUAC).

1947 On December 3, Tennessee Williams's *A Streetcar Named Desire* opens on Broadway in New York City.

1948 The Baskin-Robbins ice cream chain opens.

1948 On April 3, Congress approves $6 billion in Marshall Plan aid for rebuilding European countries.

1948 On May 14, the state of Israel is established.

1948 On May 29, the play *Oklahoma!* closes after a record 2,246 performances.

1948 On June 25, heavyweight boxing champion Joe Louis knocks out Joe Walcott for his twenty-fifth title defense; following the fight, he announces his retirement from boxing.

1948 On September 13, Margaret Chase Smith of Maine becomes the first woman elected to the U.S. Senate.

1948 On November 2, incumbent Harry S. Truman is elected president.

1949 Builder Abraham Levitt and his sons begin construction on a Long Island, New York, suburb called Levittown, which will become a symbol for the postwar housing boom.

1949 On February 10, Arthur Miller's *Death of a Salesman* opens on Broadway in New York City.

1949 On April 4, the North Atlantic Treaty Organization (NATO) is formed by the United States and twelve other mainly European countries to provide for mutual defense.

1949 On September 23, American, British, and Canadian officials reveal that the Soviet Union has successfully detonated an atomic bomb.

1949 On October 1, the Communist People's Republic of China is proclaimed.

1950 The first Xerox copy machine is produced.

1950 Miss Clairol hair coloring is introduced, making it easy for women to dye their hair at home.

1950 Desegregation continues when Charles Cooper becomes the first black player in the National Basketball Association and Althea Gibson becomes the first black woman to compete in a national tennis tournament.

1950 In March, the Boston Institute of Contemporary Art and New York's Metropolitan Museum and Whitney Museum release a joint statement on modern art opposing "any attempt to make art or opinion about art conform to a single point of view."

1950 On May 8, President Harry S. Truman sends the first U.S. military mission to Vietnam.

1950 On June 30, U.S. combat troops enter the Korean War.

1950 On October 2, *Peanuts,* the comic strip written and drawn by Charles Schulz, debuts in seven U.S. newspapers.

1951 *The Caine Mutiny,* a war novel by Herman Wouk, is published and soon becomes one of the longest lasting best-sellers of all time, holding its place on the *New York Times* list for forty-eight weeks.

1951 On April 5, Julius and Ethel Rosenberg receive death sentences for allegedly giving secret information to the Soviet Union.

1951 On June 25, CBS offers the first color television broadcast.

1951 On August 5, the soap operas *Search for Tomorrow* and *Love of Life* premiere on CBS.

1951 On October 15, the sitcom *I Love Lucy* premieres on CBS.

1951 On November 18, the news program *See It Now,* hosted by Edward R. Murrow, premieres on CBS.

1952 *Gunsmoke* debuts as a radio drama. In 1955, the Western drama moves to TV where it lasts until 1975. The show, which starred James Arness as Marshal Matt Dillon, becomes the longest running prime-time TV show with continuing characters.

1952 In January, *American Bandstand,* a popular teen-oriented music program, debuts as a local show in Philadelphia, Pennsylvania. Dick Clark, its most famous host, joins the show in 1956.

1952 On January 14, *The Today Show* debuts on NBC.

1952 In September, *The Old Man and the Sea,* a short novel by Ernest Hemingway, is printed in *Life* magazine and is the Book-of-the-Month Club's co-main selection.

1953 On October 5, the New York Yankees become the first team in history to win five consecutive World Series when they defeat the Brooklyn Dodgers.

1952 In November, *Bwana Devil,* the first 3-D movie, is released.

1952 On November 4, World War II general Dwight D. Eisenhower is elected president.

1953 *Playboy* becomes the first mass-market men's magazine and rockets to popularity when it publishes nude pictures of rising movie star Marilyn Monroe.

1953 IBM introduces its first computer, the 701.

1953 On January 1, Hank Williams, the father of contemporary country music, dies at age twenty-nine from a heart disease resulting from excessive drinking.

1953 On April 3, the first national edition of *TV Guide* is published.

1953 On July 27, the Korean War ends.

1953 On September 13, Nikita Khrushchev is named first secretary of the Soviet Union's Communist Party.

1953 In November, an eleven-day photoengravers strike leaves New York City without a daily newspaper for the first time since 1778.

1954 U.S. senator Joseph McCarthy of Wisconsin leads hearings into the presence of communists in the U.S. Army; his actions are later condemned by the Senate.

1954 *Sports Illustrated* becomes the first glossy weekly magazine about sports.

1954 Swanson Foods introduces the first TV dinners.

1954 On April 4, legendary conductor Arturo Toscanini makes his final appearance conducting the NBC Symphony Orchestra. The concert is broadcast on the radio live from New York City's Carnegie Hall.

1954 On April 4, Walt Disney signs a contract with ABC to produce twenty-six television films each year.

1954 On May 14, the Soviet Union joins with seven Eastern European countries to form the Warsaw Pact, a union of nations pledged to mutual defense.

1954 On May 17, with its *Brown v. Board of Education* decision, the U.S. Supreme Court ends segregation in public schools.

1954 In July, the Newport Jazz Festival debuts in Newport, Rhode Island.

1954 On July 19, "That's All Right, Mama" and "Blue Moon of Kentucky," the first professional records made by Elvis Presley, are released on Sun Records.

1954 On September 27, *The Tonight Show* debuts on NBC.

1954 In October and November, Hungary tries to leave the Warsaw Pact but is attacked and reclaimed by the Soviet Union.

1955 Velcro is invented.

1955 *The $64,000 Question* debuts and soon becomes the most popular game show of the 1950s.

1955 In January, Marian Anderson becomes the first black singer to appear at the Metropolitan Opera.

1955 On January 19, President Dwight D. Eisenhower holds the first televised presidential news conference.

1955 In March, *The Blackboard Jungle,* the first feature film to include a rock and roll song on its soundtrack—"Rock Around the Clock," by Bill Haley and The Comets—opens. The song becomes the country's number-one single in July.

1955 On April 12, large-scale vaccinations for polio are administered throughout the United States.

1955 On July 17, the Disneyland amusement park opens in Anaheim, California.

1955 On September 30, actor James Dean dies after his Porsche roadster slams into another car on a California highway.

1955 On October 13, poet Allen Ginsberg gives the first public reading of *Howl,* his controversial poem-in-progress.

1955 On December 5, Rosa Parks refuses to give up her seat to a white man on a bus in Montgomery, Alabama, sparking a bus boycott that will become a key moment in the Civil Rights Movement.

1956 On June 20, Loew's Inc. releases MGM's pre-1949 film library—excluding *Gone with the Wind* (1939)—for television broadcast.

1956 On November 6, President Dwight D. Eisenhower is reelected.

1956 On November 30, videotape is first used commercially on television, during the broadcast of CBS's *Douglas Edwards with the News.*

1957 On September 26, the landmark musical *West Side Story,* a modern-day adaptation of *Romeo and Juliet* by William Shakespeare, opens on Broadway at the Winter Garden Theatre in New York City.

1957 On October 5, the Soviet Union launches the satellite *Sputnik,* the first man-made satellite in space.

1958 On October 2, Leonard Bernstein begins his first season as director of the New York Philharmonic.

1958 On October 16, sponsors drop the NBC quiz show *Twenty-One* after a grand jury investigation determines that contestants were provided with pre-show answers.

1959 On January 2, revolutionary leader Fidel Castro assumes power in Cuba.

1959 On January 3, Alaska becomes the forty-ninth state.

1959 On February 3, rock and roll legends Buddy Holly, Ritchie Valens, and J. P. Richardson (known as "The Big Bopper") die in a plane crash outside Clear Lake, Iowa.

1959 On August 21, Hawaii becomes the fiftieth state.

1959 On October 21, the Solomon R. Guggenheim Museum, designed by architect Frank Lloyd Wright, opens in New York City.

1960 Designer Pierre Cardin introduces his first fashion designs for men.

1960 On January 3, the Moscow State Symphony begins a seven-week tour at New York City's Carnegie Hall, becoming the first Soviet orchestra to perform in the United States.

1960 On February 11, Jack Paar, host of *The Tonight Show,* walks off the show when an NBC censor deletes a joke from his performance without his knowledge.

1960 On February 20, black students in Greensboro, North Carolina, stage sit-ins at local lunch counters to protest discrimination.

1960 In April, the New York state legislature authorizes the City of New York to purchase Carnegie Hall, which was scheduled for demolition.

1960 On April 1, Lucille Ball and Desi Arnaz appear for the last time as Lucy and Ricky Ricardo on *The Lucy-Desi Comedy Hour.*

1960 On May 5, the Soviet Union announces the capture of American pilot Francis Gary Powers, whose U-2 spy plane was shot down over the Soviet Union.

1960 On September 26, U.S. senator John F. Kennedy of Massachusetts and Vice President Richard M. Nixon appear in the first televised presidential debate.

1960 On October 13, jazz trumpeter Louis Armstrong begins a goodwill tour of Africa, partially sponsored by the U.S. State Department.

1960 On November 8, U.S. senator John F. Kennedy of Massachusetts is elected president.

1961 On January 20, Robert Frost reads his poem "The Gift Outright" at the inauguration of President John F. Kennedy.

1961 On January 27, soprano Leontyne Price first performs at New York's Metropolitan Opera.

1961 In April, folk singer Bob Dylan makes his debut at Gerde's Folk City in New York City's Greenwich Village.

1961 On April 12, Soviet cosmonaut Yuri Gagarin becomes the first man to orbit the Earth.

1961 During the summer, Freedom Rides across the South are aimed at desegregating interstate bus travel.

1961 On August 15–17, East Germany constructs the Berlin Wall, separating communist East Berlin from democratic West Berlin.

1961 On October 1, Roger Maris sets a new single-season home run record with 61 homers.

1962 On February 10, Jim Beatty becomes the first person to run a mile in less than four minutes with a time of 3:58.9.

1962 On May 30, jazz clarinetist Benny Goodman begins a six-week, U.S. State Department–arranged tour of Russia.

1962 On July 10, the *Telstar* satellite is launched and soon brings live television pictures to American television viewers.

1962 On August 5, actress Marilyn Monroe dies from an overdose of barbiturates.

1962 On September 25, Philharmonic Hall, the first completed building of New York's Lincoln Center for the Performing Arts, is inaugurated by Leonard Bernstein and the New York Philharmonic.

1962 On September 29, *My Fair Lady* closes on Broadway after 2,717 performances, making it the longest-running show in history.

1962 In October, the United States and the Soviet Union clash over the presence of Soviet missiles in Cuba.

1962 On October 1, James Meredith becomes the first black person to enroll at the University of Mississippi as federal troops battle thousands of protesters.

1963 On January 8, *Mona Lisa,* by Leonardo da Vinci, is shown at Washington's National Gallery, the first time the painting ever has appeared outside the Louvre in Paris, France.

1963 On May 7, the Guthrie Theatre in Minneapolis, Minnesota, the first major regional theater in the Midwest, opens.

1963 On November 22, President John F. Kennedy is assassinated in Dallas, Texas, and Vice President Lyndon B. Johnson assumes the presidency.

1963 On November 24, the murder of alleged presidential assassin Lee Harvey Oswald is broadcast live on television.

1964 Ford introduces its Mustang, a smaller sporty car.

1964 On February 9, the Beatles make their first live appearance on American television, on *The Ed Sullivan Show.*

1964 On February 25, Cassius Clay (who later changes his name to Muhammad Ali) beats Sonny Liston to become the heavyweight boxing champion of the world.

1964 In May, the just-remodeled Museum of Modern Art in New York City reopens with a new gallery, the Steichen Photography Center, named for photographer Edward Steichen.

1964 On July 2, President Lyndon B. Johnson signs the Civil Rights Act of 1964, which bans racial discrimination in public places and in employment.

1964 On August 7, in the Gulf of Tonkin Resolution, Congress gives President Lyndon B. Johnson the power to use military force to protect U.S. interests in Vietnam.

1964 On November 3, incumbent Lyndon B. Johnson is elected president.

1965 In January, Bob Dylan plays an electric guitar on his new single, "Subterranean Homesick Blues."

1965 On February 21, black leader Malcolm X is murdered in Harlem, New York.

1965 On March 8, the first U.S. combat troops are sent to Vietnam.

1965 On April 26, *Symphony No. 4* by Charles Ives is performed in its entirety for the first time by the American Symphony Orchestra, conducted by Leopold Stokowski.

1965 On May 9, piano virtuoso Vladimir Horowitz returns to the Carnegie Hall stage after a twelve-year "retirement."

1965 On June 2, in a letter to President Lyndon B. Johnson, Pulitzer Prize–winning poet Robert Lowell declines an invitation to attend a White House arts festival, citing his "dismay and distrust" of American foreign policy.

1965 In July, Bob Dylan and his electric guitar are booed off the Newport Folk Festival stage.

1965 On September 29, President Lyndon B. Johnson signs into law the Federal Aid to the Arts Bill.

1965 On October 15, demonstrations against the Vietnam War occur in forty U.S. cities.

1965 On December 9, *A Charlie Brown Christmas* becomes the first *Peanuts* special to air on TV.

1966 The National Organization for Women (NOW) is established.

1966 On June 8, the National Football League and the American Football League merge.

1966 On July 12, rioting by blacks breaks out in twenty U.S. cities over racial discrimination.

1966 On August 29, the Beatles play their last live concert.

1966 On December 8, philanthropist, horse breeder, and art collector Paul Mellon donates his collection of British rare books, paintings, drawings, and prints, valued at over $35 million, to Yale University.

1967 On January 15, in the first Super Bowl, the Green Bay Packers defeat the Kansas City Chiefs, 35–10.

1967 On February 18, the National Gallery of Art arranges to purchase Leonardo da Vinci's *Ginevra dei Benci* for between $5 million and $6 million, the highest price paid to date for a single painting.

1967 In June, the Monterey International Pop Festival, an important early rock music event, is held in California.

1967 On June 20, Muhammad Ali is stripped of his boxing titles after being found guilty of tax evasion.

1967 On July 23, federal troops are called in to put a stop to rioting in Detroit, Michigan. Forty-three people are killed in the rioting, which lasts a week.

1967 On November 9, the first issue of *Rolling Stone* magazine is published. On the cover is a portrait of the Beatles' John Lennon.

1967 In December, Universal News, the last of the movie newsreel companies, closes because it is unable to compete with television news.

1968 On January 30, North Vietnam launches the Tet Offensive, escalating the war in Vietnam.

1968 On April 4, civil rights leader Martin Luther King Jr. is murdered in Memphis, Tennessee.

1968 On April 19, *Hair* opens on Broadway, at New York City's Biltmore Theatre.

1968 On June 5, presidential candidate and U.S. senator Robert F. Kennedy of New York is murdered in Los Angeles, California.

1968 On September 16, presidential candidate and former vice president Richard Nixon appears as a guest on TV's *Rowan and Martin's Laugh-In* and delivers one of the show's signature lines: "Sock it to me."

1968 On November 1, the Motion Picture Association of America inaugurates its film ratings system.

1968 On November 5, former vice president Richard Nixon is elected president.

1969 Hot pants make their first appearance.

1969 On July 20, U.S. astronaut Neil Armstrong becomes the first man to walk on the moon when the *Apollo 11* mission succeeds.

1969 On August 15–17, the Woodstock Music and Art Fair is held on a six-hundred-acre hog farm in upstate New York.

1969 On November 15, a quarter million Vietnam War protesters march in Washington, D.C.

1969 On December 6, a fan is murdered during the Altamont Rock Festival in California.

1970 Soviet cosmonauts spend seventeen days in space, setting a new record for space longevity.

1970 Across the nation, protests continue over the ongoing Vietnam War.

1970 Rock stars Jimi Hendrix and Janis Joplin die within three weeks of each other, both as a result of drug overdoses.

1970 In March, three women—Elizabeth Bishop, Lillian Hellman, and Joyce Carol Oates—win National Book Awards.

1970 On May 4, National Guard members shoot antiwar protesters at Kent State University in Ohio, killing four students.

1970 On April 10, the Beatles disband.

1970 On April 30, U.S. and South Vietnamese troops invade Cambodia, which has been sheltering North Vietnamese troops.

1970 On September 6, four airliners bound for New York are hijacked by Palestinian terrorists, but no passengers are harmed.

1970 On September 19, *The Mary Tyler Moore Show* debuts on CBS.

1970 On September 21, *Monday Night Football* debuts on ABC.

1970 On October 2, the Environmental Protection Agency (EPA) is created to regulate environmental issues.

1971 Disney World opens in Orlando, Florida.

1971 Hot pants become a fashion sensation.

1971 On January 2, cigarette advertising is banned from television and radio.

1971 On February 6, British troops are sent to patrol Northern Ireland.

1971 On February 9, the European Economic Community, a precursor to the European Union, is established.

1971 On March 8, Joe Frazier defeats Muhammad Ali to retain the world heavyweight boxing title.

1971 On April 20, the U.S. Supreme Court rules that students can be bused to end racial segregation in schools.

1971 In June, the Twenty-sixth Amendment to the Constitution lowers the legal voting age to eighteen.

1971 On June 13, the *New York Times* publishes the "Pentagon Papers," which reveal Defense Department plans for the Vietnam War.

1971 In September, a prison uprising in Attica, New York, ends with forty-three people killed, including ten hostages.

1971 On October 12, the rock musical *Jesus Christ Superstar* opens on Broadway in New York City.

1971 On October 13, the Pittsburgh Pirates and the Baltimore Orioles play in the first World Series night game.

1971 On December 25, "Christmas bombing" occurs in North Vietnam.

1972 In a sign of the cooling of Cold War tensions, East and West Germany and North and South Korea each enter into negotiations to normalize relations.

1972 *Ms.* magazine begins publication.

1972 *Pong*, the first video game available to play at home, becomes popular, as does the first video game machine, Odyssey, introduced by Magnavox.

1972 On February 14, the musical *Grease* opens on Broadway in New York City.

1972 On February 21, President Richard Nixon begins a seven-day visit to Communist China.

1972 On May 22, President Richard Nixon begins a nine-day visit to the Soviet Union.

1972 On June 17, the Watergate scandal begins with the arrest of five men caught trying to bug the Democratic National Committee headquarters at the Watergate building in Washington, D.C. The investigation soon reveals deep corruption in the Nixon administration.

1972 On July 24, the United Nations asks the United States to end its bombing of North Vietnam.

1972 On August 12, the last American combat troops leave Vietnam.

1972 On November 8, cable TV network HBO premieres in Pennsylvania with 365 subscribers.

1973 Three major American cities—Los Angeles, California; Atlanta, Georgia; and Detroit, Michigan—elect a black mayor for the first time.

1973 Investigations into the Watergate affair capture the public attention and shatter the Nixon administration.

1973 The Sears Tower (now known as the Willis Tower), at the time the world's tallest building, is completed in Chicago, Illinois.

1973 Ralph Lauren designs the costumes for the film *The Great Gatsby,* helping build his reputation.

1973 Fantasy-adventure game Dungeons and Dragons is created by Dave Arneson and Gary Gygax.

1973 The first Internet is set up by the U.S. Department of Defense as a way of connecting all the department's computers.

1973 On January 14, the Miami Dolphins win the Super Bowl and become the first professional football team to finish a season undefeated.

1973 On October 16, the Organization of Petroleum Exporting Countries (OPEC) declares an embargo (ban) on the export of oil to the United States and other Western countries.

1973 On October 23, the House of Representatives begins impeachment proceedings against President Richard Nixon.

1974 The Ramones launch the American punk movement with their performances at the New York City club CBGB.

1974 The streaking fad sweeps the country.

1974 President Richard Nixon tours the Middle East and the Soviet Union.

1974 On January 18, Israel and Egypt sign a peace accord that ends their long armed conflict.

1974 On April 8, Hank Aaron of the Atlanta Braves breaks Babe Ruth's lifetime home run record when he hits his 715th career homer.

1974 In May, screenwriter Dalton Trumbo, who had been blacklisted in the 1950s during the anticommunist crusades of U.S. senator Joseph McCarthy of Wisconsin, receives an Academy Award for the 1957 film *The Brave One.*

1974 On August 8, Richard Nixon announces that he would become the first U.S. president to resign from office, amid evidence of a cover-up of the Watergate affair.

1974 On August 9, Vice President Gerald Ford replaces Richard Nixon as president. Less than a month later, he officially pardons Nixon.

1974 On September 8, motorcycle stunt rider Evel Knievel tries to jump a rocket over the Snake River Canyon in Idaho but falls short.

1974 On October 3, Frank Robinson joins the Cleveland Indians as major league baseball's first black manager.

1974 On October 30, boxer Muhammnad Ali regains his world heavyweight boxing title by defeating George Foreman.

1974 In December, unemployment hits 6.5 percent amid a prolonged economic slump and rises to 8.9 percent by May 1975.

1975 The video cassette recorder (VCR) is invented by Sony Corporation in Japan.

1975 The first personal computer, the Altair 8800, is sold in a kit form.

1975 The cult film *The Rocky Horror Picture Show* is released.

1975 Skateboarding becomes popular, and mood rings and pet rocks are popular fads.

1975 Rock star Bruce Springsteen appears on the cover of both *Time* and *Newsweek* thanks to his popular album *Born to Run.*

1975 The Soviet Union and the United States cooperate in the manned *Apollo-Soyuz* space mission.

1975 On January 5, the all-black musical *The Wiz* opens on Broadway in New York City. It eventually tallies 1,672 performances.

1975 On April 30, Saigon, the capital of South Vietnam, is invaded by the communist North Vietnamese, ending the Vietnam War.

1975 On October 1, the Organization of Petroleum Exporting Countries (OPEC) raises crude oil prices by 10 percent.

1975 On October 11, *Saturday Night Live* debuts on NBC.

1976 The first personal computer, the Apple, is developed by Steve Jobs and Steve Wozniak. The Apple II, introduced a year later, offers color graphics.

1976 Model and actress Farrah Fawcett-Majors sets a trend with her feathered haircut and appears on millions of posters in her tiny red bathing suit.

1976 On July 4, the United States celebrates its bicentennial.

1976 On November 2, former Georgia governor Jimmy Carter is elected president.

1976 On November 6, *Gone with the Wind* is broadcast on TV for the first time.

1977 The film *Saturday Night Fever* helps make disco music popular.

1977 Studio 54 becomes New York City's hottest nightclub featuring disco music.

1977 Egyptian artifacts from the tomb of King Tutankhamen, or King Tut, draw huge audiences across the nation.

1977 Alex Haley's book *Roots* becomes a best-seller after the airing of the TV miniseries based on the book.

1977 On January 21, President Jimmy Carter signs an unconditional pardon for most Vietnam-era draft evaders.

1977 On February 8, *Hustler* magazine publisher Larry Flynt is convicted of obscenity.

1977 In April, the Christian Broadcasting Network (CBN) makes its debut.

1977 On August 16, Elvis Presley, the king of rock and roll, dies at Graceland, his Memphis, Tennessee, mansion.

1978 The Walkman personal cassette player is introduced by Sony.

1978 On July 25, the first human test-tube baby is born in England.

1978 On September 17, U.S. president Jimmy Carter hosts negotiations between Israeli prime minister Menachem Begin and Egyptian president Anwar Sadat at Camp David, Maryland.

1978 On October 13, punk rock musician Sid Vicious of the Sex Pistols is arrested for the stabbing death of his girlfriend.

1978 On November 18, Jim Jones and over nine hundred followers of his People's Temple cult are found dead after a mass suicide in Jonestown, Guyana.

1978 On December 5, the Soviet Union and Afghanistan sign a treaty of friendship, and within a year U.S. support for the Afghan government disappears.

1979 Eleven people are trampled to death at a Who concert in Cincinnati, Ohio.

1979 Jerry Falwell organizes the Moral Majority to lobby politicians regarding the concerns of Christian fundamentalists.

1979 On January 1, the United States and the People's Republic of China establish formal diplomatic relations.

1979 On March 28, a major accident in the nuclear reactor at the Three Mile Island power plant near Harrisburg, Pennsylvania, raises concerns about nuclear power.

1979 On November 4, Iranian militants seize the U.S. embassy in Tehran, Iran, and take fifty-two hostages, whom they will hold for over a year.

1979 On December 27, the Soviet Union invades Afghanistan, beginning more than two decades of war and disruption in that country.

1980 Post-it notes are created by 3M chemist Arthur Fry.

1980 On February 22, the U.S. Olympic ice hockey team wins the gold medal, sparking national celebration.

1980 On April 12, the United States votes to boycott the Summer Olympics in Moscow to protest the Soviet presence in Afghanistan.

1980 On April 21, the Mariel boatlift begins, bringing 125,000 refugees from Cuba to Florida before being halted in September.

1980 In June, the all-news CNN cable TV network debuts.

1980 On August 19, a report issued by the *Los Angeles Times* indicates that 40 to 75 percent of NBA players use cocaine.

1980 On November 4, former California governor Ronald Reagan is elected president.

1980 On November 21, the "Who Shot J.R.?" episode of *Dallas* draws the largest television audience of all time.

1980 On September 4, Iraq begins an eight-year war with Iran.

1980 On October 2, in his last fight, heavyweight boxer Muhammad Ali is defeated by World Boxing Council champion Larry Holmes.

1980 On December 8, former Beatles musician John Lennon is shot and killed in New York City.

1981 Nintendo's *Donkey Kong* is the most popular coin-operated video game.

1981 NASA launches and lands the first reusable spacecraft, the space shuttle.

1981 On January 13, the National Collegiate Athletic Association (NCAA) votes to sponsor women's championships in twelve sports after the 1981–82 season.

1981 On January 20, American hostages held at the U.S. embassy in Tehran, Iran, are released on the day of President Ronald Reagan's inauguration.

1981 On January 23, the United States withdraws support for the Marxist government of Nicaragua and begins to support antigovernment rebels known as Contras.

1981 On March 26, comedian Carol Burnett wins a $1.6 million libel lawsuit against the tabloid *National Enquirer.*

1981 On March 30, President Ronald Reagan and three others are wounded in an assassination attempt in Washington, D.C.

1981 On July 29, Great Britain's Prince Charles marries Lady Diana Spencer in an event televised around the world.

1981 On August 1, the Music Television Network (MTV) starts offering music videos that soon become as important as the actual music.

1981 On September 21, Sandra Day O'Connor is confirmed as the first woman to serve on the U.S. Supreme Court.

1982 The compact disc is introduced.

1982 The popular movie *E.T.: The Extra-Terrestrial* sets box office records.

1982 Michael Jackson's album *Thriller* is the year's most popular recording.

1982 Americans frustrate themselves trying to solve Rubik's Cube, a popular puzzle.

1982 On April 2, Argentina invades the Falkland Islands off its coast, sparking a short war with Great Britain, which claims the islands.

1982 On June 7, Graceland, the late Elvis Presley's Memphis, Tennessee, home, is opened as a tourist attraction.

1982 On July 27, acquired immune deficiency syndrome (AIDS) is officially named.

1982 On September 15, *USA Today* becomes the first national newspaper.

1982 On October 7, *Cats* opens on Broadway in New York City and will become the decade's most popular musical.

1983 First lady Nancy Reagan announces a "War on Drugs."

1983 Sally Ride becomes the first woman astronaut in space when she joins the crew of the space shuttle *Challenger.*

1983 Actor Paul Newman introduces his own line of spaghetti sauces to be sold in grocery stores; he uses the proceeds to benefit charities.

1983 On February 28, the farewell episode of the sitcom *M*A*S*H* is seen by 125 million viewers.

1983 On March 23, President Ronald Reagan proposes a space-based antimissile defense system that is popularly known as "Star Wars."

1983 On April 18, terrorists bomb the U.S. embassy in Beirut, Lebanon, killing sixty-three.

1983 On September 1, the Soviet Union shoots down a Korean Air Lines flight that has strayed into its airspace, killing 269.

1983 On October 25, three thousand U.S. soldiers invade the Caribbean island nation of Grenada to crush a Marxist uprising.

1983 In November, Cabbage Patch Kids dolls, with their soft faces and adoption certificates, become the most popular new doll of the Christmas season.

1984 Trivial Pursuit becomes the nation's most popular board game.

1984 *The Cosby Show* debuts on NBC.

1984 Rap group Run-DMC is the first rap group to have a gold album.

1984 Apple introduces a new personal computer, the Macintosh, with a dramatic advertising campaign.

1984 On November 6, Ronald Reagan is reelected president.

1984 On December 3, a Union Carbide plant in Bhopal, India, leaks poison gas that kills two thousand and injures two hundred thousand.

1985 Nintendo Entertainment System, a home video game system that has brilliant colors, realistic sound effects, and quick action, is introduced to the United States.

1985 On March 16, U.S. journalist Terry Anderson is kidnapped in Lebanon; he will be held until December 4, 1991.

1985 In April, Coca-Cola changes the formula of its popular soft drink and the public reacts with anger and dismay, prompting the company to reissue the old formula as Classic Coke.

1985 On July 13, British rock star Bob Geldof organizes Live Aid, a charity concert and album to aid the victims of African famine.

1985 On October 2, the death of handsome movie star Rock Hudson from AIDS raises awareness about the disease.

1986 Country singer Dolly Parton opens a theme park in Tennessee called Dollywood.

1986 On January 28, the space shuttle *Challenger* explodes upon liftoff, killing the six astronauts and one teacher who were aboard.

1986 On February 26, Robert Penn Warren is named the first poet laureate of the United States.

1986 On April 26, a serious meltdown at the Chernobyl nuclear power plant near Kiev, Ukraine, releases a radioactive cloud into the atmosphere and is considered a major disaster.

1986 On May 1, in South Africa, 1.5 million blacks protest apartheid (the policy of racial segregation). Around the world, foreign governments place sanctions on South Africa.

1986 On June 10, Nancy Lieberman becomes the first woman to play in a men's professional basketball league when she joins the United States Basketball League.

1986 On July 15, the United States sends troops to Bolivia to fight against drug traffickers.

1986 On July 27, Greg LeMond becomes the first American to win France's prestigious Tour de France bicycle race.

1986 In October, it is discovered that members of the Reagan administration have been trading arms for hostages in Iran and illegally channeling funds to Contras in Nicaragua. This Iran-Contra scandal will eventually be investigated by Congress.

1986 On November 22, twenty-one-year-old Mike Tyson becomes the youngest heavyweight boxing champion when he defeats World Boxing Council champ Trevor Berbick.

1987 On March 19, televangelist Jim Bakker resigns after it is revealed that he has been having an adulterous affair with church secretary Jessica Hahn.

1987 On June 25, Soviet leader Mikhail Gorbachev announces *perestroika,* a program of sweeping economic reforms aimed at improving the Soviet economy.

1987 On October 3, Canada and the United States sign a free-trade agreement.

1987 On October 17, the stock market experiences its worst crash in history when it drops 508 points.

1987 On November 11, Vincent van Gogh's painting *Irises* is sold for $53.9 million.

1988 McDonald's opens twenty restaurants in Moscow, Russia.

1988 Singer Sonny Bono is elected mayor of Palm Springs, California.

1988 On February 5, former Panamanian dictator General Manuel Noriega is charged in a U.S. court with accepting bribes from drug traffickers.

1988 On February 14, Ayatollah Khomeini of Iran calls author Salman Rushdie's book *The Satanic Verses* offensive and issues a death sentence on him. The author goes into hiding.

1988 On April 14, Soviet forces withdraw from Afghanistan after ten years of fighting in that country.

1988 On July 3, believing it is under attack, a U.S. warship shoots down an Iran Air passenger liner, killing 290 passengers.

1988 On November 8, Vice President George Herbert Walker Bush is elected president.

1988 On December 21, Pan Am Flight 747 explodes over Lockerbie, Scotland, killing 259 on the flight and 11 on the ground. Middle Eastern terrorists are eventually charged with the crime.

1989 On March 24, the Exxon *Valdez* oil tanker runs aground in Alaska, spilling 240,000 barrels of oil and creating an environmental disaster.

1989 In May, more than one million Chinese demonstrate for democracy in Beijing.

1989 In June, Chinese troops crack down on demonstrators in Tiananmen Square, drawing attention to the repressive government.

1989 On August 9, Colin R. Powell becomes the United States' first black chairman of the Joint Chiefs of Staff.

1989 On August 23, the Soviet states of Lithuania, Latvia, and Estonia demand autonomy from the Soviet Union. Later, across the former Soviet-dominated region, Soviet republics and satellite countries throw off communist control and pursue independence.

1989 On August 24, former baseball star Pete Rose is banned from baseball for life because it is believed that he bet on games in which he was involved.

1989 On October 15, Wayne Gretzky of the Los Angeles Kings becomes the National Hockey League's all-time leading scorer with his 1,850th point.

1989 On October 17, a major earthquake hits the San Francisco, California, area.

1989 On December 16, American troops invade Panama and seize dictator General Manuel Noriega. Noriega will later be convicted in U.S. courts.

1989 On December 22, the Brandenburg Gate in Berlin is officially opened, allowing people from East and West Berlin to mix freely and signaling the end of the Cold War and the reunification of Germany.

1990 The animated sitcom *The Simpsons* debuts on the FOX network.

1990 Ken Burns's documentary *The Civil War* airs on PBS.

1990 British scientist Tim Berners-Lee invents the World Wide Web.

1990 On April 25, the Hubble Space Telescope is deployed in space from the space shuttle *Discovery.*

1990 On July 26, President George Herbert Walker Bush signs the Americans with Disabilities Act, which provides broad protections for those with disabilities.

1990 On August 2, Iraq invades Kuwait, prompting the United States to wage war on Iraq from bases in Saudi Arabia. Much of this conflict, called the Persian Gulf War, is aired live on television and makes CNN famous for its coverage.

1990 On October 3, East and West Germany are reunited.

1991 Mass murderer Jeffrey Dahmer is charged with killing fifteen young men and boys near Milwaukee, Wisconsin.

1991 On March 3, U.S. general Norman Schwarzkopf announces the end of the Persian Gulf War.

1991 In October, confirmation hearings for U.S. Supreme Court justice nominee Clarence Thomas are carried live on television and feature Anita Hill's dramatic accusations of sexual harassment. Despite the charges, Thomas is confirmed.

1991 On November 7, Los Angeles Lakers basketball star Earvin "Magic" Johnson announces that he has contracted the HIV virus.

1991 On December 8, leaders of Russia and several other former Soviet states announce the formation of the Commonwealth of Independent States.

1992 On April 29, riots erupt in Los Angeles, California, following the acquittal of four white police officers in the beating of black motorist Rodney King. The brutal beating had been filmed and shown widely on television.

1992 On May 21, Vice President Dan Quayle criticizes the CBS sitcom *Murphy Brown* for not promoting family values after the main character has a child out of wedlock.

1992 In August, the Mall of America, the nation's largest shopping mall, opens in Bloomington, Minnesota.

1992 On August 24, Hurricane Andrew hits Florida and the Gulf Coast, causing a total of over $15 billion in damage.

1992 On October 24, the Toronto Blue Jays become the first non-U.S. team to win baseball's World Series.

1992 On November 3, Arkansas governor Bill Clinton is elected president, defeating incumbent George Herbert Walker Bush and strong third party candidate H. Ross Perot.

1992 On December 17, the United States, Canada, and Mexico sign the North American Free Trade Agreement (NAFTA).

1993 Jack "Dr. Death" Kevorkian is arrested in Michigan for assisting in the suicide of a terminally ill patient, his nineteenth such action.

1993 On February 26, six people are killed when terrorists plant a bomb in New York City's World Trade Center.

1993 On April 19, more than eighty members of a religious cult called the Branch Davidians are killed in a mass suicide as leaders set fire to their compound in Waco, Texas, following a fifty-one-day siege by federal forces.

1993 In July and August, the Flood of the Century devastates the American Midwest, killing forty-eight.

1994 Tiger Woods becomes the youngest person and the first black to win the U.S. Amateur Golf Championship.

1994 Special prosecutor Ken Starr is appointed to investigate President Bill Clinton's involvement in a financial scandal known as Whitewater. The investigation will ultimately cover several scandals and lead to impeachment proceedings against the president.

1994 In January, ice skater Nancy Kerrigan is attacked by associates of her rival, Tonya Harding, at the U.S. Olympic Trials in Detroit, Michigan.

1994 On May 2, Nelson Mandela is elected president of South Africa. The black activist had been jailed for decades under the old apartheid regime and became the country's first black president.

1994 On August 11, major league baseball players go on strike, forcing the cancellation of the playoffs and World Series.

1994 On November 5, forty-five-year-old boxer George Foreman becomes the oldest heavyweight champion when he defeats Michael Moorer.

1995 On April 19, a car bomb explodes outside the Alfred P. Murrah Federal Office Building in Oklahoma City, Oklahoma, killing 168 people. Following a manhunt, antigovernment zealot Timothy McVeigh is captured, and later he is convicted and executed for the crime.

1995 On September 1, the Rock and Roll Hall of Fame opens in Cleveland, Ohio.

1995 On September 6, Cal Ripken Jr. of the Baltimore Orioles breaks the long-standing record for most consecutive baseball games played with 2,131. The total reaches 2,632 games before Ripken removes himself from the lineup in 1998.

1995 On October 3, former football star O. J. Simpson is found not guilty of the murder of his ex-wife and her friend in what many called the "trial of the century."

1996 Three years after the introduction of H. Ty Warners's Beanie Babies, the first eleven toy styles are retired and quickly become collector's items.

1996 On September 26, American astronaut Shannon Lucid returns to Earth after spending 188 days in space—a record for any astronaut.

1996 On November 5, Bill Clinton is reelected to the presidency.

1997 Researchers in Scotland successfully clone an adult sheep, named Dolly.

1997 The Hale-Bopp comet provides a nightly show as it passes by the Earth.

1997 Actress Ellen DeGeneres becomes the first openly gay lead character in her ABC sitcom *Ellen.*

1997 On January 23, Madeleine Albright becomes the first woman sworn in as U.S. secretary of state.

1997 On March 27, thirty-nine members of the Heavens Gate religious cult are found dead in their California compound.

1997 On April 13, Tiger Woods becomes the youngest person and the first black to win a major golf tournament when he wins the Masters with the lowest score ever.

1997 On June 19, the play *Cats* sets a record for the longest-running Broadway play with its 6,138th performance.

1997 On June 20, four major tobacco companies settle a lawsuit with states that will cost companies nearly $400 billion.

1997 On June 28, boxer Mike Tyson is disqualified when he bites the ear of opponent Evander Holyfield during a heavyweight title fight.

1997 On July 5, the *Pathfinder* spacecraft lands on Mars and sends back images and rock analyses.

1997 On August 31, Britain's Princess Diana is killed in an auto accident in Paris, France.

1998 Mark McGwire of the St. Louis Cardinals sets a single-season home run record with seventy home runs.

1998 The final episode of the popular sitcom *Seinfeld* is watched by an estimated audience of seventy-six million.

1998 On January 22, Unabomber Ted Kaczynski is convicted for a series of mail bombings and sentenced to life in prison.

1998 On March 24, the movie *Titanic* wins eleven Academy Awards, tying the record set by *Ben-Hur* in 1959.

1998 On April 10, a new drug for male impotence known as Viagra hits the market and is a popular sensation.

1998 On August 7, terrorists explode bombs outside the U.S. embassies in Nairobi, Kenya, and Dar es Salaam, Tanzania.

1998 In November, former professional wrestler Jesse "The Body" Ventura is elected governor of Minnesota.

1998 On December 19, the House of Representatives initiates impeachment proceedings against President Bill Clinton, but the U.S. Senate acquits Clinton on two charges in early 1999.

1999 The U.S. women's soccer team wins the World Cup by defeating China.

1999 On March 24, NATO launches a bombing campaign against Serbia to stop its actions in Kosovo.

1999 On March 29, the Dow Jones Industrial Average closes above 10,000 for the first time in history thanks to a booming stock market dominated by high-tech companies.

1999 On April 20, in Littleton, Colorado, two students go on a vicious shooting spree, killing themselves and twelve other students.

1999 On September 24, *IKONOS,* the world's first commercial, high-resolution imaging satellite, is launched into space; it can detect an object on Earth as small as a card table.

2000 The world wakes up on January 1 to find that the so-called "Y2K" computer bug had failed to materialize.

2000 In May, Eminem releases his *Marshall Mathers LP,* which sells 1.76 million copies in its first week, becoming the fastest-selling album by a solo artist of all time.

2000 The fourth Harry Potter book, *Harry Potter and the Goblet of Fire,* is released in July and sets new publishing sales records.

2000 Tiger Woods becomes the youngest golfer to win all four Grand Slam golf tournaments.

2000 The first inhabitants of the International Space Station take up residence in orbit over the Earth.

2000 In November, outgoing First Lady Hillary Rodham Clinton wins a seat in Congress as a senator representing New York state.

2000 On December 12, over a month after Election Day, Texas governor George W. Bush is declared the winner of the presidential race against Vice President Al Gore after contentious vote recounting in Florida is ordered stopped by the Supreme Court. Bush takes Florida by a margin of 527 votes and edges Gore in the Electoral College by only four votes.

2000 On December 28, squeezed by "big box" retailers like Wal-Mart, Montgomery Ward announces it will be closing its doors after 128 years in business.

2001 Wikipedia is launched.

2001 On April 1, a U.S. spy plane collides with a Chinese fighter jet and is forced to land on Chinese soil, causing an international incident.

2001 The first draft of the human genome, a complete sequence of human DNA, is published.

2001 The "dot com bubble" bursts, leading to widespread bankruptcies in the software and Internet industries.

2001 On September 11, nineteen terrorists hijack four planes, flying two into the twin towers of the World Trade Center in New York City and one into the Pentagon in Arlington, Virginia. The fourth plane goes down in a field in Pennsylvania during a fight over the controls and fails to reach its intended target, believed to be the White House.

2001 In October, Afghanistan, accused of harboring terrorist training camps and 9/11 mastermind Osama bin Laden, is invaded by the United States and its allies, initiating the so-called War on Terror.

2002 Europe introduces its first universal currency, the Euro, initially accepted in twelve countries.

2002 The U.S. State Department issues its report on state sponsors of terrorism, singling out seven countries: Cuba, Iran, Iraq, Libya, North Korea, Sudan, and Syria.

2002 The United States begins detaining suspected terrorists without trial at its military base in Guantanamo Bay, Cuba.

2002 Halle Berry wins the Academy Award for best actress, becoming the first African American to win the honor.

2002 Bulgaria, Estonia, Latvia, Lithuania, Romania, Slovakia, and Slovenia, all former Soviet bloc nations, are invited to join the North Atlantic Treaty Organization (NATO).

2003 On February 1, the space shuttle *Columbia* disintegrates during reentry, scattering the craft's debris across the United States and killing all seven astronauts aboard.

2003 SARS, a new respiratory disease, first appears in Hong Kong before spreading around the world.

2003 In the face of mass global protests, the United States invades Iraq on March 19 as part of its continuing war on terror. By April 9, the capital city of Baghdad is taken. The weapons of mass destruction that were reported to be harbored by Iraqi dictator Saddam Hussein and were the publicly stated reason behind the invasion are never found.

2003 On December 13, Saddam Hussein is found hiding in a bolt hole in an Iraqi village.

2004 Online social network Facebook is founded.

2004 On March 11, Madrid, Spain, is the target of the worst terrorist attacks since September 11, 2001; 191 people are killed and 2,050 wounded in a series of coordinated train bombings.

2004 George W. Bush is elected to a second term by a wider margin than in 2000.

2004 On December 26, a tsunami caused by an earthquake measuring 9.3 on the moment magnitude scale in the Indian Ocean kills over three hundred thousand people across eleven countries in Southeast Asia and Sri Lanka.

2005 The video-sharing Web site YouTube is launched.

2005 Prince Charles, the heir to the throne of Great Britain, marries his longtime love, Camilla Parker Bowles.

2005 In June, pop star Michael Jackson is acquitted of child molestation charges.

2005 On July 7, coordinated bombings on three trains and a bus kill fifty-six people in London, England.

2005 On July 26, American cyclist Lance Armstrong wins his record seventh-straight Tour de France.

2005 On August 29, Hurricane Katrina makes landfall on America's Gulf Coast. The resulting destruction, largely centered on New Orleans, Louisiana, after the city's levee system fails, leads to billions of dollars in damage and over eighteen hundred deaths. The federal government is widely criticized for its slow reaction to the disaster, with rapper Kanye West famously declaring on live television, "George Bush doesn't care about black people."

2005 In November, French surgeons perform the world's first face transplant.

2006 The issue of global warming becomes a mainstream subject of discussion with the release of former vice president Al Gore's film *An Inconvenient Truth* and the accompanying book of the same name.

2006 The *Oxford English Dictionary* adds the verb "google" to its pages.

2006 Online social network Twitter is launched.

2006 The United States reaches a population of three hundred million only thirty-two years after hitting the two hundred million mark.

2006 Pluto is downgraded from planetary status, reducing the number of planets in the solar system to eight.

2006 On February 22, the one billionth digital song is downloaded from Apple's iTunes store.

2006 Riding a backlash against the ongoing wars in Iraq and Afghanistan and dissatisfaction with the George W. Bush administration, the Democratic Party wins back majorities in both houses of Congress for the first time in twelve years.

2006 On December 30, Iraqis execute former president Saddam Hussein.

2007 President George W. Bush announces that 21,500 more troops will be sent to Iraq as part of a "surge" to stem the ongoing guerrilla attacks being carried out against U.S. troops and Iraqi civilians by Iraqi dissidents and Arab terrorists.

2007 On the night of February 17, pop star Britney Spears, increasingly under media scrutiny for her erratic behavior, shaves her head and lashes out against paparazzi and reporters who had been tailing her.

2007 Apple introduces the iPhone.

2007 In the wake of Barry Bonds setting a new home run record amongst whispers of his use of performance-enhancing drugs, the Mitchell Report is released, detailing a year-long investigation into the widespread abuse of steroids in major league baseball.

2008 The Iraq troop surge is judged largely a success by July, eighteen months after it was implemented.

2008 On August 17, swimmer Michael Phelps sets a new Olympic record when he wins his eighth gold medal.

2008 With the September 15 collapse of lending firm Lehman Brothers, a major panic sweeps the world financial markets. Along with the collapse of the housing bubble, these are the first clear signals of the onset of the Great Recession, the worst global economic crisis since the Great Depression.

2008 On November 4, U.S. senator Barack Obama of Illinois becomes the first African American elected president of the United States.

2009 Barack Obama's historic inauguration on January 20 draws over one million people to the National Mall in Washington, D.C.

2009 Upon assuming office, President Barack Obama orders the closing of the Guantanamo Bay detention center and passes a $75 billion economic stimulus package.

2009 On April 15 (tax day), protests break out across the country, marking the beginning of the loosely affiliated Tea Party movement. Although lacking a single guiding organization or national leader, the conservative, ostensibly grassroots, movement is united by its concern over certain types of government spending and increasing federal deficit levels.

2009 On June 25, pop star Michael Jackson is found dead of an apparent prescription drug overdose. His passing ignites worldwide mourning and an outpouring of grief from hundreds of millions of fans, despite the singer's legal and personal troubles through the 1990s and the first decade of the 2000s.

2009 On October 31, jobless claims break the 10 percent barrier for the first time since the Great Recession began.

2009 With the situation in Iraq less dire and attacks by the Afghan Taliban on the rise, President Barack Obama announces a surge of thirty thousand more troops in Afghanistan.

Bowling, Beatniks, and Bell-Bottoms

Pop Culture of 20th- and 21st-Century America

1980s

Prosperity and Conservatism

When Ronald Reagan (1911–2004) won the 1980 presidential election over the president then in office, Jimmy Carter (1924–), he inherited an economy in disarray. Unemployment was high and so were prices. People were ready for a change in both the style and the substance of their leader, and Reagan gave it to them. Within a few years, the economy turned around. Inflation (the measure of the rise in prices) dropped, jobs were created, and the size of the government shrank. As Reagan told Americans during his successful 1984 re-election campaign, "America is back and standing tall" and "It's morning in America."

If you were in the right demographic—that is, if you were young, white, and well educated—it was indeed a good decade to be an American. A new social group called "young urban professionals," or yuppies, enjoyed the Reagan-era boom a great deal. As managers and professionals working in urban areas, these yuppies enjoyed rising incomes and they spent their money lavishly. Large corporations also fared well under the Reagan administration, which had cut back sharply on regulations that limited business activities. The 1980s became known for its cut-throat business climate as many companies merged or were taken over.

Although many Americans enjoyed the benefits of an improving economy, others did not. African Americans in general did not fare well in comparison to the rest of the population, and those in inner cities fared the worst. Homelessness rose dramatically in the 1980s, thanks to

1980s At a Glance

WHAT WE SAID:

Dude: Guy; also used as a conversational filler. The term was widely used in such 1980s teen movies as *Fast Times at Ridgemont High, Bill and Ted's Excellent Adventure,* and on the "Wayne's World" segments of TV's *Saturday Night Live.*

Diss: To insult someone; this term was one of many to come out of urban hip-hop culture.

Fresh: A term from hip-hop culture, used to express approval, as in "That tune is fresh."

Glass ceiling: An invisible obstacle that blocks the advancement of women or minorities in an organization. Though most legal forms of job discrimination were removed in the 1980s, many groups still felt that a glass ceiling limited their access to better jobs.

"Go ahead—make my day!": These words, originally uttered by Detective Harry Callahan (played by Clint Eastwood) in the 1983 film *Sudden Impact,* were later used by President Ronald Reagan daring lawmakers to pass a law that he wanted to veto.

"Just Say No": This anti-drug slogan launched by first lady Nancy Reagan's drug war program soon became a popular response to anything that should be avoided.

"PC": The abbreviation for "politically correct," a term used to describe someone who was careful not to offend anyone, especially a member of an ethnic or other subgroup.

"Reach out and touch someone": Accompanied by a catchy song, this advertising jingle urged Americans to use AT&T's long distance telephone service.

Sucks: Is inadequate or undesirable, as in "The rising cost of living sucks."

"Where's the Beef?": This question was barked out by an elderly lady who could not find the beef in the skimpy hamburger she bought at the leading hamburger chain. Wendy's used this humorous pitch to try to gain some ground against hamburger giant McDonald's; presidential candidate Walter Mondale also used it to question opponent Gary Hart's programs in the 1984 presidential race.

Yuppies: Literally "young urban professionals" (or "young upwardly-mobile professionals"); this somewhat derisive term referred to a class of people who got rich quick in the 1980s and flaunted their wealth.

WHAT WE READ:

***Cosmos* (1980):** Astronomer Carl Sagan's clear explanations about the evolution of the universe, and a close tie-in with a PBS-TV series of the same name, helped make his book a favorite.

***The Far Side* (1980–95):** Gary Larson's off-the-wall, single-panel comic strip was one of the most popular comic strips in America.

cuts in welfare programs. Some estimates placed the number of homeless in America as high as three million.

The Reagan administration also made changes in American foreign policy that added some proverbial "heat" to the Cold War (the long standoff between the United States and the communist Soviet Union). At the center of foreign policy was what came to be called the

***A Light in the Attic* (1981):** Shel Silverstein's collection of humorous poems and drawings is one of the best-selling children's works of all time.

***Jane Fonda's Workout Book* (1982):** This book and the videos that followed captured a popular exercise craze at its height. Women, mostly, hopped around the house doing Fonda's workout and hoped to sculpt their bodies to look like the gracefully aging movie star's.

***USA Today* (1982–):** The Gannett Company's boldly-colored paper offered itself as the first national newspaper. Critics called the paper superficial and labeled it "McPaper," but its innovations were soon copied by countless newspapers.

***Iacocca* (1984):** The best selling nonfiction book of the decade was the biography of Lee Iacocca, the auto executive who, with the help of the federal government, helped revive the nation's number three automaker, Chrysler.

***Fatherhood* (1986):** This humorous collection of anecdotes by America's favorite comedian, Bill Cosby, was helped along by the fact that Cosby played America's favorite father on the sitcom *The Cosby Show.*

***All I Really Need to Know I Learned in Kindergarten* (1988):** Offering such truisms as "play fair" and "don't hit people," self-titled philosopher Robert Fulghum offered common-sense wisdom.

***Clear and Present Danger* (1989):** The best selling fiction book of the 1980s, this novel about the CIA's involvement in the war on drugs was one of many of Tom Clancy's books to sell over a million copies.

Novels by Stephen King or Danielle Steel: Horror writer King and romance novelist Steel were the top two authors of the decade, as judged by the number of books they placed at the top of the *New York Times* best-seller list (King, twelve titles; Steel, eight).

WHAT WE WATCHED:

***60 Minutes* (1968–):** This hour-long, hard-hitting news exposé was consistently near the top in TV ratings throughout the 1980s.

***Dallas* (1978–91):** Fifty-three percent of TV viewers learned who shot evil oil baron J. R. Ewing on November 21, 1980, making the episode the most-watched in TV history.

The Empire Strikes Back* (1980) and *Return of the Jedi (1983): These two sequels to *Star Wars* (1977) continued the space saga, brought new innovations in special effects, and were accompanied by a blizzard of marketing and merchandise tie-ins.

"Reagan Doctrine," which held that any country that was an enemy of communism was a friend of the United States. With this in mind the United States backed pro-American governments in Latin America, sent Marines to Lebanon to assist in peacekeeping, and invaded the small Caribbean country of Grenada to support an anti-Marxist government. Reagan's successor to the presidency, former vice president

1980s At a Glance (continued)

***Dynasty* (1981–89):** This prime-time soap opera centered on the lives of the oil-rich Carrington family.

***Raiders of the Lost Ark* (1981):** This joint effort by filmmaking giants Steven Spielberg and George Lucas featured the adventures of Indiana Jones (played by Harrison Ford) and re-established the adventure movie as an important genre.

***E.T.: The Extra-Terrestrial* (1982):** This charming film about an alien who is stranded on Earth and wants to return home helped make director Steven Spielberg famous.

MTV (1982–): This cable TV channel offered a range of programming related to pop, rock, and rap music, including a heavy dose of music videos. The channel became a favorite of American youth and changed the way performers made music by making it vital to produce a video to support any major single.

***The Cosby Show* (1984–92):** The most popular show of the late 1980s, this sitcom focused on the daily life of the Huxtables, an African American family led by father Bill Cosby.

***The Breakfast Club* and *St. Elmo's Fire* (1985):** These movies about high-schoolers and twenty-somethings, respectively, made stars of a group of actors known as the "Brat Pack," including Emilio Estevez, Rob Lowe, Demi Moore, and Molly Ringwald.

***Wall Street* (1987):** No film better captured the spirit of corporate greed than this Oliver Stone–directed drama about the morally corrupt practices of a corporate raider played by Michael Douglas. This movie included the famous line, "Greed is good."

WHAT WE LISTENED TO:

The Police: This rock group and its lead singer Sting mixed reggae with rock to come up with some of the decade's greatest hit songs, including "Don't Stand So Close to Me" (1980) and "Every Breath You Take" (1983).

Madonna (1958–): With her albums *Madonna* (1983), *Like a Virgin* (1985), *True Blue* (1986), *You Can Dance* (1988), and *Like a Prayer* (1989), Madonna established herself as a dance pop diva and shocked people with her bold sexuality.

***1999* (1983):** This album by Prince was the dance hit of the decade, featuring the title cut and "Little Red Corvette."

***She's So Unusual* (1984):** Orange-haired Cyndi Lauper was the first female vocalist to produce four Top Five hits from her debut album. The perky artist's hits were "Girls Just Want to Have Fun," "Time After Time," "She Bop," and "All Through the Night."

George H. W. Bush (1924–), continued Reagan's policies upon his election in 1988.

Reagan's anticommunist actions and his strong anticommunist public statements put pressure on Soviet leaders that eventually led to the most important political event of the decade—the collapse of the Soviet Union. Mikhail Gorbachev (1931–) became the leader of the Soviet Union in

Run-DMC: The rap group earned the first rap gold record in 1984 and continued rising through the music charts until hitting the top in 1986 with its album, *Raising Hell.*

***Thriller* (1984):** This 1984 album by pop superstar Michael Jackson took marketing to new levels by packaging the music with a special effects–laden video that received heavy play on MTV, a barrage of advertising, and a movie about making the video.

"I Can't Live Without My Radio": LL Cool J's hit single was featured in the first rap movie, *Krush Grove,* in 1985. The charismatic LL Cool J led rappers' discouragement of the violence highlighted in so called "gangsta" rap.

"We Are the World" (1985): Featuring some of the biggest pop and rock stars of the decade, this single helped raise money for the starving in Africa and was featured at the Live Aid benefit concerts in 1985.

***Trio* (1987):** Leading country singer Emmylou Harris paired with Linda Ronstadt and Dolly Parton to create a million-selling album that revived old-time country sounds.

Milli Vanilli: This pop group received the 1989 Grammy Award for Best New Artist—then had to return the award when it was found that someone else had done the singing on their record. They are remembered now as a symbol of the triumph of style over substance in the 1980s.

WHO WE KNEW:

Jim Bakker (1940–) and his wife, Tammy Faye Bakker (1942–2007): This husband-and-wife team of televangelists came to national attention in 1987 when it was learned that Jim had paid off a church secretary to conceal their sexual liaison. The episode revealed what many felt was the hypocrisy of preachers who were getting rich off their ministries.

Jerry Falwell (1933–2007): This religious leader founded the Moral Majority in 1979, a group that pursued the political agenda of the Religious Right. Falwell used television sermons to raise millions of dollars for conservative causes throughout the 1980s.

Rock Hudson (1925–1985): When this popular sex-symbol and film star of the 1950s and 1960s died of AIDS in 1985, it helped raise the nation's consciousness about the deadly disease.

Willie Nelson (1933–): This country star released more than twenty albums in the 1980s, starred in movies, and helped organize the Farm Aid concerts to raise money for struggling American farmers.

Ronald Reagan (1911–2004): More than a president, this former Hollywood actor was a symbol of America in the 1980s. Strongly probusiness, he urged Americans to consume their way to a better life, which led to a booming economy.

1985. He scaled back Soviet commitments overseas and tried to increase the openness in the tightly controlled communist state. Soon, the changes he tried to make slipped out of his control and, over the next several years, the government collapsed. The most dramatic moment in the collapse came in 1989, when the Berlin Wall that had divided the communist East Germany from the capitalist West Germany was torn down. By 1991, the Cold War—which had lasted more than forty years—was finally over.

1980s At a Glance (continued)

Princess Diana (1961–1997) and Prince Charles (1948–): Almost one billion people around the world watched this royal British couple wed in an elaborate ceremony on July 29, 1981. Two sons (jokingly referred to as "an heir and a spare"), a divorce, and Diana's death in a car crash in 1997 followed during the subsequent sixteen years.

Dr. Ruth Westheimer (1928–): The jolly, thrice-married "Dr. Ruth" hosted a cable talk show on which the German-accented psychologist doled out sexual advice to callers.

Reagan's economic and foreign policy conservatism also encouraged political conservatism on domestic issues. A coalition of religious groups, primarily representing fundamentalist Christian churches (those who interpret the Bible literally), worked together to push their political issues. Known as the "Religious Right," they backed amendments to require school prayer and ban abortions. Though neither proposed amendment succeeded, the Religious Right was successful in shaping debate about these issues.

These larger social, economic, and political forces all had an impact on American popular culture. Perhaps the biggest impact was made by yuppies, an important demographic subgroup of the larger baby boomer generation. Knowing that yuppies and boomers were such avid consumers, American manufacturers, musicians, television programmers, and movie producers all created products suited to yuppie and boomer tastes. From the vehicles they drove (minivans and sport utility vehicles, known as SUVs), to the clothes they wore (Ralph Lauren and J.Crew), to the TV shows they watched *(Dallas, Knots Landing,* and *Murphy Brown),* to the coffee they drank (Starbucks), the yuppies' influence was felt.

As always, popular culture reflected the energy and interests of a range of Americans. Some African American performers, such as Bill Cosby (1937–) and Michael Jackson (1958–2009), appealed to mainstream tastes. Others, such as filmmaker Spike Lee (1957–), stamped their unique and even radical visions on popular culture. In music, rappers slowly made progress in popularizing their distinctive style. Some, like Run-DMC (1982–), gained real popularity, while others, like 2 Live Crew (1986–), scared white America with their vulgarity and violent lyrics. Conservatives vented their frustrations and led their crusades over the AM-radio airwaves, while liberals were assumed to be in charge of most television stations and National Public Radio. Whether American popular culture came from the center or from the fringes, it continued to contribute to the great variety and vitality of the American experience.

1980s

Commerce

After nearly a decade of slow business growth and declining consumer confidence, the American economy experienced a period of strong performance and inflating confidence beginning in 1982. The cheerleader for this decade of economic optimism was none other than the nation's president, Ronald Reagan (1911–2004). He told America that it was time to get government off of people's backs. He reduced government regulations, reduced taxes, and let businesses seek their maximum profit.

The 1980s were an era in which big businesses got even bigger. Many large companies sought to gain power by purchasing competitors. Corporate buyouts, mergers, and "leveraged buyouts"—in which a corporate raider gained control of another company's stock and forced its sale—became commonplace. This intense corporate competition was symbolic of the age, as an intense focus on profit and getting ahead seemed to be common among many Americans. Gordon Gecko, the evil hero of the 1987 film *Wall Street,* put it best when he said, "Greed is good."

For the average American, the booming economy of the 1980s meant a rise in disposable income—the money that people have to spend on items they do not need, but want. Many Americans engaged in "conspicuous consumption," purchasing luxury goods to show others that they were doing well. Others simply spent more freely on the wide range of consumer goods available. Several successful companies capitalized on the free spending of the 1980s. The Starbucks Coffee Company expanded dramatically in the 1980s when it began offering intensely flavored (and high-priced) coffee drinks at its upscale coffee shops. Retailers like J.Crew and Land's End offered stylish clothes in mail-order catalogs that filled America's mailboxes. The Home Shopping Network—a cable TV channel—offered a steady stream of discount merchandise with aggressive selling techniques. IBM, long one of the nation's leading companies, got even bigger by selling personal computers to Americans who were just learning how to use the complicated, ever more powerful machines. In short, Americans loved spending money in the 1980s.

Home Shopping Network

The Home Shopping Network (HSN) was the first major business to earn huge profits by combining two beloved American pastimes, shopping and watching **television** (see entry under 1940s—TV and Radio in volume 3). Followed by many imitators, the network has expanded from small beginnings on a Florida **radio** (see entry under 1920s—TV and Radio in volume 2) station to become a multibillion-dollar corporation that broadcasts into nearly one hundred thousand homes.

The Home Shopping Network got its start in St. Petersburg, Florida, where the company is still headquartered. In 1977, real estate developer Roy Speer (1932–) and radio broadcaster Lowell "Bud" Paxson (1935–) started a radio call-in shopping club called Suncoast Bargaineers. The club was so successful that by 1982, Speer and Paxson moved it to a local **cable TV** (see entry under 1970s—TV and Radio in volume 4) channel, renaming it Home Shopping Network. The concept of HSN was that while items were being advertised live on the air by attractive hosts, viewers could call on the telephone and order them. Home Shopping Network concentrated on selling to older middle-class and working-class Americans. Their most popular products included costume jewelry, cooking pots and utensils, house-cleaning equipment, and celebrity clothing and cosmetic lines. The idea of shopping without leaving home had great appeal to the viewing public. By 1985, HSN was carried on national cable stations and had over seventy-five thousand regular customers.

The Home Shopping Network remained the only television shopping channel until 1986, when seventeen other companies began to compete with them. One of these, QVC (the abbreviation stands for Quality, Value, Convenience), has grown to be HSN's major competitor in television sales, although QVC tends to appeal to a younger, wealthier audience than HSN. In 1995, Barry Diller (1942–), the former chairman of Fox Network, bought HSN and became its chairman. Under Diller's leadership, HSN, Inc. acquired Ticketmaster and the USA and SciFi cable networks.

However, HSN is still best known for television sales. The network's sales shows are broadcast live twenty-four hours a day, every day except Christmas. The shows reach millions of viewers and offer them not necessities, but the little luxuries of life, available with a phone call and a credit card. The shows are often hosted by sports heroes or celebrities of the past who gain new fame advertising their products on HSN. Lucky callers may even get to talk to the hosts on the air. In 1996, HSN opened the Museum of Modern Shopping in St. Petersburg to showcase their most popular products.

By 2011 HSN, Inc. operated two separate businesses, Home Shopping Network and Cornerstone, the latter of which primarily markets home and apparel brands and operates approximately twenty retail stores. Responding to technological developments and social trends, HSN became the first company of its kind to offer multiple shopping applications for mobile electronic devices such as the Apple **iPhone** (see entry under 2000s—Music in volume 6) and Verizon Android.

Tina Gianoulis

For More Information

Farah, Joseph. "Don't Flip That Dial or You'll Miss the Bargain of a Lifetime!" *TV Guide* (October 4, 1986): pp. 40–43.

Hayes, Cassandra. "Cashing in on the Home Shopping Boom." *Black Enterprise* (February 1995): pp. 120–27.

HSN. http://www.hsn.com (accessed July 5, 2011).

Motavalli, John. "Home Is Where the Mart Is." *Channels: The Business of Communications.* (Vol. 6, December 1986): pp. 77–79.

Paisner, Daniel. *Tele-shopping: A Guide to Television's Home Shopping Networks.* New York: Warner, 1987.

IBM

Founded by Charles Ranlett Flint (1850–1934) as the Computing-Tabulating-Recording Company in 1911, the company that in 1924 became known as International Business Machines (IBM) started out making shopkeepers' scales and counting machines for the U.S. Census Bureau. IBM became famous for its mainframe computers in the 1950s and 1960s when it was one of America's largest and most powerful corporations. Some say the blue suits worn by the sales staff inspired the press to nickname the company "Big Blue"; others say it was the color of the "big blue boxes," the large mainframe computers of the 1960s. Always seen as one of the safe bets of American commerce, IBM's collapse in the late 1980s sent shockwaves through the world of computing. By the late 1990s, however, Big Blue had managed to revive its reputation as a major computer manufacturer.

One of the first computers with virtual memory: the IBM System/370 mainframe. © F8 IMAGING/HULTON ARCHIVE/GETTY IMAGES.

In the early days under chief executive Thomas Watson Jr. (1914–1993), IBM concentrated on sales. Although it was later to gain a reputation as having a bullying approach to business, IBM was actually very good to its employees in its early years. In the 1930s IBM was among the first companies to offer insurance and paid vacations; it even had a fund for the widows of IBM workers killed in World War II (1939–45). Less commendably, the company has been implicated in assisting the Nazi government in Germany during the war years by supplying it with technology.

With the invention of electronic computing after World War II, IBM entered the mainframe computer market. The sharp-suited sales force enjoyed a lifetime employment policy and sold some of the most technically advanced machines of the time. IBM's domination of the computer market lasted until the 1970s, when smaller companies like **Apple Computer** (see entry under 1970s—The Way We Lived in volume 4) proved quicker to exploit the new **personal computer** (PC; see entry under 1970s—The Way We Lived in volume 4) market. Although the company made record profits of $6.6 billion in 1984—the year it was portrayed as an evil "Big Brother" in a famous advertisement aired by Apple—its dominance was beginning to fade. Barely a decade later, it reported losses of $8.5 billion.

The company rebounded in the first decade of the new century, relocating more than half of its workforce to India, selling its personal computer business to competitor Lenovo, and focusing more on research. In 2009, the company was awarded the National Medal of Technology and Innovation by President **Barack Obama** (see entry under 2000s—The Way We Lived in volume 6) for its Blue Gene supercomputer. IBM also came to the public's attention in 2011 for its artificial intelligence program, Watson, which beat human champions on the TV game show *Jeopardy!*

Over the years, IBM's image has swung from gentle giant to evil empire and back again. For most of the twentieth century, however, it was a symbol of powerful and efficient American enterprise. In 2011, after seeing a steady rise in profits throughout the economic recession of the early 2000s, IBM was ranked the seventh most profitable company in the world by *Fortune* magazine. At the start of the twenty-first century, IBM remains one of the giants among several large computing firms competing for dominance in the global market.

Chris Routledge

For More Information

Black, Edwin. *IBM and the Holocaust: The Strategic Alliance Between Nazi Germany and America's Most Powerful Corporation.* New York: Crown, 2001.

Campbell-Kelly, Martin, and William Aspray. *Computer: A History of the Information Machine.* 2nd ed. Boulder, CO: Westview Press, 2004.

Carroll, Paul. *Big Blues: The Unmaking of IBM.* New York: Crown, 1993.

Gerstner, Louis V. *Who Says Elephants Can't Dance? Inside IBM's Historic Turnaround.* New York: HarperBusiness, 2002.

IBM. http://www.ibm.com (accessed December 13, 2011).

Maney, Kevin. *The Maverick and His Machine: Thomas Watson, Sr., and the Making of IBM.* New York: Wiley, 2003.

Maney, Kevin, Steve Hamm, and Jeffrey M. O'Brien. *Making the World Work Better.* Upper Saddle River, NJ: IBM Press, 2011.

J.Crew

J.Crew, a brand of sportswear first made available in 1983, added a new dimension to casual dress in America. The brand's catalog—which in 1994 was mailed in eighteen "issues" with a circulation of four million copies per issue—presented J.Crew clothing in photographs that illustrated a particular lifestyle. Models were not pictured in standard poses against standard backgrounds as they had been in department-store catalogs for years. Instead, J.Crew models were pictured making Thanksgiving dinner with "family," spending a day at the beach, playing croquet at a garden party, or lounging in a city loft apartment.

The catalog pictures promoted more than the clothes—stonewashed **jeans** (see entry under 1950s—Fashion in volume 3), **T-shirts** (see entry under 1910s—Fashion in volume 1), and roll-neck sweaters; indeed, they promoted an approach to life. Many young adults, college students, and early career professionals adopted the J.Crew look as their own in the 1980s and 1990s.

By the start of the new millennium, the brand had become worth over $800 million. The company continued expanding or introducing new lines over the next decade, including Crewcuts for kids and Madewell, an all-denim label. The company also focused on opening retail locations throughout the decade, which totalled approximately three hundred by 2011. In 2010, J.Crew agreed to be taken private for $3 billion by two large equity firms in a management-led buyout of shareholders.

Sara Pendergast

For More Information

jcrew.com. http://www.jcrew.com (accessed July 10, 2011).
Rudolph, Barbara. "The Chic Is in the Mail." *Time* (July 17, 1989): p. 74.

Starbucks

For decades, **Dunkin' Donuts** (see entry under 1940s—Food and Drink in volume 3) franchises offered consumers the equivalent of a working man's coffee break: a simple cup of **coffee** (see entry under 1990s—The Way We Lived in volume 5), accompanied by a sweet, tasty donut. Starbucks, on the other hand, established a strong market position by portraying itself as a franchise that caters to an upscale, sophisticated coffee drinker. It features not only coffee but also specialty drinks such as latte (coffee mixed with

Starbucks is one of the world's most successful coffee franchises. © PAUL J. RICHARDS/AFP PHOTO/GETTY IMAGES.

steamed or hot milk), Frappuccino (a low-fat, blended beverage), and chai (a strong tea-based drink). Plenty of exotic coffee mixtures, along with assorted confections, pastries, mugs, and coffee-brewing equipment, can be found at Starbucks. Indeed, much of the success flavored, blended coffees and such terms as latte and chai can be traced to Starbucks.

Starbucks is based in Seattle, Washington, and has been in existence since 1971. Back then, it was a retail store, located in the city's Pike Place Market, which offered coffee beans and coffee-making products, but not prepared, ready-to-drink beverages. The firm's rise to international prominence did not begin for another fifteen years, until Howard Schultz (1954–), a company executive who was intrigued by Italy's espresso bars and coffee-house culture, opened Il Giornale, modeled after the traditional Italian coffeehouse. Schultz offered his customers various European-style coffees. Then in 1987, he bought out the company's two original founders, and began opening similar coffeehouses down the Pacific Coast, in Canada, in the Midwest and the Northeast, and, eventually in Europe and Asia. That first year, 17 Starbucks stores existed. By 1990, the number had risen to 84 stores. By 1995, the number of stores was 676; by 2000, it was over 3,300. By 2007, this number had nearly tripled to an incredible 15,000 Starbucks locations worldwide.

Starbucks is a favored daily morning pit stop for white-collar urban commuters, as well as a suburban hangout. It is both a coffee house and a retail store selling coffee beans and brewing equipment. A typical Starbucks is artfully designed, with tables and chairs of various sizes, modern fixtures, and subdued lighting. Most locations look less like a traditional coffee shop and more like a cozy living space, where patrons are encouraged to get comfortable, enjoy coffee and conversation, and listen to the folksy rock piped in over the loudspeaker. In fact, it is the Starbucks "look" that is as responsible for attracting customers as the company's product.

By the late 1990s, Starbucks had become the number-one specialty coffee outlet in the United States, yet it has attracted as many critics as fans. Its detractors view Starbucks as a glorified **fast-food** (see entry under 1920s—Food and Drink in volume 2) outlet that caters to pretentious **yuppies** (see entry under 1980s—The Way We Lived in volume 5) who believe themselves to be sophisticated and cutting-edge as they order their Frappuccinos, but instead are being sold what amounts to fast food with fancy names. Many perceive the company to be the epitome of corporate over-expansion, whose inescapable sameness is blamed for the demise of small, more unique businesses and increased homogeneity in the American marketplace.

During the economic recession that began in 2008, consumers were forced to cut back their luxury spending, and the chain saw its stock price decline by over 50 percent. Sales were further impacted by the entry of lower-priced chains such as **McDonald's** (see entry under 1940s—Food and Drink in volume 3) and Dunkin' Donuts into the gourmet coffee business. By 2009, the chain had shut down nearly one thousand of its stores, cutting eighteen thousand jobs. In the first decade of the century, Starbucks was also boycotted by groups criticizing the chain for various offenses, including oversaturating the market and wasting water and by groups demanding that it use fair-trade coffee. As of 2009, Starbucks operated a total of 16,706 locations in over fifty countries.

Rob Edelman

For More Information

Schultz, Howard. *Onward: How Starbucks Fought for Its Life Without Losing Its Soul.* New York: Rodale, 2011.

Schultz, Howard, and Dori Jones Yang. *Pour Your Heart Into It: How Starbucks Built a Company One Cup at a Time.* New York: Hyperion, 1997.

Starbucks Coffee. http://www.starbucks.com (accessed July 11, 2011).

1980s

Fashion

By the 1980s, American fashion had recovered from polyester leisure suits and hot pants—the strange fashion trends of the 1970s—and was trending towards far more tasteful conventions. Leading the way were the nation's president and first lady, Ronald Reagan (1911–2004) and Nancy Reagan (1921–). Like Jacqueline Kennedy (1929–1994), who set fashion trends in the 1960s as the first lady, the Reagans wore tasteful, expensive clothes. They held lavish parties at the White House, and they made it fashionable to be glamorous again.

The biggest factor pushing America's new love for high fashion in the 1980s was rising prosperity and the tendency of wealthier Americans to want to show off their wealth. Many did so by dressing in the latest styles offered by American and European designers. In America, designers like Donna Karan (1948–) and Ralph Lauren (1939–) offered sophisticated styles for women, including stylish clothes that could be worn to work. For men, the nicely tailored "power suit" came back into style and was the uniform of success for most business men. Late in the decade, however, a new trend toward casual clothes in the workplace emerged. Starting as "casual Fridays," by the 1990s many workplaces permitted casual clothing all the time.

Brand names became increasingly important in the 1980s. High-fashion designers such as Ralph Lauren and Calvin Klein (1942–) offered jeans and casual clothes that could be purchased by middle-class people, who liked wearing a prestige label. Izod polo shirts—featuring a distinctive alligator logo on the chest—were one of the hottest single items of the decade. The polo shirt was one of the standard garments in the preppy style, which was most popular among college-age people. On the other hand, exercise clothes—running suits and stretchy spandex tights, for example—also boomed in popularity, helped along by a brief rage for ripped sweatshirts made popular by the movie *Flashdance* (1983).

Models had always been used to show off women's clothes in fashion shows and magazines. In the 1980s, several of these women became celebrities in their own right—in fact, they became known as "supermodels." These supermodels became associated with the brands of clothing, perfume, or makeup that they sold. Their salaries and level of public recognition soared.

Goth Culture

The "gothic" look is basic black. © MAGICINFOTO/ SHUTTERSTOCK.COM.

In the late 1800s, the word "gothic" was used to describe a popular type of novel, typified by an atmosphere of mystery and romance, filled with dark foreboding and supernatural occurrences. *Frankenstein,* written by Mary Shelley (1797–1851) and published in 1818, is an example of a gothic novel. In the 1980s, a youthful subculture emerged that used the word "gothic" or "goth" to describe itself. Dressing in black, often with hair dyed black against pale skin, these modern goths share the dark, brooding tone of the gothic novels of the nineteenth century. Young people usually become goths because they feel alienated, or separate, from mainstream society. They are often rejected or ridiculed by their more "normal" peers for one reason or another. Goths embrace that rejection by dressing and acting outlandishly and forming their own separate society. The goth subculture is based not only on magic, mysticism, and a romanticization of the dark sides of life, but also on tolerance, free-thinking, and challenging traditional gender roles.

Goth culture emerged from the **punk** (see entry under 1970s—Music in volume 4) subculture of the early 1980s. Punks, too, wore distinctive clothing. They had dyed hair, and pierced body parts as well, although their style was more confrontational and angry and less mystical than the goths. In the mid-1980s, Anthony H. Wilson (1950–), the manager of a rock band called Joy Division, characterized his band as "gothic" and the term stuck and came to define a lifestyle. That lifestyle is a sort of postmodern medievalism, where devotees combine flowing Victorian clothes with metal studs and buckles, read vampire stories and fairy lore, and listen to the music of bands like Bauhaus, Siouxsie and the Banshees, and The Cure.

Adults sometimes worry about the brooding, depressed nature of many goth youth, and their obsession with death and the supernatural. There have been studies of self-harm among goths. The *British Medical Journal* concluded in 2006 that "identification as belonging to the Goth subculture was the best predictor of self harm and attempted suicide." Most goths, however, value humor and gentle theatrics over anger and revenge.

By the 2000s, goth culture had fragmented into several sub-scenes. The new generation adopted goth's dark aesthetic and nonconformist attitude in a new, minimalist culture known as **"emo"** (see entry under 2000s—Music in volume 6) and later "scene." Others, primarily the older, original goth adherents and Europeans, invested themselves in developing the "rivethead" scene, which involved industrial music and militaristic dress. The explosion of the **rave** (see entry under 1940s—TV and Radio in volume 3) scene prompted the development of a hybrid culture known as "cybergoth," which fused the neon colors and copious drug consumption of the partiers with the dark, flamboyant elements of goth.

Tina Gianoulis

For More Information

Acker, Kerry. *Everything You Need to Know about the Goth Scene.* New York: Rosen, 2000.

Baddeley, Gavin. *Goth Chic: A Connoisseur's Guide to Dark Culture.* 2nd ed. London: Plexus, 2006.

Katz, Jon. "What Hath Goth Wrought? A Much Maligned Subculture Hits the Net to Beat a Bad Rap." *Utne Reader* (No. 96, November-December 1999): pp. 104–8.

Kilpatrick, Nancy. *The Goth Bible: A Compendium for the Darkly Inclined.* New York: St. Martin's Griffin, 2004.

Preppy

The word "preppy" was originally used to describe someone who attended a private college-preparatory high school (called a "prep" school). Gradually, the term came to mean any young person who was upper class and snobbish, and also described the style of clothes such people wore. The word was widely used in the 1980s as a negative term describing the superficial values of those with a privileged lifestyle. By 2000, it was mostly found in articles about fashion. Its meaning had become less negative, simply describing the button-down collars and loafers that are considered the preppy style.

Though the word "preppy" had been used on the East Coast for many years, it was widely popularized by two books published a decade apart. *Love Story,* a novel published in 1970 by Erich Segal (1937–), tells about the romance between two college students, one an Italian American working-class woman and the other an upper-class jock. In the book, Jenny Cavilleri never lets rich Oliver Barrett forget their class differences, and she scornfully calls him a "preppy." Both the book and the film that was made from it the same year were very popular, and "preppy" entered the American vocabulary nationwide.

The "preppy" look. © MICHAEL HEVESY/JUPITERIMAGES/GETTY IMAGES.

The second book, published in 1980, was the **best-seller** (see entry under 1940s—Commerce in volume 3) *The Official Preppy Handbook,* edited by Lisa Birnbach (1957–), which was a satirical look at the lifestyle of young adults of the upper class. In an intimate style that showed how well Birnbach knew her subjects, she poked fun at those who came from "old money"; that is, the spoiled children of families who had been wealthy for a long time. Birnbach included chapters on which silly nicknames were appropriate for the children of aristocrats ("Muffy" for girls, "Chip" for boys), and how to dress casually while still showing off one's wealth.

Both *Love Story* and *The Official Preppy Handbook* achieved popularity because they ridiculed the arrogance of the upper classes. Such ridicule is the intention of those who use the silly, snappy word "preppy" to deflate those who may think their wealth or background places them above others.

Tina Gianoulis

For More Information

Austin, Stephanie. *The Preppy Problem.* New York: Fawcett, 1984.

Banks, Jeffrey. *Preppy: Cultivating Ivy Style.* New York: Rizzoli, 2011.

Birnbach, Lisa, ed. *The Official Preppy Handbook.* New York: Workman, 1980.

Birnbach, Lisa, with Chip Kidd. *True Prep: It's a Whole New Old World.* New York: Knopf, 2010.

Schoenstein, Ralph. *The I-Hate-Preppies Handbook: A Guide for the Rest of Us.* New York: Simon & Schuster, 1981.

Supermodels

For decades, models were lanky, attractive, but nameless individuals who strode down fashion-show runways wearing the latest creations of clothing designers. Their faces and bodies appeared in fashion advertisements printed in women's magazines, or on the covers of such publications. Occasionally, a model earned acclaim by becoming a movie actress. However, the rise of the "supermodel" in the 1980s and 1990s resulted in an individual model winning fame simply for being a "personality." Her earning the title "supermodel" meant that she was a superstar, as celebrated as any top film, **television** (see entry under 1940s—TV and Radio in volume 3), or sports star.

Supermodel Christie Brinkley was one of the most prominent supermodels of the 1980s.

The supermodel concept is the creation of a media eager to capitalize on a familiar and beautiful face. A supermodel mingled publicly with the rich and famous. She was cited in gossip columns, appeared on television talk shows, and partied at the trendiest nightspots. No longer anonymous, she now became famous. Supermodels such as Christie Brinkley (1954–), Cindy Crawford (1966–), Naomi Campbell (1970–), Kate Moss (1974–),

Christy Turlington (1969–), Claudia Schiffer (1970–), and Linda Evangelista (1965–) all became recognizable to the celebrity-obsessed public not just for their beauty but for their distinct personalities. Crawford exuded a confident sexuality, while the paper-thin Moss put forth a cute boyishness. A supermodel's fame allowed her to take control of her career, market herself, and earn higher fees. For example, in 1991, Turlington signed a contract with Maybelline that paid her $800,000 for twelve days' work each year. Four years later, Schiffer reportedly earned $12 million for her various modeling assignments.

Models became supermodels for a number of reasons. In the 1980s, fashion designers such as Calvin Klein (1942–) began advertising on television and billboards, resulting in the most popular models becoming more familiar to the masses. At the same time, **Hollywood** (see entry under 1930s—Film and Theater in volume 2) actresses in general became less glamorous. Even though their careers consisted of nothing more than posing, models still embraced old-style glamour, which allowed them to replace actresses as symbols of luxury and wealth. In this regard, many viewed supermodels not so much as individuals but as ideals.

In the late 1990s, opinion-makers began trumpeting the fall of the supermodel, observing that many star actresses had re-embraced traditional glamour and were winning the best modeling assignments. During the decade that followed, clothes also took a decided turn toward the casual, lessening the industry's dependence on glamour. There have been exceptions to this trend, however, beginning with the 1999 discovery of 14-year-old Gisele Bündchen (1980–) in a Brazilian **McDonald's** (see entry under 1940s—Food and Drink in volume 3). Dubbed "the sexy models," she and a succession of Brazilian models put to rest the "heroin chic" image embodied by predecessors such as Moss. In the first decade of the twenty-first century, some of these younger models, including Heidi Klum (1973–) and Tyra Banks (1973–), also created successful **reality TV** (see entry under 1990s—TV and Radio in volume 5) shows based on their lives, in their cases as *Project Runway* and *America's Next Top Model,* respectively.

Rob Edelman

For More Information

Gross, Michael. *Model: The Ugly Business of Beautiful Women.* New York: Warner Books, 1996.

Halperin, Ian. *Shut Up and Smile: Supermodels, the Dark Side.* Los Angeles: Ogo Books, 1999.

Supermodels-online.com. http://www.supermodels-online.com (accessed July 12, 2011).

1980s

Film and Theater

Special effects had begun to play a minor role in films in the 1970s, but it was in the 1980s that special effects came to be used to make a wide range of movies more exciting, spectacular, and, usually, violent. Although *E.T.: The Extra-Terrestrial* (1982) used special effects to tell the gentle story of an alien who wished to go home, it was the exception to the rule. Most of the time, special effects were used to depict on-screen violence and action. Two sequels to the popular 1977 film *Star Wars—The Empire Strikes Back* (1980) and *Return of the Jedi* (1983)—set the standard for space movies. Four *Star Trek* movies in the decade followed suit. Films like *The Terminator* (1984) and *Robocop* (1987) used special effects to tell their violent science-fiction stories.

President Ronald Reagan's (1911–2004) crusade against communism during the 1980s was helped along by a high number of patriotic films. In *Red Dawn* (1984) and *Invasion U.S.A.* (1985), resourceful action heroes fight off Soviet invaders. *Missing in Action* (1984) and *Rambo: First Blood Part II* (1985) send action heroes to Vietnam to win victories that American forces could not win in the real war. Lighter movies like *Top Gun* (1986) made fighting for America seem so glamorous and fun that the military used the movie for recruiting. Not all films shared this rosy vision of the American military, however. The films *The Killing Fields* (1984), *Full Metal Jacket* (1987), and *Born on the Fourth of July* (1989) all presented serious and heartfelt criticisms of war.

Horror films grew in popularity during the decade, dominated by the "slasher" film *Friday the 13th* (1980) and its many sequels; the suspenseful *A Nightmare on Elm Street* (1984) franchise; and by sequels to the 1978 film *Halloween.* Many of these films centered around a psychotic male killer stalking and killing women, which feminists said revealed many Americans' hostility towards the achievements of women.

Comedies released during the decade showed Hollywood's lighter side. Stars like Eddie Murphy (1961–), Bette Midler (1945–), Steve Martin (1945–), Whoopi Goldberg (1955–), and Robin Williams (1952–) all starred in popular comedies. Some of the most notable comedies of the decade were "dumb comedies" like *Airplane!* (1980), *Caddyshack* (1980), *Fast Times at Ridgemont High* (1982), and *Naked Gun* (1988). Unlike mainstream comedies, which relied on witty wordplay and quick timing between actors, the dumb comedies featured seemingly stupid characters and lots of physical humor.

Theater enjoyed a boom during the 1980s as well, thanks in large part to big productions that were launched on Broadway and then toured around the world. Big budget shows like *Cats* (which opened in New York in 1982), *Les Misérables* (1987), and *The Phantom of the Opera* (1988) ran for years and were promoted with original cast albums and merchandise. The New York theater scene was also helped by the fact that many Hollywood stars returned to the stage in this decade for limited—and very popular—performances.

Airplane!

Airplane! (1980) was a new kind of motion-picture comedy. It skillfully satirized a popular film genre, one that was dramatic and serious in nature yet at the same time ripe for parody. In the case of *Airplane!,* the genre to be made fun of was the **disaster movie** (see entry under 1970s—Film and Theater in volume 4), set on board a commercial airplane or an ocean liner. In such films, the plane or ship becomes imperiled in mid-journey and is in danger of crashing or sinking.

Airplane! may be most directly linked to *Zero Hour* (1957), scripted by Arthur Hailey (1920–) and based on his **television** (see entry under 1940s—TV and Radio in volume 3) play "Flight Into Danger" (1955). However, the film's most celebrated film ancestors are *Airport* (1970), based on a best-selling novel by Hailey, and its three sequels: *Airport 1975*

"Surely, you can't be serious": Julie Hagerty (left), Lorna Patterson, Leslie Nielsen, and Peter Graves in the 1980 comedy Airplane! © PARAMOUNT/ THE KOBAL COLLECTION/ART RESOURCE, NY.

(1974); *Airport '77* (1977); and *The Concorde—Airport '79* (1979). The standard storyline in such films first involves the introduction of the characters, from pilots to stewardesses, passengers to airport personnel. Their personalities and interpersonal relationships are revealed: A pilot might be romantically involved with a stewardess, for example, or a key member of the airport staff might be overworked and overstressed. At first, the flight that becomes the film's centerpiece is ordinary, like any one of thousands of others. Then peril enters the picture. In *Zero Hour,* the pilots are stricken with food poisoning; in *Airport,* a disturbed man is intent on blowing up himself and the plane. The tension then increases. Will a pilot or other able-bodied individual somehow manage to safely land the plane? How will the different passengers respond to the danger at hand? Will there be heroes? Will there be cowards? Who will live? Who will die? Indeed, will the plane crash, and will all those on board perish?

Such scenarios are dramatic in nature, but they also may be seen as essentially corny, making them ripe for parody. In *Airplane!,* the main characters are a former military pilot (played by Robert Hays, 1947–), whose experiences in battle have made him terrified of flying, and his ex-girlfriend (Julie Hagerty, 1955–), a stewardess who has ended their relationship because of his inability to overcome his trauma. The gags become increasingly sillier and pile up continually, as he pursues her on board her flight and then must operate the plane after the pilots can no longer fly it.

Airplane! established the careers of its director-creators, Jim Abrahams (1944–), Jerry Zucker (1947–), and David Zucker (1950–). Adding to the overall sense of mirth was their inspired casting of veteran performers such as Lloyd Bridges (1913–1998), Leslie Nielsen (1922–2010), Robert Stack (1919–2003), and Peter Graves (1925–2010). All these people, who had earned stardom as dramatic actors, went about parodying just the sort of roles they often played on screen. Because of his success in *Airplane!,* Nielsen enjoyed a second career playing bumbling police detective Frank Drebin in the television comedy series *Police Squad* (1982) and its big-screen follow-ups: *The Naked Gun: From the Files of Police Squad!* (1988); *The Naked Gun 2½: The Smell of Fear* (1991); and *Naked Gun 33⅓: The Final Insult* (1994). All satirized police dramas in the same manner that *Airplane!* made fun of disaster films. The Zucker brothers were the creators of *Police Squad,* and David Zucker directed the initial two *Naked Gun* features.

Rob Edelman

For More Information

Aronsky, Rory. "Airplane!" *Airodyssey.net.* http://www.airodyssey.net/ (accessed July 13, 2011).

Sklar, Robert. *Movie-Made America: A Cultural History of American Movies.* Rev. ed. New York: Vintage Books, 1994.

Blade Runner

Set in a futuristic Los Angeles, California, *Blade Runner* (1982) combines the genres (categories) of science fiction and the detective story. Director Ridley Scott (1937–) helmed this high-tech thriller about humans, androids (robots that look like human beings), and the relationships between them. The film is based on a short story by science fiction writer Philip K. Dick (1928–1982).

Rick Deckard (Harrison Ford, 1942–) is a former cop and an expert "blade runner"—someone who hunts down renegade androids and destroys them. The androids, known in the movie as "replicants," are almost human. They are stronger and faster but are made with strictly limited lifespans. Replicants were originally created to be slave labor "off-world," but some rebel, which is why blade runners exist.

The film opens with Deckard being pressed back into service by the Los Angeles Police Department (LAPD). Five murderous outlaw replicants have returned to Los Angeles, their location and purpose unknown. Deckard is ordered to find and terminate them.

As he carries out his assignment, Deckard begins to question the supposed distinctions between replicants and humans. The more he learns, the more uneasy he becomes with a system that designates replicants as nonhuman, fit only for slavery and early death. Deckard's confusion and disillusionment grow with each of the replicants he hunts down. His doubts reach their peak as he confronts Roy (Rutger Hauer, 1944–), the last of the group and the most dangerous. Roy has the chance to kill Deckard but spares his life. Then Roy's own built-in clock ticks its last. Even after Roy is dead, Deckard learns that he is not quite done with androids—his lover, Rachael (Sean Young, 1959–), is a replicant, too.

The film offers a depressing version of the future. Deckard's Los Angeles is a crowded, polluted, rainy neon jungle where many species of plants and animals exist only in replicant form, the originals having become extinct long ago. Overpopulation is so great that neon billboards everywhere tout the virtues of emigrating "off-world."

Director Scott later re-edited his film, and the revised version was released to theaters in 1993. The biggest changes involved eliminating the Deckard "voice-over" that narrated the original, and a new ending that was bleaker and less hopeful.

Justin Gustainis

For More Information

BRmovie.com. http://www.brmovie.com (accessed April 1, 2002).

Dick, Philip K. *Do Androids Dream of Electric Sheep?* New York: Ballantine Books, 1982.

Kerman, Judith. *Retrofitting Blade Runner.* 2nd ed. Madison: University of Wisconsin Press, 1997.

Sammon, Paul M. *Future Noir: The Making of Blade Runner.* 2nd ed. London: Gollancz, 2007.

Do the Right Thing

The 1989 film *Do the Right Thing* dealt with one of the most sensitive topics in American life: relations between the races. The controversial comedy-drama wowed movie critics, became a surprise hit at the box

Director and actor Spike Lee and actors Danny Aiello, Richard Edson, and John Turturro in a scene from the 1989 film Do the Right Thing.

office, and made writer and director Spike Lee (1957–) one of the most popular filmmakers in **Hollywood** (see entry under 1930s—Film and Theater in volume 2).

Set in New York City, *Do the Right Thing* featured a talented cast of actors. Danny Aiello (1936–) played Sal, a gruff Italian American pizza-parlor owner. John Turturro (1957–) played his headstrong son, Pino. Giancarlo Esposito (1958–) played Buggin' Out, an African American activist. Lee himself appeared as Mookie, a pizza deliveryman struggling to make ends meet. The film takes place on the hottest day of the summer in Brooklyn's Bedford-Stuyvesant neighborhood. Tensions are running high between Sal, who decorates his pizza parlor with photos of famous Italian celebrities, and his African American patrons, who prefer rap music over **Frank Sinatra** (1915–1998; see entry under 1940s—Music in volume 3). Sal's customers begin to question why all the businesses in the neighborhood are owned by whites or Asians. When

Buggin' Out starts a campaign to boycott Sal's pizzeria, the crisis reaches a boiling point. Violence erupts at the end, with Mookie, who struggles to see things from all points of view, caught in the middle.

Do the Right Thing raised a number of important questions, particularly in inner-city communities. For instance, why are there so few black-owned businesses in black neighborhoods? And at what point—and by what means—should the residents of those communities take action to address their grievances? The film does not offer any easy answers. In fact, it ends with quotes from two African American leaders of the **civil rights movement** (see entry under 1960s—The Way We Lived in volume 4), Martin Luther King Jr. (1929–1968) and Malcolm X (1925–1965), superimposed on the screen. One quote favors nonviolence; the other calls for resistance "by any means necessary."

Lee's powerful script earned him an Oscar nomination for Best Screenplay. Aiello was also nominated for his performance as Sal. Critics praised Lee's direction, particularly his use of handheld cameras. The rap group Public Enemy (1982–) contributed the film's memorable theme song, "Fight the Power." Today, *Do the Right Thing* is considered a classic. Lee moved on to other successful projects like *Malcolm X* (1992), *He Got Game* (1998) and *Inside Man* (2006).

Robert E. Schnakenberg

For More Information

Hardy, James Earl. *Spike Lee.* New York: Chelsea House, 1996.

Haskins, James. *Spike Lee: By Any Means Necessary.* New York: Walker and Co., 1997.

Lee, Spike, with Kaleem Aftab. *Spike Lee: That's My Story and I'm Sticking to It.* New York: Norton, 2005.

McDaniel, Melissa. *Spike Lee: On His Own Terms.* New York: Franklin Watts, 1998.

Parish, James Robert. *Today's Black Hollywood.* New York: Pinnacle Books, 1995.

Reid, Mark A. *Spike Lee's Do the Right Thing.* London: Cambridge University Press, 1997.

E.T.: The Extra-Terrestrial

Few commercial films succeed at mining box-office gold while still deeply touching the hearts of viewers, young and old. *E.T.: The Extra-Terrestrial* (1982) is one such motion picture. Directed by Steven Spielberg

Actor Henry Thomas as Elliott and his new alien friend, E.T., in a scene from the beloved 1982 film E.T.: The Extra-Terrestrial.

(1947–), *E.T.* spotlights the evolving relationship between a space alien and a bright, sensitive middle-class suburban ten-year-old named Elliott.

At the film's outset, a spaceship lands in the woods near Elliott's home. After being scared off by the presence of humans, who from the aliens' point of view are menacing, the aliens return to their craft and head back into space. However, one of them accidentally is left behind. The terrified creature, who comes to be known as E.T., is befriended by Elliott. The two communicate by instinct, and Elliott soon becomes painfully aware that his little pal is homesick and wishes to return to his own planet.

Within the realm of the science fiction (sci-fi) movie genre, *E.T.* was a new kind of film. Before *E.T.,* the aliens in most sci-fi dramas were villains. Generally the technology of the aliens, who were intent on invading and destroying Earth, was far superior to that of earthlings. Most of the classic "doom-and-gloom" sci-fi films were produced during the 1950s, at the height of the **Cold War** (1945–91; see entry under

1940s—The Way We Lived in volume 3), when the threat of a nuclear war with the Soviet Union loomed large.

At the time of its release, *E.T.* became the number-one moneymaking film in history, a record that has since been eclipsed, first by another Spielberg hit, ***Jurassic Park*** (see entry under 1990s—Print Culture in volume 5), in 1993. The film was rereleased in 2002, upon the occasion of its twentieth anniversary. *E.T.* is at once funny and exciting, clever and moving, magical and memorable. Arguably, it remains Spielberg's all-time most beloved film.

Rob Edelman

For More Information

Baxter, John. *Steven Spielberg.* London: HarperCollins, 1996.
Brode, Douglas. *The Films of Steven Spielberg.* Rev. ed. New York: Citadel Press, 2000.
Conklin, Thomas. *Meet Steven Spielberg.* New York: Random House, 1994.
Connolly, Sean. *Steven Spielberg.* Des Plaines, IL: Heinemann Library, 1999.
E.T.: The Extraterrestrial (film). Universal Pictures, 1982.
E.T.: The Extraterrestrial. The 20th Anniversary. http://www.et20.com (accessed December 14, 2011).
Ferber, Elizabeth. *Steven Spielberg: A Biography.* New York: Chelsea House, 1996.
Knight, Bertram T. *Steven Spielberg: Master of Movie Magic.* Parsippany, NJ: Crestwood House, 1999.
Mathison, Melissa, and Linda Sunshine. *E.T., the Extra-Terrestrial from Concept to Classic.* New York: Newmarket Press, 2002.
McBride, Joseph. *Steven Spielberg: A Biography.* 2nd ed. Jackson: University Press of Mississippi, 2010.
Powers, Tom. *Steven Spielberg: Master Storyteller.* Minneapolis: Lerner Publishers, 1997.
Rubin, Susan Goldman. *Steven Spielberg: Crazy for Movies.* New York: Abrams, 2001.
Schoell, William. *Magic Man: The Life and Films of Steven Spielberg.* Greensboro, NC: Tudor Publishers, 1998.
Taylor, Philip M. *Steven Spielberg: The Man, His Movies, and Their Meaning.* 3rd ed. New York: Contiuum, 1999.

Fatal Attraction

This 1987 film by director Adrian Lyne (1941–) was seen by some social critics as a warning about the dangers of adultery. Others called it an example of a backlash against feminism. Still others saw it simply as a first-class thriller.

Glenn Close has a disagreement with Michael Douglas in a scene from the 1987 thriller Fatal Attraction. © PARAMOUNT/ THE KOBAL COLLECTION/ART RESOURCE, NY.

Michael Douglas (1944–) plays Dan Gallagher, a lawyer whose work brings him into contact with wealthy, beautiful Alex Forrest, played by Glenn Close (1947–), in a departure from her usual role of nurturing mother figure. The two are instantly attracted to one another. Although Gallagher is married, and Alex knows it, the two engage in a brief, passionate affair.

When Gallagher tries to end the encounter (as both of them had agreed), Alex becomes enraged, revealing severe mental instability. She tells Gallagher that the affair is not over, and his going back to his wife and daughter will not make any difference to her.

Alex begins stalking Gallagher and his family. At first, she seems only intent on making Gallagher uncomfortable. When Gallagher refuses to return to her bed, however, Alex begins to escalate the harassment. She breaks into the Gallaghers' home and kills the family's pet rabbit. She takes the daughter for a terrifying roller-coaster ride. She tells Gallagher that she is pregnant with his child. Finally, Alex turns violent.

The film was financially successful and also generated considerable discussion across America about adultery, obsession, and the high cost of adventure.

Justin Gustainis

For More Information

Conlon, James. "The Place of Passion: Reflections on *Fatal Attraction.*" *Journal of Popular Film and Television* (Winter 1989): pp. 148–55.

Holmlund, Chris. "Reading Character with a Vengeance: The *Fatal Attraction* Phenomenon." *Velvet Light-Trap* (Spring 1991): pp. 25–36.

Leonard, Suzanne. *Fatal Attraction.* Malden, MA: Wiley-Blackwell, 2009.

Rohrkemper, John. "'Fatal Attraction': The Politics of Terror." *Journal of Popular Culture* (Winter 1992): pp. 83–89.

Friday the 13th

Originally dismissed as a low-budget "slasher flick," *Friday the 13th* has surprised its many critics by producing a long line of sequels, a host of imitators, and a lasting impact on America's popular culture.

The initial 1980 film was made on a shoestring budget of $600,000 by producer Sean S. Cunningham (1941–), who also directed and co-wrote the script. Costs were kept low by hiring a cast of unknown actors, with the exception of Betsy Palmer (1929–), an actress who made a number of films in the 1950s and who played Mrs. Voorhees in *Friday the 13th.*

The script, which was written in only two weeks, places a group of teenaged camp counselors at isolated Camp Crystal Lake, to prepare it for reopening after twenty years. The camp had been closed after inattentive counselors allowed young attendee Jason Voorhees to drown. The teenagers tease each other with legends of Jason's vengeful ghost—until an unseen figure starts killing them off. Most of the counselors are murdered in various gory ways (stabbing, impaling, and so on) until the last few survivors confront and kill the maniac, who turns out to be Mrs. Vorhees, insanely vengeful over her son's death, even after all this time. All is well, apparently—except Jason never drowned, and now he wants revenge for his mother's death.

The bloody dispatch of a series of teenagers has become a staple of the series, but it is only with the first sequel (1981's *Friday the 13th*

Part 2) that all the conventions fall into place. Jason, the murderous, hockey mask-wearing stalker, is apparently a supernatural creature who cannot be destroyed. In any given film in the series, Jason will be "killed" several times, but he always returns for more. In the climactic scene, Jason will appear to be *really* dead—until the next film, which will bring him back again, usually with no effort to explain the "resurrection."

Over the years, the producers have sought new contexts for Jason and his victims. Part 7 (*The New Blood*) pits Jason against a girl with psychokinetic powers (the ability to move physical objects with one's mind), similar to the main character in the film *Carrie* from the novel by Stephen King (1947–). Part 8 (*Jason Takes Manhattan*) moves the carnage to New York City, whereas 2002's *Jason X* sets the slaughter on a space station.

Justin Gustainis

For More Information

Bracke, Peter M. *Crystal Lake Memories: The Complete History of "Friday the 13th."* Los Angeles: Sparkplug Press, 2005.

Dika, Vera. *Games of Terror: "Halloween," "Friday the 13th," and the Films of the Stalker Cycle.* East Rutherford, NJ: Fairleigh Dickinson University Press, 1990.

Friday the 13th: The Website. http://www.fridaythe13thfilms.com (accessed July 14, 2011).

Grove, David. *Making "Friday the 13th": The Legend of Camp Blood.* Guildford, England: FAB, 2004.

Mayo, Mike. *VideoHound's Horror Show: 999 Hair-Raising, Hellish, and Humorous Movies.* Detroit: Visible Ink Press, 1998.

Ghostbusters

The 1984 film *Ghostbusters* offers a lighthearted take on the struggle between humans and supernatural evil. It represents a humorous counterpart to such "serious" films as *The Haunting* (1963) and *The Legend of Hell House* (1973).

The script was written by Dan Aykroyd (1952–) and Harold Ramis (1944–), who played the title characters (along with Bill Murray, 1950–, and Ernie Hudson, 1945–). Ivan Reitman (1946–) directed this "action comedy," which opens with three parapsychologists (researchers into the paranormal) played by Aykroyd, Ramis, and Murray, being fired from their academic jobs. They start a private firm, "Ghostbusters," hire a colleague (Hudson) and a secretary (Annie Potts, 1952–), and take jobs ridding New York of pesky ghosts.

Ernie Hudson (left), Bill Murray, Dan Aykroyd, and Harold Ramis on duty in New York City in a scene from the 1984 comedy Ghostbusters. © COLUMBIA/THE KOBAL COLLECTION/ART RESOURCE, NY.

After clearing out the apartment of Dana Barrett (Sigourney Weaver, 1949–), the Ghostbusters realize that her building is being used to summon the ancient Babylonian God, Gozer—an event that could bring on the end of the world. The terrible creature finally shows up and the Ghostbusters go to work. The film's title song (which included the oft-repeated "Who ya gonna call? Ghostbusters!"), by Ray Parker Jr. (1954–), was a hit single and a popular music video.

The hugely successful film was followed by *Ghostbusters II* in 1989. Director Reitman and the original cast returned to combat another supernatural threat to the world. New York's sewers are filling with pink slime, a sign of impending spiritual doom. The Ghostbusters determine that the spirit of a dead wizard, Vigo the Carpathian, is seeking to be reborn so that he can use sorcery to rule the world. For his reincarnation, Vigo targets the infant son of Dana Barrett. Aykroyd, Murray, and company are called to save the day once again.

The popular movies gave rise to the usual cultural artifacts: action figures, **video games** (see entry under 1970s—Sports and Games in volume 4), and trading cards. They also inspired an animated-cartoon television series, which ran from 1986 to 1991. *The Real Ghostbusters* took the main characters from the films and put them in humorously scary situations with ghosts and ghouls, not unlike those seen in the *Scooby-Doo* cartoon series.

Justin Gustainis

For More Information

Brown, Christopher. *The Official Ghostbusters Training Manual: A Guide to Catching Ghosts.* Yellow Springs, OH: Antioch, 1984.

Ghostbusters.net: Your Guide to Ghostbusters. http://www.ghostbusters.net/ghostbusters (accessed July 14, 2011).

Shay, Don, ed. *Making "Ghostbusters": The Screenplay.* New York: Zoetrope, 1985.

Indiana Jones Movies

The three *Indiana Jones* films were inspired by both the **James Bond** (see entry under 1960s—Film and Theater in volume 4) series and the "cliffhanger serials" popular in American theaters during the 1930s and 1940s. Directed by Steven Spielberg (1946–) and produced by George Lucas (1944–), the enormously successful films helped define popular moviemaking in the 1980s. Thanks to the combination of state-of-the art special effects, nonstop action, and a touch of religious mysticism, the original film resulted in several spinoffs that kept interest in Indiana Jones alive well into the 1990s.

Raiders of the Lost Ark (1981) introduces Indiana Jones (played by Harrison Ford, 1942–), globetrotting archaeologist and treasure hunter. Set in 1936, the film finds "Indy" competing with Nazi agents to locate the Ark of the Covenant, a powerful religious artifact. *Indiana Jones and the Temple of Doom* (1984) strands the hero in rural India, where he helps a village recover a sacred stone stolen by a renegade Hindu priest who practices black magic and human sacrifice. *Indiana Jones and the Last Crusade* (1989) introduces Indy's archaeologist father (Sean Connery, 1930–). Together, they foil a Nazi plot to find the Holy Grail, the legendary cup used by Jesus at the Last Supper.

Actor Harrison Ford has portrayed adventurer Dr. Henry "Indiana" Jones in four films. © COLUMBIA/ THE KOBAL COLLECTION/ART RESOURCE, NY.

The films inspired a series of adventure novels built around the Indiana Jones character as well as novelizations of the original movie scripts. Several **comic book** (see entry under 1930s—Print Culture in volume 2) series were also published; the longest of these were by **Marvel Comics** (1983-86; see entry under 1960s—Print Culture in volume 4) and Dark Horse Comics (1991-96). A computer adventure game, *Indiana Jones and the Infernal Machine,* was released in 1998, and other games followed. A **television** (see entry under 1940s—TV and Radio in volume 3) series, *Young Indiana Jones,* ran on ABC from 1991 to 1993. The series sent young Indy adventuring through the first two decades of the twentieth century, encountering real-life historical figures along the way. A fourth film in the franchise, *Indiana Jones and the Kingdom of the Crystal Skull*, was released in 2008, nearly two decades after the one preceding it. This film, set in the 1950s to explain the change in the 64-year-old Ford's appearance, has the hero fighting Cold War enemies. This film brought in more money at the box office than any of the three films preceding it and became the second-highest grossing film of 2008.

Justin Gustainis

For More Information

Kiernan, Bernard P. *The Indiana Jones Handbook.* Philadelphia: Quirk Books, 2008.

Luceno, James. *Indiana Jones: The Ultimate Guide.* New York: DK, 2008.

Madsen, Dan. *The Young Indiana Jones Chronicles: On the Set and Behind the Scenes.* New York: Bantam Books, 1992.

Rinzler, J. W., and Laurent Bouzereau. *The Complete Making of "Indiana Jones": The Definitive Story Behind All Four Films.* New York: Del Rey, 2008.

Vaz, Mark Cotta, and Shinji Hata. *From "Star Wars" to "Indiana Jones": The Best of the Lucasfilm Archives.* San Francisco: Chronicle Books, 1994.

Rambo

John Rambo was first introduced in the 1972 Vietnam war novel by David Morrell (1943–), *First Blood.* Rambo has just returned from serving in the Vietnam War (1954–75). While working with the elite Special Forces, he had been captured by the Viet Cong. He eventually escaped but was psychologically damaged by the experience. Drifting through Kentucky, he is harassed and arrested by a local sheriff. In response, Rambo snaps and reverts to a killing machine, with tragic results.

The novel was moderately successful and became a film in 1981. In the film version, Rambo, played by Sylvester Stallone (1946–), is still a Special Forces veteran of Vietnam, but his deadly skills are much more restrained. In the novel, Rambo kills without mercy; for him, it is war. But Stallone's is a kinder, gentler Rambo. He wounds many people, but kills no one, conforming to the mold of the "good guy" hero.

In 1985, *Rambo: First Blood Part II* sends the hero on a mission for the U.S. Central Intelligence Agency (CIA), which believes that American

Actor Sylvester Stallone has portrayed Vietnam War veteran John Rambo in four films. © CAROLCO/THE KOBAL COLLECTION/ART RESOURCE, NY.

prisoners may remain in Vietnam. Rambo's assignment: sneak in and find out for certain. Once in Vietnam, Rambo is betrayed, captured by the Vietnamese, and tortured by their Russian "advisors." He eventually escapes, to slaughter every Vietnamese and Russian soldier in the vicinity. The film was a huge financial success. For some, however, Rambo represented the kind of "kill-the-Commies" machismo (exaggerated masculinity) that had involved the United States in Vietnam in the first place.

In 1988, *Rambo III* finds Stallone's character meditating in a Thai monastery, where he is visited by his former commanding officer,

Colonel Sam Trautman. The Green Beret colonel has the dangerous mission of helping Afghan guerrillas combat the Soviet invaders of their country. Trautman asks for assistance, but Rambo refuses. Trautman goes in alone and is captured. Rambo rushes to Afghanistan, rescues his friend, and helps him mow down the Russians. Surprisingly, the film lost money, at least in its U.S. release. In 2008, twenty years after the previous film in the franchise, a fourth film was released, simply entitled *Rambo.* Directed and co-written by Stallone himself, this installment takes our hero to Burma, where he saves a group of missionaries captured by a military regime. Stallone claimed that the film, which was by far the most violent in the series with an estimated 263 kills (the others featured 1 kill, 69 kills, and 132 kills, respectively), was intended to draw the world's attention to Burma's longstanding humanitarian crisis.

A number of toy companies were licensed to produce Rambo action figures, as well as plastic guns and knives modeled after those used in the films. The Rambo character also saw action briefly as a **Saturday morning cartoon** (see entry under 1960s—TV and Radio in volume 4) character in the 1980s.

Justin Gustainis

For More Information

Morrell, David. *First Blood.* New York: M. Evans and Co., 1972.

Walsh, Jeffrey, and James Aulich, eds. *Vietnam Images: War and Representation.* Hampshire, UK: Macmillan Press, 1989.

1980s

Music

One of the biggest music stories of the 1980s actually involved a television network. A specialized cable channel, MTV (which stands for Music Television) went on the air in 1981. The cable channel soon made the music video an essential element of selling a hit song. Almost single-handedly, MTV made stars of Madonna (1958–), Michael Jackson (1958–2009), and the group Duran Duran. It helped bring rap music to the mainstream when it offered shows centered around this emerging musical form.

Rap music had been an underground musical form until the mid-1980s, but the band Run-DMC reached a mass audience with its first album in 1982. Its 1985 album *King of Rock* was an even bigger hit and helped make the band a regular feature on MTV. Other popular male rappers of the decade were LL Cool J (1969–) and Tone Loc (1966–); female rap artists included Salt-N-Pepa (1985–) and Queen Latifah (1970–). There were even white rappers such as the Beastie Boys. Even though many rappers and rap groups reached mainstream audiences, the controversy over the music of some groups, such as Public Enemy and 2 Live Crew (which was charged with obscenity), made it clear that rap music still had a dangerous edge.

The single best-known performer of the 1980s was Michael Jackson. His 1983 album *Thriller,* with its singles "Billie Jean" and "Beat It," made the former child star one of the richest performers in America and helped MTV establish itself. Jackson also helped pioneer trends in dance and dress. Other music sensations of the 1980s included Whitney Houston (1963–2012), who had seven consecutive number-one hits; Madonna, whose song "Material Girl" (1985) defined a generation of preteen girls who looked up to Madonna as an idol; Prince (1958–), an androgynous (showing both masculine and feminine tendencies) funk-rock player who had a smash hit with the album *1999* (1983) and a popular movie and album called *Purple Rain* (1984); and Bruce Springsteen (1949–), whose song "Born in the U.S.A." nearly became an alternative national anthem after its release in 1984. The popularity of several of these stars showed that both African Americans and women could easily reach the pinnacle of musical success.

Country music enjoyed a real resurgence in the 1980s, launching a number of new stars—Randy Travis (1959–), Ricky Skaggs (1954–), Reba McEntire (1955–), and Wynonna Judd (1964–) and Naomi Judd (1946–). Some older stars, such as Willie Nelson (1933–), Dolly Parton (1946–), George Jones (1931–), Waylon Jennings (1937–2002), and Merle Haggard (1937–), saw their careers revived. Several jazz musicians also reached mainstream audiences. Perhaps the best known were Sade (1959–), Wynton Marsalis (1961–), and Kenny G (1959–).

Compact Disc

Throughout the history of recorded sound, technological changes have periodically reshaped the music industry. One such change was the introduction of the 33 1/3-rpm long-playing record (LP; see entry under 1940s—Music in volume 3) and the 45-rpm "single" in 1948, which replaced the earlier 78 rpm record. Recorded at speeds of thirty-three and one-third and forty-five revolutions per minute, vinyl records improved the way people listened to music and they offered new opportunities for musical innovation. The introduction of the compact disc (CD) in 1983 was another momentous change. By the late 1980s, the compact disc had almost completely replaced vinyl records, which could become scratched or worn out. Compact discs used digital technology to take sound and convert it to samples that could be read by a laser beam of light. The digital coding could then be placed on a 4½ inch disc.

The compact disc (CD) was viewed as superior to the long-playing record (LP) because more music could fit on a CD, which was much smaller and more durable. © SILVER-JOHN/SHUTTER.STOCK.COM.

A number of factors are responsible for the success of CDs: they are portable, they do not wear out like vinyl, and each disc can hold much more music than previous media. Digital technology allows people to take a lot of music with them since discs are light and easy to carry. Many discs can hold eighty minutes of music or more. Electronics manufacturers soon introduced portable CD listening devices such as Sony's **Walkman** (see entry under 1970s—Music in volume 4), which were first used for cassette tapes but were later adapted for CDs. CDs can also be put into car stereos, allowing the original recording a consumer buys to move easily from the home stereo to the portable stereo to the car stereo. CDs are also more durable than vinyl records. Only the laser beam touches the disc, so the disc can be played indefinitely without wearing out like vinyl records. The discs also never develop the pops and hiss of vinyl records.

Compact discs added a much-needed jolt to the music industry. Many people, impressed by the sound quality, durability, and portability of CDs, repurchased many of their old records on disc. The popularity of the new medium also led record companies to mine their collections and release CD box sets of older music, much of which had disappeared from record shelves. These box sets reinvigorated people's interest in older music. Often the box sets came with elaborate packaging that contained detailed histories of the artists and information about the music. By the late 1980s, the CD had become the dominant form of music technology and an important part of American culture. By the twenty-first century, however, downloading songs onto MP3 players such as the **iPod** (see entry under 2000s—Music in volume 6) became the norm.

Timothy Berg

For More Information

Millard, Andre. *America on Record: A History of Recorded Sound.* 2nd ed. New York: Cambridge University Press, 2005.

Farm Aid

Many American farmers were in trouble during the 1980s. Because of an economic downturn, they faced bankruptcy, the loss of family farms, and the possibility that they might have to give up farming. Thanks to a number of musicians who came to their aid, many of these farmers were able to go on with their way of life. Beginning in 1985, these musicians held a number of benefit concerts to help America's family farmers stay in business. The concerts were known as Farm Aid.

Musician **Bob Dylan** (1941; see entry under 1960s—Music in volume 4) got the idea for Farm Aid from **Live Aid** (see entry under 1980s—Music in volume 5), a benefit concert held in 1985 to raise money for starving people in Africa. Dylan wanted to hold a similar concert for American farmers. Musicians Willie Nelson (1933–), John Mellencamp (1951–), and Neil Young (1945–) organized the first Farm Aid concert in Champaign, Illinois, in 1985. Eighty thousand people attended that concert and the organizers raised more than $7 million. That success prompted more Farm Aid concerts, held in various cities, including Austin, Texas; Lincoln, Nebraska; Dallas, Texas; and New Orleans, Louisiana. Some of the biggest names in rock music have performed at annual Farm Aid benefits, which have continued into the twenty-first century, including—in addition to Dylan, Nelson, Mellencamp, and

Country singer Willie Nelson, performs at Farm Aid in Columbia, South Carolina, October 12, 1996. Nelson was one of the organizers of the benefit concerts. © PHOTOFEST, INC.

Young—Elton John (1947–), Ringo Starr (1940–), Tom Petty (1950–) and the Heartbreakers, the **Beach Boys**, and the **Grateful Dead** (see last two entries under 1960s—Music in volume 4). All of the original founders have remained on the Farm Aid board except for Dylan (who was replaced by Dave Matthews in 2001), although the 2011 concert lineup included Dylan's son Jakob. Nelson has remained at the forefront of the cause, acting as its spokesman and doing his own version of Farm Aid concerts on tour.

In addition to raising money at concerts, Farm Aid created a permanent organization that addressed other agricultural issues. Farm Aid helped pass the Agricultural Credit Act. Designed to help family farmers, the act raised money for farmers victimized by the Mississippi River floods of 1993. Farm Aid has continued to act as an advocacy group for farmers for the past twenty-five years. In 2011, the group's focus was on preserving family farms both by encouraging grassroots action and working to change government policy on the local and national levels. Like other benefit concerts, Farm Aid has proved again and again how the power of music and celebrity can bring new attention to neglected causes.

Timothy Berg

For More Information

Farm Aid: Keep America Growing. http://www.farmaid.org (accessed July 18, 2011).

Nelson, Willie, with Bud Shrake. *Willie: An Autobiography.* New York: Simon & Schuster, 1988.

Heavy Metal

Detroit native Alice Cooper thrilled audiences with his theatrical rock. © EBET ROBERTS/GETTY IMAGES.

With its loud, distorted **electric guitars** (see entry under 1950s—Music in volume 3), powerful vocals, and often-dark style, heavy metal music became an important style of **rock and roll** (see entry under 1950s—Music in volume 3) starting in the 1970s. Amid the pop-rock and psychedelic rock of the late 1960s, musicians and groups such as Deep Purple and **Led Zeppelin** (see entry under 1970s—Music in volume 4) incorporated a harder, louder tone coupled with mystical imagery that went far beyond anything else heard on mainstream **radio** (see entry under 1920s—TV and Radio in volume 2) in the late 1960s. Heavy metal music is all about aggression, power, and pushing the boundaries of "respectable" music. Its critics are many, but its fans outnumber them because heavy metal music speaks to raw human emotions.

As the genre (category) got going in the 1970s, it produced a number of important artists who took the sound to new levels. Black Sabbath, led for a long time by singer Ozzy Osbourne (1948–), reached many fans with their songs that touched on teenage insecurities. Alice Cooper (1948–) hit on a similar theme with the song "I'm Eighteen" and later brought fantastic theatrical productions to his concerts, with fake blood, smoke and fire, and the trademark loud and distorted heavy metal sound. **KISS** (see entry under 1970s—Music in volume 4), perhaps the most successful heavy metal band of the 1970s, wore elaborate makeup and produced theatrical rock concerts that made them fan favorites. Their songs "Dr. Love" and "Rock and Roll All Nite" expressed the desire for good times, another essential heavy metal theme.

In the 1980s, heavy metal became even more successful. Bands like Judas Priest and Iron Maiden continued the early, raw sound. More melodic, radio-friendly heavy metal bands like Bon Jovi and Def Leppard reached an even wider market and scored a number of hits during the 1980s. "Speed metal" and "thrash" bands that fused heavy metal and **punk** (see entry under 1970s—Music in volume 4), the most famous of which was Metallica, rose in popularity throughout the 1980s, along with sub-genres including death metal, black metal, and power metals. Heavy metal became the subject of a hit show on **MTV** (see entry under 1980s—Music in volume 5) and of a hit movie, *This Is Spinal Tap* (1984), that both spoofed and celebrated the genre in a mock documentary about a fictional heavy metal band.

Heavy metal music has also been in the limelight for more controversial reasons. In the 1980s, critics, led by the Parents Music Resource Center, founded by Tipper Gore (1948–), wife of then–U.S. senator and later vice president Al Gore (1948–), charged that heavy metal music was spreading bad messages that had an evil influence on children. These critics charged that some heavy metal songs contained satanic messages or focused on violence and death, causing negative reactions in children. Throughout the 1990s and into the first decade of the twenty-first century, several shooting sprees in the United States and Canada, such as the one at Columbine High School in Colorado, were attributed by critics to the teenage killers' admiration for heavy metal, although this connection was never proved. Despite these charges, heavy metal has continued to attract a loyal fan base.

Metallica remained at the top of the charts during the 1990s, joined by a few straightforward metal bands, but many bands fell into new, softer categories of "groove metal" or "alternative metal," such as White Zombie, Jane's Addiction, and Alice in Chains. Other hugely successful bands of the 1990s, such as Nine Inch Nails and Ministry, fused metal with a primarily industrial sound. By the mid-2000s, new metal bands were mainly coming out of western Europe, although American "metalcore," a fusion of metal and hardcore, as practiced by bands such as Shadow Falls and Killswitch Engage, reached the top of *Billboard*'s chart in 2004.

Timothy Berg

For More Information

Arnett, Jeffrey Jensen. *Metalheads: Heavy Metal Music and Adolescent Alienation.* Boulder, CO: Westview Press, 1996.

Bangs, Lester. "Heavy Metal." *The Rolling Stone Illustrated History of Rock 'n' Roll.* 3rd ed. Edited by Anthony DeCurtis, James Henke, and Holly George-Warren. New York: Random House, 1992.

Bukszpan, Daniel. *The Encyclopedia of Heavy Metal.* New York: Barnes & Noble, 2003.

Christe, Ian. *Sound of the Beast: The Complete Headbanging History of Heavy Metal.* New York: HarperEntertainment, 2003.

Walser, Robert. *Running with the Devil: Power, Gender, and Madness in Heavy Metal Music.* Hanover, NH: Wesleyan University Press, 1993.

Michael Jackson (1958–2009)

Most preteen show business personalities fade from the spotlight upon reaching adolescence. This was not the case with Michael Jackson. He first earned fame during the late 1960s as the lead singer of The Jackson Five, a pop group featuring Michael and four of his five brothers. The Jackson Five enjoyed a series of smash-hit records. Young Michael—still in elementary school—was acknowledged as among the era's finest **rhythm and blues** (R&B; see entry under 1940s—Music in volume 3) vocalists.

While barely out of his teens, Jackson began to be marketed as a solo performer. He appeared as the scarecrow in the 1978 screen adaptation of *The Wiz.* A hit Broadway musical, *The Wiz* was an all-black-cast version of the classic **Hollywood** musical ***The Wizard of Oz*** (1939; see last two entries under 1930s—Film and Theater in volume 2). Hit singles and albums followed. His 1983 album *Thriller* became the best-selling album of all time, and produced two classic number-one singles, "Billie Jean" and "Beat It." Jackson cemented his fame by stealing the show while appearing on the **television** (see entry under 1940s—TV and Radio in volume 3) special *Motown 25* (1983), on which he performed his groundbreaking, breathtaking dance steps and famous "moonwalk," a trademark move in which he spins and perches on his toes. His thirteen-minute-long *Thriller* (1983) still is acknowledged by many as the all-time-greatest music video.

Michael Jackson performs at the Capital Center in Landover, Maryland, on October 13, 1988. © LUKE FRAZZA/AFP/GETTY IMAGES.

Despite his musical successes, Jackson was a controversial pop-culture figure, as celebrated for his weird behavior as for any professional accomplishment. He used his fingers to eat his food in restaurants. He traveled with a pet boa constrictor. His face was dramatically altered by plastic surgery, with his skin color becoming noticeably lighter. As the years passed, he came to be regarded by some as a freak and an oddity. Despite all these peculiarities, Michael Jackson—particularly during his prime early 1980s years—became an entertainment-industry legend.

In the 1990s, Jackson went on to record numerous best-selling albums, including *Dangerous* (1991) and *HIStory* (1995). In 1992 the singer founded the Heal the World Foundation, through which he donated millions of dollars to charities that help children in need worldwide. In 1993, however, Jackson was accused of child molestation, the first of a series of similar scandals; although no charges were filed, Jackson settled out of court with the boy's family for $22 million. That same year, Jackson married Lisa Marie Presley (1968), daughter of famed singer **Elvis Presley** (1935–1977; see entry under 1950s—Music in volume 3). Jackson divorced Presley in 1995, and two years later the singer married Deborah Rowe, a nurse. They had two children, of whom he retained full custody after their divorce. In 2009, plagued with millions of dollars in debts, Jackson embarked on a world tour, his first since 1997. Three weeks before the first concert, the singer died of cardiac arrest brought on by drugs administered by his personal physician, Conrad Murray (1953–), who was later convicted of involuntary manslaughter.

Michael Jackson sold more records, won more awards, and broke more world records than any musician in history. He was inducted twice into the Rock and Roll Hall of Fame, once for his work with the Jackson 5 and once as a solo performer, and won thirteen Grammy Awards. In the year following his death, the singer sold thirty-five million albums. Jackson is considered to have single-handedly rewritten the history of pop music.

Rob Edelman

For More Information

Campbell, Lisa D. *Michael Jackson: The King of Pop.* Boston: Branden Books, 1993.

George, Nelson. *Thriller: The Musical Life of Michael Jackson.* New York: Da Capo Press, 2010.

Graves, Karen Marie. *Michael Jackson.* San Diego: Lucent Books, 2001.

"Jackson Sells 35 Million Albums Since Death." Msnbc.com. http://today.msnbc.msn.com/id/37957972/ns/today-entertainment/ (accessed July 18,2011).

Michaeljackson.com. http://www.michaeljackson.com (accessed July 18, 2011).

Nicholson, Lois P. *Michael Jackson.* New York: Chelsea House, 1994.

Taraborrelli, J. Randy. *Michael Jackson: The Magic and the Madness.* Rev. ed. London: Pan Books, 2004.

Vogel, Joseph. *Man in the Music: The Creative Life and Work of Michael Jackson.* New York: Sterling, 2011.

Karaoke

Karaoke (pronounced kear-ee-OH-kee) is a popular form of entertainment in which amateur singers sing along with pre-recorded **pop music** (see entry under 1940s—Music in volume 3) songs stripped of their vocal tracks. The word "karaoke" is a combination of two Japanese words: *kara,* meaning empty, and *oke,* meaning orchestra. Recorded music on a cassette tape or a **compact disc** (CD; see entry under 1980s—Music in volume 5) provides the instrumental track of a band or an orchestra, with the singer's voice stripped out, to be filled by anyone brave enough to hold the microphone at a party or a karaoke bar.

Invented by Kisaburo Takagi of the Nikkodo Company, karaoke originated in a bar in Kobe, Japan, in 1972. By 1976, the first home karaoke machines were marketed to the Japanese public. Performing karaoke-style fit perfectly with the popular Asian custom of singing at public events. Even before karaoke, it was not unusual in Asian culture for amateurs to rise and offer a song at a wedding or other gathering. The point of this was not to demonstrate excellence in singing, but rather to show good will and comradeship. The introduction of the karaoke machine allowed singers to choose from a wide variety of songs and to read the words from a song sheet. Video karaoke added lyrics on the screen with a bouncing ball to help the whole audience sing along. Soon after its introduction, karaoke spread not only in Japan but through Korea and Southeast Asia.

Karaoke first came to the United States in Asian restaurants. Non–Asian Americans were introduced to the new fad by **Johnny Carson** (1925–; see entry under 1960s—TV and Radio in volume 4) on ***The Tonight Show*** (see entry under 1950s—TV and Radio in volume 3) on NBC in 1986. Soon karaoke bars opened all over the United States. Americans do not have a long tradition of performing for each other, but they do often have a hunger for the spotlight, and karaoke offered amateurs a moment on center stage. Although the first karaoke venues were bars and restaurants, home karaoke machines became more popular in the 1990s.

Karaoke continues to thrive as a form of self-expression and amusement in bars and homes throughout the world. In 1999, it was even taken to the Balkan town of Kosovo to entertain refugees in the war-torn city, perhaps proving true the words of Nikkodo executive Akihiko Kurobe, quoted in *Transpacific:* "Karaoke has no boundaries or prejudices. It is ageless and impartial to gender. It will last forever. Karaoke is like your family or lover. It makes sadness half and happiness double."

Karaoke technology improved steadily throughout the first decade of the twenty-first century with versions adapted for Microsoft's Xbox and karaoke services for cell phones. Hundreds of Web sites also sprang up providing karaoke, along with software enabling singers to hear one another over the Web. Karaoke contests have been in existence since at least 2003, the year in which the first Karaoke World Championship was held.

Tina Gianoulis

For More Information

Gonda, Thomas A., Jr. *Karaoke: The Bible: Everything You Need to Know about Karaoke.* Oakland, CA: G-Man Publishing, 1993.

"Karaoke = Kurobe." *Transpacific* (Vol. 9, no. 6, October 1994): pp. 24–26.

Karaoke Scene. http://www.karaokescene.com/ (accessed July 19, 2011).

Wolpin, Stewart. "High-Tech Hootenanny: Can Karaoke Conquer America?" *Video Magazine* (Vol. 16, no. 1, April 1992): pp. 30–36.
Xun Zhou, and Francesca Tarocco. *Karaoke: The Global Phenomenon.* London: Reaktion, 2006.

Live Aid

The Live Aid concerts took place on July 13, 1985, at Wembley Stadium in London, England, and at JFK Stadium in Philadelphia, Pennsylvania. The concerts raised almost $140 million for the starving in Africa, the most money ever raised for charity by a single event. The combined concerts remain the biggest music event ever held, attended by roughly 170,000 people.

Live Aid was the brainchild of rock singer Bob Geldof (1954–) of the Boomtown Rats. Moved by images of starving Ethiopian children on a **television** (see entry under 1940s—TV and Radio in volume 3) documentary, he decided something had to be done. Two charity records—Geldof's *Do They Know It's Christmas?* in Britain and *We Are the World,* written by Michael Jackson (1958–2009) and Lionel Ritchie (1949–), in the United States—were released for the Christmas season in 1984. Live Aid was Geldof's real triumph. Comprising sixteen hours of music, it became one of the key cultural moments of the 1980s.

Watched by almost two billion people on television around the world, Live Aid brought together some of the biggest names in the history of rock and pop music, including **Led Zeppelin** (see entry under 1970s—Music in volume 4), Queen, U2, Mick Jagger (1943–), Tina Turner (1938–), **Bob Dylan** (1941–; see entry under 1960s—Music in volume 4), and Phil Collins (1951–) of Genesis. Collins's involvement was noteworthy in that he appeared at both sites, assisted by a trip on the Concorde. At the center of it all, though, was Geldof, who persuaded most of the biggest stars of the time to perform without compensation and convinced several major corporations to donate their services.

Chris Routledge

For More Information

Clinton, Susan. *Live Aid.* Chicago: Children's Press, 1993.
Geldof, Bob. *Geldof in Africa.* London: Century, 2005.

Gray, Charlotte. *Bob Geldof: The Pop Star Who Raised $140 Million for Famine Relief in Ethiopia.* Milwaukee: Gareth Stevens, 1988.

Hillmore, Peter. *Live Aid: World Wide Concert Book.* Parsippany, NJ: Unicorn, 1985.

Live Aid: The Greatest Show on Earth. http://www.herald.co.uk/local_info/live_aid.html (accessed July 20, 2011).

LL Cool J (1969–)

LL Cool J is the stage name of rapper James Todd Smith. The name stands for "Ladies Love Cool James," a reference to the music superstar's good looks and charming personality. LL Cool J rode those attributes, and his flair for rhyming, to the top of the charts in the 1980s. He became one of **rap and hip-hop** (see entry under 1980s—Music in volume 5) music's biggest crossover success stories.

LL Cool J performs in Chicago, on July 2, 1987. © PAUL NATKIN/WIREIMAGE/GETTY IMAGES.

Born in Queens, New York, in 1969, LL Cool J was easily recognized by his Kangol hat, gold chains, and Adidas sweats. He began rapping as a teenager and recorded his debut album, *Radio*, with Rick Rubin (1963–), producer of **Run-DMC** (see entry under 1980s—Music in volume 5). The album melded LL's boasting rhymes with aggressive beats and **rock and roll** (see entry under 1950s—Music in volume 3) guitars and became one of rap's first classic recordings. In the 1990s, LL continued to break new ground, appearing with a full band on a memorable installment of the live **MTV** (see entry under 1980s—Music in volume 5) music show *MTV Unplugged.* The rapper released albums that went gold or platinum throughout the decade and won a Grammy Award in 1995. LL embarked on a movie and television career, appearing in films such as *Krush Groove* (1985) and *The Hard Way* (1991). These performances led to a starring role in a 1995 television series, *In the House*, which in turn led to many other TV and film appearances. The singer has also continued to release new albums approximately every two years. Rappers who have gone on to great fame often cite the trail-blazing "Mr. Smith" as an inspiration.

Robert E. Schnakenberg

For More Information

"Bands A-Z: LL Cool J." *MTV.com.* http://www.mtv.com/bands/az/ll_cool_j/artist.jhtml (accessed December 16, 2011).

Baughan, Brian. *LL Cool J.* Broomall, PA: Mason Crest, 2006.

Juzwiak, Richard. *LL Cool J.* New York: Rosen, 2006.

LL Cool J. *I Make My Own Rules.* New York: St. Martin's, 1997.

"LL Cool J." *Def Jam Recordings.* http://www.islanddefjam.com/artist/home.aspx?artistID=7309 (accessed December 16, 2011).

Shekell, Dustin > *LL Cool J: Hip-Hop Stars.* Philadelphia: Chelsea Publishing House, 2007.

Madonna (1958–)

In the 1980s, Madonna, born Madonna Louise Ciccone, burst upon the national landscape and became a focus of both intense adoration and controversy. Madonna—as singer, dancer, and actress—conveyed a provocative sexuality and fiery ambition that challenged sexual, racial, and religious values.

From small-town Michigan origins, singer/actress Madonna has made a name for herself worldwide. © DAVID MCGOUGH/DMI/TIME LIFE PICTURES/GETTY IMAGES.

Madonna portrayed herself as a "Boy Toy" and "Material Girl" who enjoyed life's hedonistic (sensual) pleasures. She courted fame and celebrity with her suggestive lyrics, naughty-girl persona, controversial behavior, and brief marriage to "bad-boy" actor Sean Penn (1960–). Her legion of (mostly female) fans viewed Madonna as a symbol of female empowerment.

Madonna's willingness to defy conventions and political correctness earned her criticism from conservatives and liberals alike. She remained a rock superstar and pop icon throughout the 1990s. However, her attempts at a film career were less satisfactory. Her best films include: *Desperately Seeking Susan* (1985), *Dick Tracy* (1990), and *Evita* (1998). Madonna's 1998 album *Ray of Light* reflected the singer's newfound interest in Eastern mysticism and contained several dance hits that expanded her popularity among her diverse fan base.

In 2000, Madonna married British director Guy Ritchie (1968–). The pair had two children (Madonna also had a daughter from a previous relationship); they divorced in 2008. Madonna continued to release hugely successful albums. She was proclaimed the number-one selling female recording artist in history by the *Guinness Book of World Records*. Her music remains popular and still often fuels the flames of controversy.

Charles Coletta

For More Information

Cross, Mary. *Madonna: A Biography.* Westport, CT: Greenwood Press, 2007.

Easlea, Daryl, and Eddi Feigel. *Madonna.* New York: Sterling, 2010.

Madonna.com. http://www.madonna.com (accessed July 21, 2011).

Metz, Allan, and Carol Benson, eds. *The Madonna Companion: Two Decades of Commentary.* New York: Schirmer Books, 1999.

Taraborrelli, J. Randy. *Madonna: An Intimate Biography.* New ed. London: Pan, 2008.

MTV

Since its start in 1981, Music Television (MTV) has proved to be one of the most important **television** (see entry under 1940s—TV and Radio in volume 3) channels of the late twentieth and early twenty-first centuries. As its name implies, MTV pulled together the two most important popular-culture developments of the post–World War II era: **rock and roll** (see entry under 1950s—Music in volume 3) and television. To its millions of viewers scattered across the globe, MTV is the foremost media representative of global youth culture. The channel offers an intoxicating mix of music, post-modern imagery, consumer goods, and original programming. To its owner, the cable-television giant Viacom, MTV is a highly profitable **cable TV** (see entry under 1970s—TV and Radio in volume 4) channel that offers advertisers unparalleled access to a youthful audience. Critics, however, complain that MTV corrupts youth, encourages mindless consumerism, and degrades the music that it supposedly celebrates.

MTV was launched at midnight on August 1, 1981, playing a music video by the Buggles called "Video Killed the Radio Star." MTV began as a twenty-four-hour-a-day music cable channel. MTV's audience grew

MTV's first logo in 1981.
© EVERETT COLLECTION.

from just over two million at the end of four months to twenty-two million by 1984. With its low production costs, the channel soon earned large profits, as advertisers proved willing to pay top dollar to reach this audience of young consumers.

The first videos to air on MTV were rough and awkward but quality improved fairly rapidly, thanks in no small part to the performer who would come to be called the "King of Pop," **Michael Jackson** (1958–2009; see entry under 1980s—Music in volume 5). Jackson's 1982 release *Thriller* featured three videos—"Thriller," "Billie Jean," and "Beat It"—that helped shape the growing art of making a video. The video for "Thriller," for example, was filmed in a graveyard and cost an estimated $1.1 million.

Beginning in the late 1980s, MTV moved away from playing a constant stream of music videos and began creating its own programs. In this way, MTV hoped to become a more traditional TV channel. New shows introduced included *Club MTV* (dance videos), *The Week in Rock* (news related to the world of rock and roll), and *Yo! MTV Raps* (a compilation of rap videos by black artists). By the mid-1990s, **rap and hip-hop** (see entry under 1980s—Music in volume 5) became MTV mainstays. MTV continued its experiments with content into the 1990s, offering such shows as ***The Real World*** and ***Beavis and Butt-Head*** (see these entries under 1990s—TV and Radio in volume 5). In *The Real World,* a group of college-aged strangers were thrown together in a beautiful house and a camera filmed every moment of their attempts to learn to live together. More controversial was *Beavis and Butt-Head,* a cartoon about two teenage slackers who exhibited gross, dangerous, and often hilarious behavior.

MTV also spread its influence around the world in the late 1980s and 1990s. MTV debuted in Europe in 1987, in Brazil in 1990, and throughout Latin America beginning in 1993. MTV executive Sara Levinson claimed that "Music is the global language. We want to be the global rock n' roll village where we can talk to the youth worldwide." By the mid-1990s, MTV reached 270 million households in more than 125 countries scattered across five continents. MTV also expanded along with technology in the early 2000s, developing a Web site, MTV.com, that broadcasts new and archived videos, and is available via the Internet and cellular devices. Critics of MTV claim that the channel spreads mindless consumerism around the world, but fans praise the channel for continually offering fresh music and programming for the world's young people.

Tom Pendergast

For More Information

Banks, Jack. *Monopoly Television: MTV's Quest to Control the Music.* Boulder, CO: Westview Press, 1996.

Denisoff, R. Serge. *Inside MTV.* New Brunswick, NJ: Transaction Books, 1988.

Goodwin, Andrew. *Dancing in the Distraction Factory: Music Television and Popular Culture.* Minneapolis: University of Minnesota Press, 1992.

Kaplan, E. Ann. *Rocking Around the Clock: Music Television, Postmodernism, and Consumer Culture.* New York: Methuen, 1987.

Marks, Craig, and Rob Tannenbaum. *I Want My MTV: The Uncensored Story of the Music Video Revolution.* New York: Dutton, 2011.

McGrath, Tom. *MTV: The Making of a Revolution.* Philadelphia: Running Press, 1996.

McGrath, Tom. *Video Killed the Radio Star: How MTV Rocked the World.* New York: Villard Books, 1994.

MTV.com. http://www.mtv.com (accessed July 21, 2011).

Temporal, Paul. *The Branding of MTV: Will Internet Kill the Video Star?* Hoboken, NJ: Wiley, 2008.

Rap and Hip-hop

Rap and hip-hop culture emerged out of the street-gang culture of poor black youths in the Bronx, New York, in the 1970s. Hip-hop culture and its signature music, rap, have grown in less than thirty years to be a major part of popular culture around the world. This youth culture has been criticized and condemned by concerned adults from parents to law enforcement officials. Supporters, however, think that hip-hop gives a voice and a sense of power to poor youth around the world who otherwise often feel powerless and unheard.

Hip-hop describes a distinctive style of dress (extremely baggy clothes, backwards baseball caps), a slang that is almost impossible for those outside the culture to understand, and an attitude of cool toughness and rebellion. Hip-hop culture includes a love of break dancing (athletic street dancing), flamboyant—and illegal—graffiti, rap music (fast rhymes spoken to a rhythmic beat, often with political content), and DJing (using a turntable as an instrument by manipulating songs and creating sounds while spinning vinyl records on the turntable).

From its beginnings in the Bronx, hip-hop spread quickly to Manhattan and Los Angeles, California, and then around the United

States and the rest of the world. Underprivileged youth everywhere responded to the tough social criticism contained in the rappers' poetic lyrics, and wealthier white youth imitated the rebellious hip-hop style. While U.S. rap had emerged from African rhythms and oral storytelling traditions, British rappers of East Indian descent drew from the traditional melodies of India. French rappers were often poor immigrants from the Middle East and West Africa. In Japan, women broke traditional gender barriers by becoming rappers.

As rap became the voice of poor youth during the 1980s, it gained in commercial popularity, making some performers rich and famous. Rappers like Will Smith (1968–) and **LL Cool J** (1968–; see entry under 1980s—Music in volume 5) had a clean-cut image and were acceptable to mainstream audiences, but other rappers began to produce harsh, angry songs, full of the violence that was often part of black urban poverty. In the early 1990s, rappers like Tupac Shakur (1971–1996), Ice T (1959–), and Snoop Dogg (1972–) created a kind of rap music that came to be called "gangsta rap." Even more than early rap, gangsta rap horrified some listeners with the violent and sexist language of its lyrics. The violent deaths of several gangsta rappers like Shakur and The Notorious B.I.G. (Christopher George Latore Wallace, a.k.a. Biggie Smalls; 1972–1997) convinced many adults that rap music was dangerous.

Although many crusaders have tried to quiet the loud, insistent voice of rap music, rap has continued to gain fans. In 1987, the music industry gave rap its own category, alongside the **rhythm and blues** (R&B; see entry under 1940s—Music in volume 3) and **jazz** (see entry under 1900s—Music in volume 1) that were its ancestors. In 1999, rap became the top-selling music genre in the United States. In the summer of 2000, Harlem's Apollo Theater introduced the first hip-hop musical, titled *Echo Park.*

The early 2000s saw a greater influx of white and female artists into hip-hop and rap genres, such as the top-sellers **Eminem** (1972–; see entry under 2000s—Music in volume 6) and Queen Latifah (1970–). While alternative forms developed due to regional variations and became popular in the United States during the next decade, traditional rap and hip-hop continued to gain fans mainly in the United Kingdom and Europe and to influence music around the globe.

Tina Gianoulis

For More Information

Ayazi-Hashjin, Sherry. *Rap and Hip Hop: The Voice of a Generation.* New York: Rosen, 1999.

Bynoe, Yvonne. *Encyclopedia of Rap and Hip-Hop Culture.* Westport, CT: Greenwood Press, 2006.

Charnas, Dan. *The Big Payback: The History of the Business of Hip Hop.* New York: New American Library, 2010.

George, Nelson, et al. *Fresh: Hip Hop Don't Stop.* New York: Random House, 1985.

Greenberg, Keith Elliot. *Rap.* Minneapolis: Lerner, 1988.

Jones, K. Maurice. *Say It Loud!: The Story of Rap Music.* Brookfield, CT: Millbrook Press, 1994.

Kinnon, Joy Bennett. "Does Rap Have a Future?" *Ebony* (June 1997): pp. 76–79.

Price, Emmett George. *Hip Hop Culture.* Santa Barbara, CA: ABC-CLIO, 2006.

Rapstation. http://www.rapstation.com (accessed July 21, 2011).

Rose, Tricia. *Black Noise: Rap Music and Black Culture in Contemporary America.* Hanover, NH: University Press of New England, 1994.

Run-DMC

Run-DMC took **rap and hip-hop** (see entry under 1980s—Music in volume 5) music to the top of the charts in the 1980s by collaborating with the hard-rock band Aerosmith on a remake of the 1970s **rock and roll** (see entry under 1950s—Music in volume 3) hit "Walk This Way." The Queens, New York–based hip-hop "posse" followed up that single with the smash 1986 album *Raising Hell,* which blended loud rock guitar and rap beats to great effect.

Run-DMC was named for two of its founding members, Joseph "Run" Simmons (1964–) and Daryl "DMC" McDaniels (1964–). Simmons and McDaniels hooked up with a disc jockey named Jason "Jam Master Jay" Mizell (1965–) and recorded their first single, "It's Like That," in 1983. Its success led to other minor hits like "Sucker MCs" and "King of Rock," paving the way for mainstream acceptance. After *Raising Hell,* Run-DMC's brand of rap-rock fell out of fashion and the group released a series of disappointing follow-up albums. They returned to prominence in 1993, however, with an album of born-again Christian rap, *Down with the King,* which featured other prominent rappers such as Q-Tip (1970–) and A Tribe Called Quest and brought the band a new generation of fans. After a series of break-ups and reconciliations

Run-DMC band members in 1988: Joseph "Run" Simmons (left), Darryl "D.M.C." McDaniels, and DJ Jason "Jam Master Jay" Mizell. © FRANK MICELOTTA/IMAGEDIRECT/ GETTY IMAGES.

Run-DMC disbanded for good. In 2002 Jam-Master Jay was murdered in Queens; the killer was never identified. Run-DMC continues to receive tributes from rappers who have followed in their hit-making footsteps.

Robert E. Schnakenberg

For More Information

Adler, Bill. *Tougher Than Leather: The Authorized Biography of Run-DMC.* New ed. Los Angeles: Consafos Press, 2002.

McDaniels, Daryl. *King of Rock: Respect, Responsibility and My Life with Run-DMC.* New York: St. Martin's Press, 2001.

Run-DMC. http://rundmc.com (accessed December 16, 2011).

Simmons, Joseph. *It's Like That: A Spiritual Memoir.* New York: St. Martin's Press, 2000.
Slavicek, Louise Chipley. *Run-DMC.* New York: Chelsea House, 2007.

2 Live Crew

This Miami, Florida, hip-hop band rocketed to fame in 1989 on the basis of a free-speech controversy sparked by their album *As Nasty as They Wanna Be.* 2 Live Crew formed in the mid-1980s, just as **rap and hip-hop** music (see entry under 1980s—Music in volume 5) was enjoying its first hints of mainstream success. The band's first album, *2 Live Crew Is What We Are* (1986), featured danceable rap tunes dealing with sexual subjects and sprinkled with profanity, making it hard for the group to get **radio** (see entry under 1920s—TV and Radio in volume 2) airplay. The Crew's third album, *As Nasty as They Wanna Be,* brought the band great notoriety when, in June 1990, the song "Me So Horny" was deemed legally obscene by a Florida judge, forcing many stores to refrain from selling it. The group appealed the judge's decision and eventually won.

The controversy spurred sales of 2 Live Crew's album, which sold over two million copies. The group rode the wave of attention for several more years and released the first live album in rap music in 1991, *Live in Concert.* Perhaps 2 Live Crew's finest moment came when it recorded a mocking version of the song "Born in the U.S.A." by Bruce Springsteen (1949–). Entitled "Banned in the U.S.A.," the song poked fun at the group's legal woes. Unfortunately, without controversy to sustain them, 2 Live Crew soon faded from prominence. Band leader Luther Campbell (1960–) filed for bankruptcy in 1995.

Robert E. Schnakenberg

For More Information

Campbell, Luther, and John R. Miller. *As Nasty as They Wanna Be: The Uncensored Story of Luther Campbell of the 2 Live Crew.* New York: Barricade Books, 1992.
Lacayo, Richard. "The Rap Against a Rap Group." *Time* (June 25, 1990): p. 18.
Light, Alan. "2 Live Crew Beats the Rap." *Rolling Stone* (November 29, 1990): p. 27.
Soocher, Stan. "2 Live Crew, Taking the Rap." *Rolling Stone* (August 9, 1990): pp. 19–22.

1980s

Print Culture

The publishing industry was very much affected by the trends affecting other areas of popular culture in the 1980s—the concentration of power in large corporations and the public thirst for status through consumption. The concentration of power in publishing took two forms. First, the number of book publishers decreased as large publishers bought up smaller ones. These big publishing houses were driven by profit, so they tended to publish books by known writers and offered fewer chances to new talent. They also tended to be engaged in publishing magazines, music, and videos, so they often looked for ideas that could be cross-promoted. Second, booksellers also got bigger. Small, independent book stores were pushed out of business by large chains like Barnes & Noble and Borders. These book chains worked hand in hand with the big publishers to promote the most popular authors; increasingly, they also offered music, wrapping paper, coffee, and other gifts.

These changes in the publishing and selling market helped shape what was published. The biggest sellers were called "blockbusters" because they were written by big-name authors like Stephen King (1947–), Danielle Steel (1947–), Robert Ludlum (1927–2001), or James Michener (1907–1997), whose works promised to sell. Many of these books were sold with built-in movie or television deals.

The wealth and thirst for status that were associated with the decade also became subjects of fiction. A set of young authors made a big splash with books that both glamorized and condemned the thirst for drugs, brand-name goods, and business success of the decade's young urban professionals (yuppies). *Bright Lights, Big City* (1984) by Jay McInerney (1955–) and *Less Than Zero* (1985) by Bret Easton Ellis (1964–) were two of the best-known such books. *The Bonfire of the Vanities* (1987), by noted "new journalist" Tom Wolfe (1931–), was the sensation of the decade, however. *The Bonfire of the Vanities* was serialized (divided into parts and published in succeeding issues) in *Rolling Stone* magazine. The book simultaneously satirized Wall Street greed, the American legal system, and glory-hungry black activists.

Magazines and newspapers also changed in the 1980s. The big news among newspapers was the introduction of *USA Today* in 1982. The first national newspaper started slowly but soon stole readers from major city papers and pioneered new styles of journalism. Magazines, on the other hand, continued to grow more and more specialized. While once there had been just two fashion magazines in the United States, in the 1980s, fashion magazines were started for hip teens (*Sassy*), middle-aged women (*Mirabella*), older women (*Lears*), and even plus-sized women (*It's Me*). Other specific markets were targeted by magazines, including young black males, Hispanics, college students, food enthusiasts, and sports fans of all sorts. It seems that in the 1980s there was a magazine for every market. Not surprisingly, because each market is limited to a certain kind of reader, most such magazines published for only a few years.

The Bonfire of the Vanities

During the 1980s, few novels were as widely read or praised as *The Bonfire of the Vanities* (1987), a witty examination of contemporary American culture by Tom Wolfe (1931–). First published in serialized form in ***Rolling Stone*** (see entry under 1960s—Print Culture in volume 4) magazine, the novel explores many social levels through the experiences of bond salesman Sherman McCoy. McCoy sees himself as a "master of the universe" due to the millions of dollars he is able to manipulate. In a nightmarish scene, McCoy and his mistress become lost in the South Bronx, where they are confronted by the poor, minorities, and the underclass—groups McCoy's fortune allowed him to avoid. For more than six hundred pages, Wolfe examines the fallout of McCoy being implicated in the hit-and-run traffic death of a young black boy. The novel spent many weeks on the **best-seller** (see entry under 1940s—Commerce in volume 3) lists and was praised for capturing the flavor of 1980s New York.

Tom Wolfe first came to the public's attention in the 1960s as an exponent of the "new journalism," a form of nonfiction reporting that combines detailed descriptions, analysis, dialogue, and a strong sense of the writer's presence. He coined phrases like "radical chic" and "the Me Decade." Among his most significant pre-*Bonfire* writings are *The Electric Kool-Aid Acid Test* (1968) and *The Right Stuff* (1979). Wolfe is also known for always appearing in public in a perfectly tailored white suit.

White-suited author and man-about-town Tom Wolfe, author of The Bonfire of the Vanities. © ROSE HARTMAN/ GETTY IMAGES.

With *The Bonfire of the Vanities,* his first novel, Wolfe gave readers a tale through which they could examine and decipher the major cultural elements and icons of the 1980s. In *Conversations with Tom Wolfe,* he explained the origin of the novel: "Two things that are so much a part of the eighties—and I couldn't believe nobody else was writing about this in book form somewhere—are the astounding prosperity generated by the investment banking industry, and the racial and ethnic animosity." Some praised the novel for its accuracy, as it depicted racial, ethnic, and political hostilities that were occurring in the real New York. Others called Wolfe racist and criticized his unique style.

In 1990, the film version of Wolfe's novel, starring Tom Hanks (1956–) and Bruce Willis (1955–), premiered and was deemed a flop. **Hollywood** (see entry under 1930s—Film and Theater in volume 2) demanded so many revisions in order to appeal to the mass audience that the finished movie bore little resemblance to Wolfe's masterpiece.

Charles Coletta

For More Information

Salamon, Julie. *The Devil's Candy: "The Bonfire of the Vanities" Goes to Hollywood.* Boston: Houghton Mifflin, 1991.

Scura, Dorothy, ed. *Conversations with Tom Wolfe.* Jackson: University Press of Mississippi, 1990.

Wolfe, Tom. *The Bonfire of the Vanities.* New York: Farrar Straus Giroux, 1987.

The Far Side

The single-panel comic strips of Gary Larson (1950–) gained millions of fans with their use of the absurd, the bizarre, and the downright weird to poke fun at human nature. Produced between 1981 and 1995, the strip became hugely successful, with spinoffs into books, greeting cards, posters, **T-shirts** (see entry under 1910s—Fashion in volume 1), mugs, and **television** (see entry under 1940s—TV and Radio in volume 3) specials.

Larson had no formal training in art or drawing. He grew up in Tacoma, Washington, and as a child showed far more interest in science than in cartooning. Much of Larson's humor is derived from his portrayal of nonhumans (such as animals, insects, or bacteria) with distinctly human qualities. In *The Far Side,* squirrels seek psychotherapy, parakeets read the newspapers lining their cages, dogs consult with canine realtors, and bears daydream about owning their own cars.

The Far Side had its debut in the *San Francisco Chronicle* on January 1, 1980. It soon became widely popular. By the time Larson retired from daily cartooning in 1995, his work was appearing in nineteen hundred newspapers, in forty countries, and in seventeen different languages. The strip gave rise to twenty-two paperback collections, each of which reached the *New York Times* **best-sellers** (see entry under 1940s—Commerce in volume 3) list. Larson's animated film, *Gary Larson's Tales from the Far Side,* was broadcast on CBS in 1994. A second film, *Gary Larson's Tales from the Far Side II,* was released in 1997.

Larson received the "Cartoonist of the Year" award in 1990 and again in 1994. In honor of his frequent use of insects as characters in his strip, Larson had a bug—*Strigiphilus garylarsoni*—named after him.

Since retiring from daily cartooning, Larson has been very protective of his copyright and has blocked the publication of his strips online. In 1998, he came briefly out of retirement to publish a book for children, *There's a Hair in My Dirt! A Worm's Story.* The story uses humor to make a serious point about the way that each element in nature is dependent on others for its existence. A thorough compilation of *The Far Side* comics was released in 2003, with a foreword by comedian Steve Martin (1945–).

Justin Gustainis

For More Information

Bernstein, Fred. "Loony 'toonist Gary Larson Takes Millions for a Daily Walk on *The Far Side*." *People Weekly* (February 4, 1985): pp. 103–6.

The Far Side. http://www.thefarside.com (accessed July 22, 2011).

Kelly, James. "All Creatures Weird and Funny; Cartoonist Gary Larson Views Man and Beast from *The Far Side*." *Time* (December 1, 1986): p. 86.

Richmond, Peter. "Creatures from the Black Cartoon: In Gary Larson's Wildly Funny Comic Strip, *The Far Side,* Animals Act Like Humans and Humans Act Like Animals." *Rolling Stone* (September 24, 1987): pp. 79–82.

Sassy

Direct and outspoken, *Sassy* magazine was the attempt of a group of idealistic editors and writers to change the nature of publications directed at teenage girls. First published in March 1988, *Sassy* was different from other girls' magazines, which were often filled with gushing articles about film and rock stars along with tips about fashion, makeup, and weight loss. *Sassy*'s writers wrote thoughtful articles about a wide range of real life topics, without preaching or talking down to their readers. Although constantly threatened by boycotts organized by right-wing critics and by advertisers who demanded they print less controversial articles, *Sassy* became an important source of information and support for the young women who read it. Though founding editor Jane Pratt (1962–) sold the magazine in 1996, and it stopped publishing for good in 1997, *Sassy* is still mourned by thousands of fans who have found little to replace its honest approach to teen journalism.

Pratt graduated from Oberlin College in Oberlin, Ohio, and worked as an intern at *McCall's* and *Teenage* magazines before deciding to start her own magazine for young women. She envisioned a publication that would have a respectful tone and would take its young readers more seriously than the usual teen magazine. Along with writers like Christina Kelly and Mary Kaye Schilling, Pratt began to publish *Sassy,* including articles with titles like "How My Brother Came Out," about gay issues, and "My Rainforest Odyssey," about protecting the environment. Instead of the usual mainstream pop-culture icons like the Backstreet Boys, *Sassy* informed its readers about the **alternative rock** (see entry under 1990s—Music in volume 5) scene, putting Kurt Cobain (1967–1994) of **Nirvana** (see entry under 1990s—Music in volume 5) and Courtney Love (1964–) of **Hole** on its cover. Even *Sassy*'s celebrity interviews contained a depth and complexity not found in the usual "What's your favorite color?" interviews found in teen magazines.

The editors and writers of *Sassy* endeared themselves to their readers by using only first names on their articles, creating the effect of a group of friends talking about the issues that were important in their lives. Circulation soon climbed to eight hundred thousand. Many critics did not appreciate *Sassy*'s frankness, however, and right-wing groups like the Moral Majority and the American Family Association led a year-long boycott of the magazine. Advertisers, too, tried to control *Sassy*'s content. Tampax, for example, successfully pressured the editors into not printing a reader's article about her experience with toxic shock syndrome, a rare condition caused by tampon use.

Finally, exhausted by constant struggles with advertisers, Pratt sold *Sassy* to Peterson Publishing, which published the more traditional *Teen* magazine. Though Peterson continued to publish a magazine called *Sassy* for another year, the format had changed so much that many former readers felt betrayed. In 1997, *Sassy* was reduced to a section in *Teen* magazine and soon disappeared altogether.

Tina Gianoulis

For More Information

Crossen, Cynthia. "Sexual Candor Marks Magazine for Teen Girls." *Wall Street Journal* (February 17, 1988): pp. 27, 31.

Jesella, Kara, and Meltzer, Marisa. *How "Sassy" Changed My Life: A Love Letter to the Greatest Teen Magazine of All Time.* London: Faber and Faber, 2007.

Keller, Sarah. "Sass Education." *Mother Jones* (April 1989): pp. 14–15.

Udell, Rochelle. "Jane Pratt." *Interview* (June 1992): pp. 80–83.

USA Today

USA Today is a daily general-interest newspaper circulated across America. It first hit newsstands on a limited basis in 1982; the paper did not go national until the following year. Its success changed the face of the newspaper business, altering both the way newspapers look and the scope and content of news stories and features.

Initially, the format of *USA Today,* published by the Gannett Company, was mocked by media critics and the newspaper industry. Its articles were considered too short and general in nature, with in-depth reporting kept to a minimum; furthermore, celebrity pieces and "upbeat" coverage took precedence over hard news. For example, the first issue of *USA Today* headlined the death of Princess Grace of Monaco, the former motion-picture star Grace Kelly (1928–1982). The assassination of Lebanese president-elect Bashir Gemayel (1947–1982) was noted in a single paragraph on the front page; the coverage of a plane crash in Spain focused on the "miracle" of its 327 survivors, rather than on the 55 passengers who were killed.

Additionally, news stories were accompanied by endless charts and tables, which tended to visualize—and trivialize—issues. The paper also placed a high value on publishing lists, poll results, and sidebars. *USA Today* was mockingly compared to fast food, earning the nickname "McPaper."

The paper sparked controversy in 1992 when its sports staff learned that tennis-great Arthur Ashe (1943–1993) was suffering from **AIDS** (see entry under 1980s—The Way We Lived in volume 5). Ashe was informed that *USA Today* was planning a piece on his health. In response, he held an emotional news conference in which he informed the world of his plight. Was Ashe's health situation a legitimate news story, given his celebrity status? Or was it a private matter that was none of the public's business?

For better or worse, many of *USA Today*'s approaches to journalism have become standard practice in the newspaper industry. Today, poll results have virtually taken over the news. The most private issues involving a celebrity's life have become media issues for public discussion. The paper's format also had an impact on the industry. *USA Today* comes in four sections: "News," "Life," "Money," and "Sports," with full-color photographs printed on the front pages of each. Previously, most newspapers were not divided into separate sections on a daily basis and shunned using color. These practices became popular with *USA Today* readers and were eventually adopted by other papers. Additionally, *USA Today*'s publication of expanded box scores in its sports section and nightly television listings for national cable channels found their way into other publications.

In the early 1990s, *USA Today* began increasing its reporting and editing staffs and emphasizing editorial content over presentation. By mid-decade, many of its critics had altered their views of the paper. In 1982, media reporter Ben Bagdikian (1920–) had called the paper a "mediocre piece of journalism [presenting] a flawed picture of the world every day." In 1997, he noted, "It has become a much more serious newspaper.... I don't think it's a joke anymore."

In the early 2000s, an era in which newspaper circulation across the United States was in general decline, *USA Today* came to enjoy the second highest circulation of any paper in the country. As of 2010, its circulation was roughly 2 million, second only to the *Wall Street Journal.*

Rob Edelman

For More Information

Neuharth, Al. *Confessions of an S.O.B.* New York: Doubleday, 1989.

Prichard, Peter S. *The Making of McPaper: The Inside Story of USA Today.* New York: Andrews, McMeel & Parker, 1987.

USA Today. http://www.usatoday.com (accessed July 22, 2011).

Zines

There is a thriving, if little-known, community of individuals in modern society who believe that they are taking part in a communications revolution. It is not driven by phone lines or cables and does not rely on large corporations or expensive equipment. Instead, it is created on **personal computers** (see entry under 1970s—The Way We Lived in volume 4) or by hand, photocopied and stapled and sold or traded on the **Internet** (see entry under 1990s—The Way We Lived in volume 5) or through alternative bookstores. This communications phenomenon is the "zine" (pronounced ZEEN), a small, handmade publication providing commentary, news, and information on any subject its creator chooses to explore.

Though modern zines began to appear in the 1980s, zines have a long and distinguished history. Ever since the invention of the printing press in the fifteenth century, people with opinions have found a way to get them into print and distribute them. The *Poor Richard's Almanac,* published by Benjamin Franklin (1706–1790) in the 1700s, was a kind of zine. So were the broadsides of the late sixteenth and early seventeenth centuries, poems or songs printed on single sheets of paper and sold by their authors to passerbye on the street for a few pennies each. Popular science-fiction magazines developed in 1930s reflected sci-fi fans' obsession with their genre (category) of writing. These fan magazines were called by the abbreviated slang, "fanzine," and it is from these fanzines that modern zines took their name. The underground press of the 1960s and 1970s, full of radical politics, X-rated cartoons, and the counterculture lifestyle, were another step in the evolution of the zine.

Self-publishing has long been a way for voices out of the mainstream to be heard. A number of specific factors contributed to the rise of self-published zines in the 1980s, though. The development of the personal computer, desktop publishing software, and inexpensive photocopying made printing easier and cheaper than ever before. Ease of printing, coupled with the slow economy and the consumerist values of the 1980s, led young people to search for independent creative outlets. Though not all publishers of zines are young, zine culture has a special appeal for youth, who are not often given a forum to express their views. Youth of the 1980s were often faced with unemployment or dead-end jobs and were stereotyped as lazy and unconcerned with important social issues. Because of adult fears of drugs and crime, there were fewer places for young people to gather, especially youth of color. For many young people in the 1980s, zines became that gathering place.

With names like *Baby Fat, Poppin' Zits!* and *Ben is Dead,* zines began to appear around the country, attempting to fulfill young people's need to communicate with each other. Unimpressed by the mainstream media's view of the world, the creators of zines put forth an alternative vision, where youth was no longer seen as unimportant or bad.

In the fall 1997 issue of *Social Justice,* Witknee Hubbs, publisher of the zine *AWOL, Youth for Peace and Revolution,* echoed the feelings of the typical zine reader: "when i walk into the grocery store and stare at the magazine rack all i see is propaganda: lies and standards set by people in power … and i'll walk out empty-handed and run home to my mailbox to see what new zines i got that day. i'll curl up in my room, free from all the people that tell me i'm just a kid/i'm just a girl/i can't change the world, and read.… i'll read the truths of so many kids that finally have an uncensored forum to yell and cry and heal and inform and incite, free from the burdens of adultism.… so while your average jane/joe teenager is out partying all night, there are a whole slew of kids overtaking the copy shops and crowding mail boxes for the love of the zine and the hope and action it inspires."

The subjects of zines are as widely varied as their creators. There are zines about **AIDS** (see entry under 1980s—The Way We Lived in volume 5), kite flying, new-wave comics, and every type of poetry, art, and music. A zine called *8 Track Mind* chronicled the history and availability of **eight-track tapes** (see entry under 1960s—Music in volume 4). *K Composite* featured interviews with the publisher's friends rather than with celebrities. *Snack Bar Confidential* highlighted food packaging and advertising of the 1960s and 1970s. *Bitch* billed itself as a feminist response to popular culture. There are thousands of zines in print, and more ezines on the Internet. Many are "perzines": personal statements of the publisher's view of life and the world, and all bear the mark of handmade individuality. The zine phenomenon represents a reaction to modern mainstream media, which many zine publishers view as slick, overhyped, and deceptive.

With the ever-present rise of the Internet among young people in the early 2000s, paper zines dwindled in popularity, with some disappearing and many others transforming themselves into Web sites and blogs. In either format, a major difference between zine culture and mainstream media is lack of ownership. Few zines are copyrighted, and there is little competition between publishers of zines. Instead, those who make zines encourage their readers to become creators and publish their own zines. Though some critics denounce zines as self-centered and amateurish, zine publishers accept the criticism cheerfully. A good zine, they say, is supposed to be self-centered and amateurish. Zines bypass the "professionalism" of the corporate world and create a vibrant place where real people exchange ideas.

Tina Gianoulis

For More Information

Austin, Bryn. "The Irreverent (Under)World of 'Zines." *Ms.* (Vol. 3, no. 4, January-February 1993): pp. 68–69.

The Book of Zines: Readings from the Fringe. http://www.zinebook.com (accessed July 22, 2011).

Chu, Julie. "Navigating the Media Environment: How Youth Claim a Place Through Zines." *Social Justice* (Vol. 24, no. 3, Fall 1997): pp. 71–86.

Gross, David M. "Zine But Not Heard: Underground, Homemade 'Fanzine' Magazines." *Time* (Vol. 144, no. 10, September 5, 1994): pp. 68–70.

Gunderloy, Mike, and Cari G. Janice. *The World of Zines: A Guide to the Independent Magazine Revolution.* New York: Viking Penguin, 1992.

Pore, Jerod. "Invisible Literature." *Whole Earth Review* (No. 75, Summer 1992): pp. 20–26.

Shea, Christopher. "The Zine Scene: Homemade Magazines Flourishing." *Chronicle of Higher Education* (Vol. 40, no. 11, November 3, 1993): pp. 37–39.

Todd, Mark, and Esther Watson. *Whatcha Mean, What's a Zine?: The Art of Making Zines and Minicomics.* Boston: Graphia, 2006.

1980s

Sports and Games

Professional and major collegiate sports continued to expand in popularity during the decade, and they continued to be lavishly funded by television programmers eager to attract an audience. Television coverage became critical to sports, for it provided the money that made huge salaries possible or, in the college world, allowed major football and basketball programs to build state-of-the-art facilities for their athletes. Televised sports received a big boost through the 1980s with the growing popularity of the ESPN cable-television station, which played an important role in popularizing a variety of sports. Even the Olympics fell under the spell of TV money; ABC paid a record $225 million to broadcast the 1984 Los Angeles summer games.

Not everyone appreciated the role that TV played in sports. One critic claimed that TV "helps make money-grubbing freaks of its heroes. It even modifies and distorts the way sports are played." Athletes no longer stuck with a team for years; instead, they jumped from team to team as they received offers for more money. The fact that many pro and college athletes were involved in drug-use scandals in the decade also helped ruin the image of the athlete as a role model.

Pro baseball in the 1980s suffered through a number of problems, including a player's strike, allegations of drug use, and the Pete Rose (1941–) betting scandal that saw the former Cincinnati Reds star banned from the game. The National Football League (NFL) was also plagued with two strikes in the 1980s. A more notable story in football was the end of the domination of the season-capping Super Bowl by American Football Conference (AFC) teams. Beginning in 1985, National Football Conference (NFC) teams dominated the game, thanks to strong performances by the Washington Redskins, San Francisco 49ers, Chicago Bears, and New York Giants—and to the almost yearly Super Bowl collapse of the Denver Broncos, who lost the Super Bowl in 1987, 1988, and 1990.

Professional basketball recovered from its slump in the 1970s thanks to the spirited play of rising stars Larry Bird (1956–) of the Boston Celtics and Earvin "Magic" Johnson (1959–) of the Los Angeles Lakers. Johnson led the Lakers to eight championship series in the decade, and the team won five of them. Challenging the Lakers for dominance were the Celtics and, late in the decade, the "bad boy" Detroit Pistons, led by point guard Isiah Thomas (1961–). College basketball became a national obsession in the 1980s, thanks in large part to the popularity of the championship playoff series known as "March Madness."

Pro hockey featured the amazing Wayne Gretzky—"the Great One." He electrified the National Hockey League, leading his Edmonton Oilers to four Stanley Cups. Meanwhile, the World Wrestling Federation exploded in popularity, as did such games as Trivial Pursuit, Rubik's Cube, and the video game *Pac-Man.*

Wayne Gretzky (1961–)

Wayne Gretzky—The Great One—is one of the finest and most celebrated hockey players who ever lived. He holds sixty-one individual **National Hockey League** (NHL; see entry under 1910s—Sports and Games in volume 1) records. On ten occasions, he was the league's scoring champ. On nine occasions, he was named the league's Most Valuable Player (MVP). He was voted to the NHL All-Star team eighteen times, and three times was the All-Star game's MVP.

Gretzky began skating when he was two-and-a-half years old. At age ten, he scored 378 goals while playing for a peewee team in his hometown of Brantford, Ontario, Canada. In 1978, when he was seventeen, he signed his first professional contract with the Indianapolis Racers of the upstart World Hockey Association (WHA) but played in just eight games before being sold to the Edmonton Oilers. Following the merger between the WHA and the more established NHL, Gretzky won the NHL Rookie-of-the-Year award with the Oilers in the 1979–80 season. He followed up by breaking the league's single-season points record. In the 1981–82 season he bested the previous season's performance with an amazing 92 goals and 212 points. Gretzky led the Oilers to the Stanley Cup in 1984, 1985, 1987, and 1988.

"The Great One," Canadian hockey player Wayne Gretzky, skates for the Los Angeles Kings during the 1988–89 season. © MIKE POWELL/ALLSPORT/ GETTY IMAGES.

In 1988, Gretzky was dispatched to the larger-market Los Angeles Kings in exchange for $15 million and various players and draft choices. His presence on a major-city American team helped to raise the profile of hockey in the United States. In 1996, he was traded to the St. Louis Blues and soon after signed with the New York Rangers, from which he retired in 1999. From 2001 to 2009, Gretzky had various roles with the NHL's Phoenix Coyotes, including part-owner, head of hockey operations, and head coach. He also was the executive director of Team Canada's men's hockey team in the 2002 and 2006 **Olympics** (see entry under 1900s—Sports and Games in volume 1), winning a gold medal in 2002. In 2010, he had the honor of lighting the Olympic cauldron at the opening ceremonies in Vancouver, British Columbia, Canada.

Rob Edelman

For More Information

Doeden, Matt. *Wayne Gretzky.* Minneapolis: Twenty-First Century Books, 2008.

Dryden, Steve, ed. *Total Gretzky: The Magic, the Legend, the Numbers.* Toronto: McClelland and Stewart, 1999.

Gretzky, Wayne. *Gretzky: An Autobiography.* New York: HarperCollins, 1990.

Gretzky, Wayne, and John Davidson. *99: My Life in Pictures.* New York: Total Sports, 1999.

McConnell, Terry, J'lyn Nye, with Peter Pocklington. *I'd Trade Him Again: On Gretzky, Politics, and the Pursuit of the Perfect Deal.* Toronto: Fenn, 2009.

Messier, Mark, Walter Gretzky, Brett Hull, et al. *Wayne Gretzky: The Making of the Great One.* New York: Beckett, 1988.
Podnieks, Andrew. *The Great One: The Life and Times of Wayne Gretzky.* Chicago: Triumph, 1999.

Pac-Man

Long before Sony PlayStation and Lara Croft, a yellow pizza with a slice missing ruled the video-game arcades. *Pac-Man* appeared in Japan in 1980, produced by Namco. Legend has it that its creator, Toru Iwatani (1955–), was inspired by a night out at a local **pizza** (see entry under 1940s—Food and Drink in volume 3) restaurant. He invented a game that would dominate the **video game** (see entry under 1970s—Sports and Games in

A Pac-Man *video game.* © DENNIS HALLINAN/GETTY IMAGES.

volume 5) market for several years. To today's gamers, *Pac-Man* looks simple and unexciting, but for many serious players it has remained the game to beat for three decades. A perfect *Pac-Man* score was not achieved until 1999.

Pac-Man is the simplest of games. The hero of the game is trapped in a maze littered with dots and occasional pieces of fruit. His task is to "eat" all the dots and fruit without being destroyed by the ghosts "Clyde," "Blinky," "Inky," and "Pinky." Once all the dots are consumed, the player goes on to a new level, which runs faster and behaves differently. "Power Pellets" allow the hero to eat the ghosts.

Originally called *Puckman,* the American arcade game of 1981 became *Pac-Man* to avoid problems with graffiti. The game was so popular that it inspired variations such as *Ms. Pac-Man* and *Baby Pac-Man Pac-Man* merchandise—ashtrays, playing cards, whoopie cushions, soft toys, and so on—soon appeared. In the early 1980s, *Pac-Man* pasta and breakfast cereal even appeared. The song "Pac-Man Fever" reached number nine on the American charts, while the *Pac-Man* **television** (see entry under 1940s—TV and Radio in volume 3) cartoon was also a big hit. *Pac-Man* was named "Game of the Century" at Classic Gaming Expo '99. By the twenty-first century, it was estimated that *Pac-Man* had been played over ten billion times, becoming the highest-grossing video game in history. On May 21–23, 2010, workers' productivity around the globe was noticeably decreased when Google changed the logo on its homepage to a *Pac-Man* game in commemoration of *Pac-Man*'s thirtieth anniversary.

Chris Routledge

For More Information

Herz, J. C. *Joystick Nation: How Videogames Ate Our Quarters, Won Our Hearts, and Rewired Our Minds.* Boston: Little, Brown, 1997.

Poole, Steven. *Trigger Happy: Videogames and the Entertainment Revolution.* New York: Arcade Publishing, 2000.

Trueman, Doug. "The History of Pac-Man." *Gamespot.* http://videogames.gamespot.com/features/universal/hist_pacman/index.html (accessed July 24, 2011).

Rubik's Cube

The multi-colored puzzle known as Rubik's Cube became a worldwide sensation in the 1980s, inspiring clubs, books, newsletters, and even a **Saturday morning cartoon** (see entry under 1960s—TV and Radio in volume 4).

Between 1980 and 1982, an estimated one hundred million Rubik's Cubes were sold worldwide. © FIXER00/ALAMY.

Hungarian architecture professor Erno Rubik (1944–) came up with the idea for the cube in the early 1970s as a teaching tool for his students. Always interested in geometry, Rubik devised a six-sided puzzle with fifty-four colored squares. The object of the puzzle was to get each side to line up entirely as one solid color. It sounded simple, but users quickly discovered how difficult it was. Mathematicians have calculated that there are 43,252,003,274,489,856,000 possible combinations to Rubik's Cube, but only *one* correct solution. The deceptive simplicity of the puzzle proved to be a large part of its appeal.

Rubik's Cube developed a cult following in Europe in the late 1970s. College students and schoolchildren were especially attracted to the device, which won prizes for outstanding invention. Rubik's idea really took off when the Ideal Toy Company began marketing Rubik's Cube in the United States and around the world. Between 1980 and 1982, an estimated one hundred million Rubik's Cubes were sold worldwide. It is difficult to say just how many were sold because of the number of imitation cubes that hit toy shelves around the same time. Some sixty books were published offering strategies and shortcuts for solving the puzzle. Clubs were formed around the globe so that cube enthusiasts could share their tricks and techniques. By 1982, Rubik's Cube had become such a household term that it became part of the *Oxford English Dictionary.*

Rubik's Cube fever peaked around that time, although a Saturday morning cartoon series, *Rubik the Amazing Cube,* ran until 1985. The game has continued to attract new players throughout the decades: 350 million cubes had been sold by 2009, making Rubik's Cube the best-selling toy in history. Novel challenges such as solving the puzzle blindfolded, one-handed, or using only one's feet have proliferated in international contests run by the World Cube Association. The world record for "speedcubing"—5.66 seconds—was set in 2011.

Robert E. Schnakenberg

For More Information

Lawless, Ken. *Dissolving Rubik's Cube: The Ultimate Solution.* New York: Putnam Publishing Group, 1982.

Rubik, Erno. *Rubik's Cubic Compendium.* New York: Oxford University Press, 1987.

Rubik's: The Only Official Site. http://www.rubiks.com/ (accessed July 24, 2011).

Slocum, Jerry. *The Cube: Secrets, Stories and Solutions of the World's Best-Selling Puzzle.* New York: Black Dog & Leventhal, 2009.

Shah, Neil. *Unlocking the Rubik's Cube.* Victoria, BC, Canada: Trafford, 2008.

Taylor, Don. *Mastering Rubik's Cube.* New York: Holt, Rinehart and Winston, 1981.

Trivial Pursuit

Although board games have lost a great deal of popularity to their digital counterparts, a few continue to capture the public's imagination and leisure time. Toward the end of the twentieth century, none was more successful than *Trivial Pursuit.*

As the name suggests, the game tests players' knowledge of obscure facts. In the basic game (known as the "Genus Edition"), the facts are divided into five categories: Art and Literature, History, Sports and Leisure, Geography, and Science and Nature. A die roll moves each

The general knowledge board game Trivial Pursuit was the hit board game of the 1980s. © ART DIRECTORS & TRIP/ALAMY.

player around a circular board, each square of which represents one of the five categories. Questions are contained on pre-printed cards, and a player must correctly answer a question in each category to have a chance of winning. Various supplementary sets of questions may be purchased, all of which can be used with the basic board.

The game was conceived in 1979 by Chris Haney and Scott Abbott, two young journalists in Montreal, Quebec, Canada. They had a friend do the artwork for the board, borrowed money wherever they could, and finally launched the game in 1981. Initial interest among distributors was limited, and the fledgling enterprise lost money. However, the game eventually caught the attention of the Selchow and Righter Company, a major American toy-and-game manufacturer. It bought the rights, marketed the game, and by 1983 *Trivial Pursuit* was an undeniable success, selling three-and-a-half million units. In the next year, sales reached twenty million.

Other sets of cards followed, which allowed the manufacturer to appeal to players with different interests. The first variant was the "Silver Screen Edition," which focused on movies. It was followed by the "Baby Boomer Edition" (dealing with events since 1950) and a "Sports Edition," among others. Recent years have seen the release of the "Millennium Edition" and the "Warner Brothers Edition."

Trivial Pursuit games are now available in nineteen languages and thirty-three countries. They can also be played on the **Internet** (see entry under 1990s—The Way We Lived in volume 5) and in a handheld electronic version, although the boxed version continued to sell well, reaching 88 million sold by 2004. New editions of the game cards are constantly under development.

Justin Gustainis

For More Information

Bernikow, Louise. "Trivia Inc." *Esquire* (March 1985): pp. 116–18.

Hasbro. "The World of Trivial Pursuit." http://www.trivialpursuit.com (accessed July 24, 2011).

Orbanes, Philip. *The Game Makers: The Story of Parker Brothers from Tiddledy Winks to Trivial Pursuit.* Boston: Harvard Business School Press, 2004.

Silver, Marc. "The Endless Pursuit of All Things Trivial." *U.S. News and World Report* (November 6, 1989): p. 102.

Tarpey, John P. "Selchow and Righter: Playing Trivial Pursuit to the Limit." *Business Week* (November 26, 1984).

World Wrestling Federation

Although it reached new levels of popularity in the late 1990s, the World Wrestling Federation (WWF) has actually been around since the early 1960s. The professional wrestling circuit, which bills itself as the world's "highest form of sports entertainment," has grown into a multibillion-dollar empire thanks to its unique mix of violent mayhem and soap opera. Stars who emerged from the WWF ranks include Hulk Hogan (1973–), Dwayne "The Rock" Johnson (1972–), and "Stone Cold" Steve Austin (1964–).

The World Wrestling Federation, at first known as the Worldwide Wrestling Federation, began in 1963 as an offshoot of another wrestling

World Wrestling Entertainment Smackdown Live Tour in 2011. © GALLO IMAGES/ALAMY.

circuit, the National Wrestling Alliance (NWA). The owner and promoter of the new organization was Vince McMahon Sr. (1915–1984). By developing such stars as Bruno Sammartino (1935–), Andre the Giant (1946–1993), and Haystacks Calhoun (1933–1989), McMahon was able to turn the floundering business of professional wrestling into a regional powerhouse. Some critics complained about the violence in professional wrestling or charged that the "sport" was actually staged, but millions of fans crowded into large arenas like New York's Madison Square Garden to cheer on the WWF's stars.

In the 1980s, McMahon's son Vince Jr. (1945–) took over the WWF and began to promote the sport nationally. He developed new stars like Hulk Hogan and Sgt. Slaughter (1948–), who brought a more cartoonish element to the matches. McMahon also used the power of **television** (see entry under 1940s—TV and Radio in volume 3), putting WWF matches on pay-per-view TV and making millions in the process. The WWF's Wrestle-mania events drew enormous crowds—ninety thousand people attended one evening of matches at the Silverdome in Pontiac, Michigan. A number of wrestling stars, like Hogan and Jesse "The Body" Ventura (1951–), went on to movie careers.

In the 1990s, a scandal involving steroid drug use by wrestlers almost toppled the WWF. The resourceful McMahon bounced back with a new breed of wrestling stars, led by Austin and later by Johnson. The level of violent content on WWF shows like *Smackdown!* rose dramatically, as wrestling cards became elaborate soap operas with ongoing storylines—often involving McMahon himself. By the end of the 1990s, wrestling was so popular that one former star—Ventura—was even elected governor of Minnesota.

In 2002, partly due to pressure from the World Wide Fund for Nature, which also held a trademark on the initials WWF, the company inaugurated its "Get the F Out" campaign, rebranding itself as World Wrestling Entertainment. As of 2011, WWE broadcasts its shows to nearly 150 countries in 30 languages.

Robert E. Schnakenberg

For More Information

Assael, Shaun, and Mike Mooneyham. *Sex, Lies, and Headlocks: The Real Story of Vince McMahon and World Wrestling Federation.* New York: Crown, 2002.

Cohen, Dan. *Wrestling Renegades: An In-Depth Look at Today's Superstars of Pro Wrestling.* New York: Pocket Books, 1999.

Greenberg, Keith Elliot. *Pro Wrestling: From Carnivals to Cable TV.* Minneapolis: Lerner, 2000.

Keith, Scott. *The Buzz on Professional Wrestling.* New York: Lebhar-Friedman Books, 2001.

Shields, Brian, and Keith Sullivan. *WW Encyclopedia.* New York: DK, 2009.

1980s

TV and Radio

The "big three" networks—ABC, CBS, and NBC—continued to dominate American television in the 1980s, although their dominance was increasingly challenged by cable TV providers and by a fourth network, FOX, created in 1985. With their market share declining, the networks tried to offer more challenging fare and to expand their broadcast hours. In general, however, network programming remained safe and noncontroversial. The exception to this rule was *Roseanne* (1988–1997), a situation comedy (sitcom) about a working-class family that addressed issues of class, race, and sexuality. Along with *Roseanne,* the most popular shows of the decade were *The Cosby Show* (1984–92), *Dallas* (1978–91), *Cheers* (1982–93), *Miami Vice* (1984–89), *Dynasty* (1981–89), and *Knots Landing* (1979–93).

Cable television became an even more important influence on TV programming in the 1980s. The availability of telecommunications satellites made it possible for more cable channels to broadcast nationwide. More and more Americans gained access to cable programming during the decade. Cable programmers such as HBO, Showtime, The Movie Channel, ESPN, MTV, VH1, and many others offered increasing competition to the big three networks. CNN revolutionized TV news broadcasting beginning in 1980 when it began offering news coverage twenty-four hours a day. By the end of the decade, CNN was known for being first on the scene at many major news events.

Radio remained a popular source of news and entertainment. In fact, a survey conducted in the 1980s revealed that 99 percent of American households owned a radio (as compared with 98 percent owning a television) and that the average American household had 5.5 radios, not including car radios. Thanks to their better sound quality, FM radio stations became the most popular in the 1980s. Many cities had FM stations that offered every possible variety of music, from jazz to classical, rock and roll to country. Increasingly, AM stations offered "talk shows." These shows tended to become polarized along political lines during the 1980s. Conservative talk show host Rush Limbaugh (c. 1951–) got his start in the 1980s. The more liberal National Public Radio (NPR) was the single most successful national radio network in the 1980s, reaching more Americans than any other network.

The A-Team

"In 1972," the gravel-voiced narrator of the **television** (see entry under 1940s—TV and Radio in volume 3) action series *The A-Team* explained, "A crack commando unit was sent to prison by a military court for a crime they didn't commit." The men soon escaped from the maximum-security stockade in which they were incarcerated, the narrator continued. He further explained that, although they were still wanted by the U.S. government, "If you have a problem, if no one else can help, and if you can find them, maybe you can hire the A-Team."

That opening voiceover perfectly set the tone for this exciting mix of action and macho fellowship, which aired on NBC from 1983 to 1987. Inspired by films like *The Dirty Dozen* (1967) and *Kelly's Heroes* (1970), *The A-Team* confronted the commandos with a new and dangerous mission every week and usually ended with a firefight or an explosion. The show proved a blockbuster hit, especially with young male audience members. The show also made a cult hero out of one of its cast members, the hulking, bejeweled former bodyguard known as Mr. T, famous for his many gold chains.

Four men formed the core of the A-Team and remained with the series for the entire five-season run. Veteran leading man George Peppard (1928–1994) played John "Hannibal" Smith, the cigar-chomping leader of the group. His signature line, uttered in almost every episode, was "I love it when a plan comes together." Dwight Schultz (1947–) played the wild man of the group, H. M. "Howlin' Mad" Murdock, a flaky former pilot who was constantly being committed to the insane asylum. Dirk Benedict (1945–) played the team's romantic rogue, Templeton "Faceman" Peck. The good-looking con artist was often called upon to charm his way into (or out of) dangerous situations.

Bodyguard-turned-actor Laurence Tureaud worked under the name of Mr. T on The A-Team *as mechanic B. A. Baracus.* © NBC-TV/ THE KOBAL COLLECTION/ART RESOURCE, NY.

By far the most popular member of *The A-Team* was its hulking mechanic, Bosco "Bad Attitude" Baracus. A muscular black man with a Mohawk hairstyle and a curious fear of flying, "B. A.," as he was called, was a mechanical genius who could fix anything or build a tank out of bamboo if the occasion called for it. Playing B. A. was one-time **Hollywood** (see entry under 1930s—Film and Theater in volume 3) bodyguard Laurence Tureaud (1952—), who adopted the professional name Mr. T. The gentle giant quickly captured the imagination of the show's viewers and began appearing on lunch boxes, in action figures, and in movies such as *Rocky III* (1982). After a much-publicized battle with cancer in the 1990s, Tureaud began a show business comeback as a commercial pitchman in the early twenty-first century. In 2010, a feature film titled *The A-Team* was released by 20th Century Fox. Starring four actors who reprised the show's original heroes, the film's context was updated to reference the first Gulf War. The original *A-Team* lives on in reruns.

Robert E. Schnakenberg

For More Information

The A-Team Site. http://www.buyersmls.com/americantv/ateam.htm (accessed July 25, 2011).

Corliss, Richard. "A B-Plus for the A-Team." *Time* (June 12, 2010).

T., Mr. *Mr. T: The Man with the Gold.* New York: St. Martin's Press, 1984.

Cheers

Cheers, the **sitcom** (situation comedy; see entry under 1950s—TV and Radio in volume 3) that aired on NBC from 1982 to 1993, was one of the most critically and popularly acclaimed programs on **television** (see entry under 1940s—TV and Radio in volume 3). Created by writers Glen Charles (1943–), Les Charles, and James Burrows (1940–), the series focused on the eccentric staff and customers of Cheers, a bar in Boston, Massachusetts. When it premiered in 1982, NBC was the lowest-rated broadcast network with no series among television's top twenty programs. *Cheers* barely survived its initial season. It remained on the air only because of the persistence of network executives who believed the quality show would eventually attract an audience. In 1985, NBC became the dominant network based largely on the success of

The cast from Cheers *later in the show's eleven-year run: (front row) George Wendt, Kirstie Alley, Ted Danson, John Ratzenberger; (back row) Rhea Perlman, Woody Harrelson, Kelsey Grammer, and Bebe Neuwirth.* © PARAMOUNT TV/THE KOBAL COLLECTION/ ART RESOURCE, NY.

Cheers and other popular sitcoms in its Thursday night "Must See TV" lineup like ***The Cosby Show*** (1984–92; see entry under 1980s—TV and Radio in volume 5) and *Family Ties* (1982–89).

Cheers was populated by a number of characters who have become television icons. The early seasons concentrated on the on-again-off-again romance between Sam Malone (Ted Danson, 1947–), a womanizing former pitcher for the Boston Red Sox who owned the bar, and snobbish waitress Diane Chambers (Shelley Long, 1949–). Tending bar was befuddled Ernie "Coach" Pantusso (Nicholas Colasanto, 1924–1985). When Colasanto died in 1985, the equally dim-witted farm boy Woody Boyd (Woody Harrelson, 1961–) replaced his character. Carla Tortelli (Rhea Perlman, 1948–) was a mean-spirited waitress with many children. The cast was rounded out by tavern regulars Norm Peterson (George Wendt, 1948–), an accountant; Cliff Clavin (John Ratzenberger, 1947–), a trivia-spouting mailman; and Frasier Crane (Kelsey Grammar, 1955–), a pompous psychologist. In 1986, Bebe Neuwirth (1958–) joined the cast as the brusque, humorless Lilith Sternin, Frasier's rival psychologist, then love interest, then wife; in 1987, Kirstie Alley (1955–) took over as the lead female character, Rebecca Howe, when Long left the series.

Cheers is considered to be one of television's most sophisticated and witty comedies. Its characters were more than stereotypes and developed into fully rounded figures over the show's 11 seasons and 269 episodes. When the series concluded in 1993, its final episode became a national event. The Sam and Diane romance was renewed as Long returned for a guest appearance. The couple contemplated reconciliation, but eventually realized they were not destined to be together. After the series ended, a number of its characters returned to television for guest appearances on the *Cheers* spin-off, ***Frasier*** (1993–2004; see entry under 1990s—TV and Radio in volume 5). *Cheers* continues to attract legions of fans in syndication (the re-release of programs to independent TV stations) as viewers continue to visit the bar "where everybody knows your name."

Charles Coletta

For More Information

Bjorklund, Dennis. *Toasting Cheers: An Episode Guide to the 1982–1993 Comedy Series with Cast Biographies and Character Profiles.* Jefferson, NC: McFarland, 1997.

Greenberg, Keith Elliot. *Charles, Burrows, & Charles: TV's Top Producers.* Woodbridge, CT: Blackbirch Press, 1995.
Wenger, Mark. *The Cheers Trivia Book.* Secaucus, NJ: Carol Publishing, 1994.

CNN

On June 1, 1980, **television** (see entry under 1940s—TV and Radio in volume 3) journalism was changed forever with the premiere of the Cable News Network (CNN). Television executive Reese Schonfeld and Ted Turner (1938—), a flamboyant Southern businessman and sportsman, founded the twenty-four-hour cable-news service on the belief that the growing **cable-TV** (see entry under 1970s—TV and Radio in volume 4) audience would support an all-news channel. Most in the mainstream media predicted the enterprise was doomed to failure and labeled CNN the "Chicken Noodle Network." However, CNN emerged as one of the most influential and important networks in television history.

It is estimated that approximately fifteen million Americans watch CNN at least once a day. That number of viewers further increases if CNN's foreign viewership is included. The network's main attraction is the immediate and continuous coverage of the day's most important events that it offers its viewers. Steven Stark (1951–), in *Glued to the Set,* writes, "CNN would cut to any event, anywhere, at any time. Over the years, those attributes would remain the hallmark of the network in both its approach to news and the reaction of the public." Only CNN provided live coverage of the *Challenger* space shuttle disaster in January 1986. Its reputation was further enhanced by its coverage of the Persian Gulf War (1991), as it provided extensive reports on all aspects of the conflict. By the mid-1990s, many spoke of the "CNN effect," which described world leaders' acknowledgement of CNN's importance and their shaping of events in order to appear in a more positive light on the network.

The success of CNN led to the creation of the twenty-four-hour news cycle, as viewers became accustomed to watching news coverage at any hour, rather than just during the networks' traditional evening newscasts. CNN scored its highest ratings with its live coverage of breaking events like the fall of the Berlin Wall (1989), the Tiananmen Square massacre (1989), and the **O. J. Simpson** (1947–; see entry under 1990s—The Way We Lived in volume 5) murder trial (1995). On

September 11, 2001, CNN was the first network to cover the events live at the World Trade Center (see 9/11 entry under 2000s—The Way We Lived in volume 6). Critics sometimes complained that CNN spent too much of its time and resources on these live, continuing stories solely to attract a mass audience.

By the late 1990s, CNN faced increased competition from other cable-news networks like MSNBC and Fox News, as Americans increasingly wanted their news on demand. In 1995, however, CNN began broadcasting over the Internet and by 2009 the network was the number three online news site in the United States. CNN's television presence has also remained strong, broadcasting into 100 million American homes and to 212 countries through its CNN International division by 2010. CNN's commitment to constant, global news coverage has changed how Americans and citizens all over the world both receive and respond to the news.

Charles Coletta

For More Information

CNN.com. http://www.cnn.com (accessed July 26, 2011).

Diamond, Edwin. *The Media Show: The Changing Face of the News, 1985–1990.* Cambridge, MA: MIT Press, 1991.

Flournoy, Don, and Robert Stewart. *CNN: Making News in the Global Market.* Luton, UK: University of Luton, 1997.

Schonfeld, Reese. *Me and Ted Against the World: The Unauthorized Story of the Founding of CNN.* New York: Cliff Street Books, 2001.

Stark, Steven. *Glued to the Set.* New York: Free Press, 1997.

Whittemore, Hank. *CNN: The Inside Story.* Boston: Little, Brown, 1990.

The Cosby Show

Until *The Cosby Show* (1984–92) came to **television** (see entry under 1940s—TV and Radio in volume 3), the relatively few sitcoms (situation comedies; see entry under 1950s—TV and Radio in volume 3) featuring all–African American casts highlighted characters who were working-class or who were struggling to make it in inner-city America. Unlike such contemporaries, *The Cosby Show* was something else altogether. The Huxtable clan, the show's centerpiece family, was headed by a father, Dr. Heathcliff "Cliff" Huxtable (played by Bill Cosby, 1937–), who was an obstetrician, and a mother, Clair (Phylicia Rashad, 1948–),

The Huxtable family cast from The Cosby Show*: (front) Lisa Bonet, Bill Cosby, Keshia Knight Pulliam, and Phylicia Rashad; (back) Sabrina Le Beauf, Tempestt Bledsoe, and Malcolm-Jamal Warner.* © CARSEY-WERNER CO./ EVERETT COLLECTION.

who was a legal-aid attorney. Both parents were strict but fair disciplinarians and positive role models for their five children, who at the show's outset ranged in age from five years to young adulthood. Most important of all, the Huxtables were comfortably upper-middle-class. They reflected the reality that all African Americans were not undereducated and uncultured. They used correct English grammar. They were not on welfare or employed in dead-end professions. They did not all come of age in single-parent households.

The Cosby Show, which aired on NBC, was TV's top-rated program for most of its run. The most established African American–oriented sitcom before *The Cosby Show* was ***Amos 'n' Andy*** (1951–53), which was based on a long-running radio series (1928–1955). *Amos 'n' Andy* focused not on the title characters but on a buffoonish con man named George Stevens, who was always scheming to make a fast buck. Other pre–*Cosby Show* African American TV comedies included *Good Times* (1974–79), about a low-income family living in the South Side Chicago **ghetto** (see entry under 1960s—The Way We Lived in volume 3), and *Sanford and Son* (1972–77), spotlighting the antics of a junkman and his offspring. George Jefferson (Sherman Hemsley, 1938–), on *The Jeffersons* (1975–85), may have been upwardly mobile; he had transformed a modest dry-cleaning business into a chain of stores. Yet he was loud and uncouth and was as small-minded as any white bigot.

As it portrayed a rock-solid family unit in which the parents prevailed in their wisdom, *The Cosby Show* had more in common which such classic 1950s sitcoms as ***The Adventures of Ozzie and Harriet*** (1952–66; see entry under 1950s—TV and Radio in volume 3) and *Father Knows Best* (1954–63), both of which featured middle-class white families. While *The Cosby Show* Huxtables were a part of the American mainstream, in no way were they ignorant of their roots. Through the course of the series, all the Cosby kids were shown to be well aware of the sacrifices of their predecessors, who had fought for and won civil rights for African Americans. Eldest daughter Sondra eventually married and delivered twins, who were named for Nelson Mandela (1918–), the South African who fought against his country's racist apartheid policies and who eventually became his country's president, and his then-wife Winnie Mandela (1936–). At the same time, because the situations presented on *The Cosby Show* were familiar to anyone attempting to sustain a marriage and raise children, the show appealed to audiences of all races and economic backgrounds. Indeed, the child-rearing philosophies explored on *The Cosby Show* reflected Cosby's knowledge of current theories of education in the United States. Cosby earned a doctorate in education at the University of Massachusetts in the 1970s.

For most of his career, Bill Cosby has been a groundbreaking entertainer. After starting out as a nightclub comedian, he became one of the first African Americans to have a starring or costarring role on an American television series, playing secret agent Alexander Scott on *I Spy* (1965–68). Three times he earned Emmy Awards as Best Actor in a Drama Series. After appearing in several short-lived programs—*The Bill Cosby Show* (1969–71), *The New Bill Cosby Show* (1972–73), and *Cos*

(1976)—he created *The Cosby Show.* Since then, Cosby has appeared in *The Cosby Mysteries* (1994–95) and *Cosby* (1996–2000). He is also well known for his educational programming, including the beloved cartoon *Fat Albert and The Cosby Kids,* and for his appearances in **Jell-O** (see entry under 1900s—Food and Drink in volume 1) pudding commercials. *The Cosby Show* engendered one spin-off, *A Different World,* which aired from 1987 to 1993 and featured Huxtable daughter Denise during the first season as she attends Hillman College, the fictional school that was her parents' alma mater.

Rob Edelman

For More Information

Adler, Bill. *The Cosby Wit: His Life and Humor.* New York: Carroll & Graf, 1986.

BillCosby.com: The Unofficial Fan Site. http://www.billcosby.com/ (accessed July 26, 2011).

Cosby, Bill. *Cosbyology: Essays and Observations from the Doctor of Comedy.* New York: Hyperion, 2001.

Cosby, Bill. *Fatherhood.* Rev. ed. Syracuse, NY: Signal Hill, 1993.

Cosby, Bill. *Time Flies.* New York: Doubleday, 1987.

Kimble-Ellis, Sonya. *Bill Cosby: Entertainer and Activist.* New York: Chelsea House, 2010.

Smith, Ronald L. *Cosby: The Life of a Comedy Legend.* Rev. ed. Amherst, NY: Prometheus Books, 1997.

Dallas

In 1978, the prime-time soap opera *Dallas* (1978–91) premiered and soon became one of the most watched and discussed programs in **television** (see entry under 1940s—TV and Radio in volume 3) history. The series revolved around the Ewings, a fabulously wealthy family whose fortune came from oil. For more than a decade, audiences tuned in to view the clan's many excesses and their exploits in both the boardroom and the bedroom. *Dallas* popularized the serial format of daytime **soap operas** (see entry under 1930s—TV and Radio in volume 2) with the prime-time audience. The show relied on melodramatic plots and season-ending cliffhangers to captivate viewers.

Larger-than-life characters who constantly battled to control the Texas oil industry, wore designer fashions, faced intense personal tragedies, and were interested in sex populated *Dallas.* Many of the

J. R. Ewing, as portrayed by actor Larry Hagman on Dallas, *"the man America loved to hate."* © LORIMAR/ THE KOBAL COLLECTION/ART RESOURCE, NY.

stories occurred at Southfork, the Ewings' huge ranch where the family all lived despite their rivalries. The cast was large and provided each episode with a number of steamy sub-plots. However, the most important character was J. R. (Larry Hagman, 1931–), the eldest Ewing son, whose sleazy personal behavior and backstabbing business ethics made him the man America loved to hate. He reveled in his unscrupulous practices and was featured on the cover of ***Time*** (see entry under 1920—Print Culture in volume 2), which called him a "human oil slick." J. R.'s corrupt nature often caused him to clash with his youngest brother, Bobby (Patrick Duffy, 1949–), who was known for his morals and integrity. In 1980, one of the most-watched episodes in TV history answered the cliffhanger question, "Who Shot J. R.?" Attempting to deduce the identity of the assailant became a popular culture phenomenon. Viewers eventually discovered the shooter was Kristin Shepard (Mary Crosby, 1959–), J. R.'s sister-in-law, whom he had framed for prostitution.

Dallas was a success throughout the world. Some critics stated its popularity was due to the viewers' desire to see that even the wealthiest individuals could lead lives more miserable than that of the average citizen. Others believed the program reflected the 1980s' emphasis on greed. *Dallas* inspired a number of similar programs like *Knots Landing* (1978–93), *Dynasty* (1981–89), and *Falcon Crest* (1981–90). All these shows glorified big business and conspicuous consumption (buying pricey items to show off wealth). Although the series ended in 1991, the cast later reunited for several TV movies, in which the Ewings still lived in luxury and J. R. continued to scheme.

In July 2011, TNT, a branch of Warner Brothers Television, announced the debut of a "continuation" series, also to be called *Dallas*, which was projected to premiere in the summer of 2012. The plot was to revolve around John Ross Ewing III, son of the original J. R., and Christopher Ewing, son of J. R.'s brother, Bobby.

Charles Coletta

For More Information

Corliss, Richard. "TV's *Dallas:* Whodunit?" *Time* (August 11, 1980): pp. 60–66.

Curran, Barbara A. *"Dallas": The Complete Story of the World's Favorite Prime-Time Soap.* Nashville, TN: Cumberland House, 2005.

Kalter, Suzy. *The Complete Book of "Dallas."* New York: Abrams, 1986.

Liebes, Tamar, and Elihu Katz. *The Export of Meaning: Cross-Cultural Readings of "Dallas."* 2nd ed. Cambridge, UK: Polity Press, 1993.

Marschall, Rick. *History of Television.* New York: Gallery Books, 1987.

Stark, Steven. *Glued to the Set.* New York: Free Press, 1997.

Ultimate Dallas. http://www.UltimateDallas.Com (accessed July 26, 2011).

Van Wormer, Laura. *Dallas.* Garden City, NY: Doubleday, 1985.

David Letterman (1947–)

An original in late-night television, comedian and talk-show host David Letterman. © WORLDWIDE PANTS INC./THE KOBAL COLLECTION/ART RESOURCE, NY.

David Letterman revitalized television's late-night talk-show format beginning in the 1980s. His irreverent and ironic humor, sometimes abrasive celebrity interviews, and wild antics won Letterman the reputation as one of TV's most popular and innovative personalities. Born in Indiana, Letterman idolized **Johnny Carson** (1925–2005; see entry under 1960s—TV and Radio in volume 4) and dreamed of being a broadcaster from childhood. In 1975, he moved to **Hollywood** (see entry under 1930s—Film and Theater in volume 2) to pursue a career as a stand-up comedian and comedy writer.

NBC offered Letterman a late-night show in the 12:30 AM time slot. *Late Night with David Letterman* (1982–93) was a perfect showcase for its host's offbeat wit. Letterman continued the traditional talk-show format of a monologue (an opening series of jokes), followed by celebrity interviews. He also added an edgy sensibility to the traditional format. Audiences could expect all sorts of unusual activity on the show. He often tangled with guests, participated in outrageous stunts, and developed a series of routines like the Top Ten Lists and Stupid Pet Tricks that kept audiences glued to the set.

Disappointed over losing out to Jay Leno (1950–) as successor to Carson when he retired from his position hosting ***The Tonight Show*** (see entry under 1950s—TV and Radio in volume 3) in 1992, Letterman moved to CBS in 1993, where the show remained for nearly two decades. When Carson died in 2005, Letterman did an opening monologue consisting solely of jokes written by his idol. Letterman has remained a strong television presence into the twenty-first century and has been nominated for fifty-two Emmy Awards.

Charles Coletta

For More Information

Carter, Bill. *The Late Shift: Letterman, Leno, and the Network Battle for the Night.* New York: Hyperion Books, 1994.
"Late Show with David Letterman." *cbs.com.* http://www.cbs.com/latenight/lateshow/ (accessed July 26, 2011).
Lefkowitz, Frances. *David Letterman.* New York: Chelsea House, 1997.
Lennon, Rosemarie. *David Letterman: On Stage and Off.* New York: Pinnacle, 1994.

Miami Vice

The popular one-hour police drama *Miami Vice* aired on NBC from 1984 to 1989. *Miami Vice* combined elements from traditional "cop shows" with an emphasis on high fashion, exotic locations, and music-video sequences. The show depicted an interracial pair of detectives who

"MTV cops": actors Don Johnson and Philip Michael Thomas as police detectives Sonny Crockett and Ricardo Tubbs on Miami Vice. © UNIVERSAL TV/THE KOBAL COLLECTION/ART RESOURCE, NY.

battled the narcotics trade in southern Florida. The series starred Don Johnson (1949–) and Philip Michael Thomas (1949–) as undercover detectives Sonny Crockett and Ricardo Tubbs. Miami's glamorous beaches and resorts were contrasted with the city's underbelly of corruption, violence, and tragedy that resulted from drug trafficking.

Miami Vice was the brainchild of NBC executive Brandon Tartikoff (1949–1997), who envisioned a show about "MTV cops." Michael Mann (1943–) executed Tartikoff's idea and crafted a series where style was more important than substance. The detectives' clothing, cars, and romances were more important than the standard "cops and robbers" plots. The series was filmed on location in Miami and made expert use of the city's unique architecture, geography, and Latin flavor. Johnson emerged as a sex symbol and sparked a casual-chic fashion trend. It became common to see men who, like Johnson on the show, wore expensive Italian sports jackets over **T-shirts** (see entry under 1910s—Fashion in volume 1) along with baggy linen slacks and slip-on shoes without socks. Johnson's perpetual "five o'clock shadow" (beard stubble) became his trademark and was copied by many men during the mid-1980s. *Miami Vice* also helped Miami reclaim its title as a playground for the rich and famous.

During the third season ratings fell as viewers grew tired of the *Miami Vice* fad. Producer Mann attempted to recapture the public's attention by abandoning the pastel color scheme for darker tones that reflected more intense plotlines. This surface change was unsuccessful, and Crockett and Tubbs left the air in 1989. *Miami Vice* is now recalled as a cultural artifact showcasing what was most hip and trendy in 1980s America.

Miami Vice aired in reruns from 1996 to 1999 in the United States on the FX cable channel, then again from 2006 to 2007 on the TV Land cable network. The show remains popular among TV viewers in Europe and the Arab world. In 2006 a film adaptation written, directed, and produced by Mann was released. Starring Jamie Foxx (1967–) as Tubbs and Colin Farrell (1976–) as Crockett, the film opened to mixed reviews but did well at the box office and in subsequent DVD sales.

Charles Coletta

For More Information

Benedek, Emily. "Inside *Miami Vice*." *Rolling Stone* (March 28, 1985): pp. 56–62, 125.

Buxton, David. *From "The Avengers" to "Miami Vice": Form and Ideology in the Television Series.* New York: Manchester University Press, 1990.
Feuer, Jane. *Seeing Through the Eighties: Television and Reaganism.* Durham, NC: Duke University Press, 1995.
Janeshutz, Trish, and Bob MacGregor. *The Making of "Miami Vice."* New York: Ballantine, 1986.
Miami Vice Chronicles. http://www.wildhorse.com/MiamiVice/ (accessed July 26, 2011).
Sanders, Steven. *Miami Vice.* Detroit: Wayne State University Press, 2010.

Roseanne

During its ten-year run during the late 1980s and 1990s, the television sitcom (situation comedy; see entry under 1950s—TV and Radio in volume 3) *Roseanne* consistently pushed the boundaries of **television** (see entry under 1940s—TV and Radio in volume 3), both in

The Conner family from the hit sitcom Roseanne*: (in front of couch) Sara Gilbert; (on couch) Michael Fishman, John Goodman, and Roseanne Barr.* © UNIVERSAL TV/THE KOBAL COLLECTION/ART RESOURCE, NY.

its portrayal of working-class characters and in its discussion of previously taboo subjects such as sex and socioeconomic status. Based on the personality and stand-up comedy act of Roseanne Barr (1952–; also known as Roseanne Arnold, and then simply Roseanne), the show centered around Roseanne and her blue-collar family, the Conners, with John Goodman (1952–) as her husband, Dan. Roseanne's wise-cracking and often biting humor, and the interplay between her and her family, seemed very real to the show's many viewers. The show earned top ratings in the early 1990s.

The Conner family's lives in the fictional Midwestern town of Lanford were often beset by hard times, and their economic problems provided the backdrop for the social commentary that came from the show. Unlike previous shows that had often made fun of blue-collar workers, *Roseanne* celebrated them even as it refused to gloss over the hardships of their lives. The show took on large social issues such as how economic recessions hurt ordinary working people, the unwillingness of politicians to deal with their problems, sexism and gender inequalities, unionization, and corporate power. Even more provocative were personal issues such as sex, birth control, abortion, homosexuality, teen pregnancy, and drug use, all of which were discussed on the show. The show's willingness to tackle these complex issues helped open them up to wider discussion in society. The political and social commentary on *Roseanne* was in marked contrast to other family-comedy sitcoms of the time such as ***The Cosby Show*** (1984–92; see entry under 1980s—TV and Radio in volume 5) and *Family Ties* (1982–1989). It also brought back some of the elements of earlier, more political sitcoms such as ***All in the Family*** (1971–79; see entry under 1970s—TV and Radio in volume 4) that had largely been missing from prime-time comedy sitcoms.

These social and political issues would not have gone very far were it not for the high-quality writing and acting in the series. Not surprisingly, when good comedy focused on realistic family lives and issues, viewers responded, making the series one of the most popular and important shows in the 1980s and 1990s. Reruns aired continuously in syndication on TBS, Nick at Nite, and TV Land throughout the early 2000s. Roseanne Barr has gone on to author three books, release DVDs for children, and to tour internationally with a new stand-up comedy act. In 2011, she premiered *Roseanne's Nuts*, a TV show about her new life running a macadamia nut farm in Hawaii.

Timothy Berg

For More Information

Arnold, Roseanne. *My Lives.* New York: Ballantine, 1994.

Barr, Roseanne. *Roseanne: My Life as a Woman.* New York: Harper & Row, 1989.

Mayerle, Judine. "Roseanne: How Did You Get Inside My House?: A Case Study of a Hit Blue-Collar Situation Comedy." *Journal of Popular Culture* (Vol. 24, no. 4, 1991): pp. 71–88.

Roseanne World. http://www.roseanneworld.com/blog/home.php (accessed July 27, 2011).

Watson, Mary Ann. *Defining Visions: Television and the American Experience in the 20th Century.* 2nd ed. Malden, MA: Blackwell, 2008.

Shock Radio

Shock radio describes an aggressive kind of **radio** (see entry under 1920s—TV and Radio in volume 2) programming that first gained popularity during the 1980s. Usually hosted by outspoken **disc jockeys** (see entry under 1950s—Music in volume 3) with strong personalities and strong opinions, the aim of shock radio is to surprise audiences by using language, opinion, and humor that many find offensive. "Shock jocks," as the hosts of these programs are called, often find themselves in trouble with the Federal Communication Commission (FCC) for their coarse language and off-color jokes. However, some audiences, especially white men between the ages of twenty-five and fifty-four, find their raunchy humor irreverent and refreshing. Regular listeners tune in to hear the latest outrageous joke.

Many people see shock radio as a reaction to the political activity and awareness of the 1960s and 1970s. During that time, many people, especially political liberals, became sensitive to the effect of racial slurs and demeaning ethnic jokes. As a result, they tried to change their language and humor to make them less offensive. This **political correctness** (see entry under 1980s—The Way We Lived in volume 5), as it came to be called, was irritating to many, especially conservative white men, who felt that it limited their freedom of speech. Listening to radio shock jocks tell sexual, racial, and ethnic jokes allowed audiences to laugh once again at forbidden topics.

One of the first and most famous shock jocks was New Yorker Howard Stern (1954–). Stern began his radio career in 1976, but he did not develop his shock-jock persona until 1981 when he worked for a Washington, D.C., radio station. His crude and insulting humor was so successful that he was soon earning $200,000 per year at New York's WNBC, and his show was sold to radio stations around the country. Dozens of other shock jocks have followed Stern, including Don Imus (1940–) in New York, Drew and Mike (Drew Lane and Mike Clark) in Detroit, and Doug Tracht (1950–; known as the Greaseman) in Washington, D.C., though none go to the extremes that Stern has typically gone.

Although shock jocks usually laugh off public criticism of their outrageous approach to entertainment, some have been punished for going too far. During his career, Stern and his radio station have been charged almost $3 million in fines by the FCC for indecency. In 1999, Tracht was fired from his job for making a racist joke about a hate crime in which a black man was killed. In 2004, Stern's show was cancelled by several Clear Channel Communications stations after the shock jock's remarks cost them nearly $500,000 in fines; Stern then transferred his show in 2006 to satellite radio, which is exempt from certain FCC rules. In April 2007, Don Imus was fired from CBS Radio for describing the Rutgers women's basketball team as "nappy-headed hos," though he returned to the airwaves on ABC Radio in December.

Tina Gianoulis

For More Information

Ahrens, Frank. "Don Imus, the Shock Jock We Hate to Love." *Washington Post* (May 26, 2000): p. C1.

Awkward, Michael. *Burying Don Imus: Anatomy of a Scapegoat.* Minneapolis: University of Minnesota Press, 2009.

Kunen, James S. "Howard Stern: New York's Mad-Dog Deejay May Be the Mouth of the '80s; He's Leader of the Pack That's Made Radio Raunchy." *People Weekly* (October 22, 1984): pp. 110–14.

Kurtz, Howard. *Hot Air: All Talk, All the Time.* New York: Times Books, 1996.

Mintzer, Richard. *Howard Stern: A Biography.* Santa Barbara, CA: Greenwood Press, 2010.

Reed, Jim. *Everything Imus.* Secaucus, NJ: Carol Publishing, 1999.

Zolgin, Richard. "Shock Jock." *Time* (November 30, 1992): pp. 72–74.

The Simpsons

Cartoonist Matt Groening (1954–) created the Simpsons family in 1986, during which they appeared in short segments of the FOX **television** (see entry under 1940s—TV and Radio in volume 3) network's *The*

On the air since 1986, the Simpson family keeps families everywhere laughing. Seen here from a May 2004 episode, father Homer Simpson as "Pie Man" and son Bart as his sidekick, "The Cupcake Kid." © PHOTOFEST, INC.

Tracy Ullman Show (1987–90). The characters' popularity quickly grew. In 1989, they got their own half-hour weekly TV series, *The Simpsons.* In addition to being the longest running animated TV show in history, *The Simpsons* is notable for providing some of the funniest criticism of American life and culture ever made.

The show's title family is a traditional situation comedy, or **sitcom** (see entry under 1950s—TV and Radio in volume 3) family. Homer, the oafish dad, works at a nuclear power plant. Marge is a doting housewife. Bart is a devilish third grader; Lisa, the second-grade middle child, favors reading and vegetarianism over television and bacon; and Maggie, the speechless infant, constantly sucks on her "Neglecto"-brand pacifier. The characters are crudely drawn, with strange hair (especially Marge's very tall and blue bouffant hairdo) and bright yellow skin. The show is a cartoon, but its humor appeals to both children and adults. While much of what happens is exaggerated, viewers cannot help but recognize kernels of truth in the actions of the show's various characters.

The show's animated format allows it to avoid the conventions of reality. The characters take all kinds of punishment but remain standing, and the show abounds with sly visual jokes. For example, in one episode Bart goes to France as a foreign-exchange student. As he gets off the plane, he immediately walks through a series of famous impressionist paintings, none of which he recognizes, though the audience is sure to. Furthermore, the show frequently incorporates events from past and contemporary popular culture into its storylines. Take, for instance, the mayor of Springfield, Joe Quimby, a corrupt politician who drinks and womanizes and whose face and Boston accent suggest a parallel with the famous Kennedys.

The plots of popular films of all eras—including such movies as ***Citizen Kane*** (1941; see entry under 1940s—Film and Theater in volume 3), ***The Graduate*** (1967; see entry under 1960s—Film and Theater in volume 4), and *Cape Fear* (1991)—are also often parodied. The debate over the effects of television violence on children is frequently alluded to in episodes of *Itchy and Scratchy,* an unbelievably violent cartoon that Bart and Lisa adore and watch religiously. Another popular character is Krusty the Klown, Bart's hero and the star of his favorite TV show, *The Krusty the Klown Show.* Krusty has allowed the licensing of his name for just about any product imaginable, from Krusty Alarm Clocks to Krusty Brand Bacon. Similarly, in real life, *The Simpsons* name has been used to sell countless products, from **video games** (see entry under 1970s—Sports and Games in volume 4) and books to **compact discs** (CDs; see entry under 1980s—Music in volume 5) and **coffee** (see entry under 1990s—The Way We Lived in volume 5) cups.

The characters on *The Simpsons* have pervaded American popular culture. Almost every American recognizes the images of Homer or Bart Simpson. (Homer's famous exclamation, "D'oh!" recently is now included in the *Oxford English Dictionary.* The dictionary defines it as a word "expressing frustration at the realization that things have turned out badly or not as planned, or that one has just said or done something foolish.") The main characters are widely recognized, and so too are many of the colorful group who make up the show's stock troupe: Barney, Homer's alcoholic best friend; Moe, the seedy barkeep of Homer's favorite bar, Moe's Tavern; Mr. Burns, the owner of the Springfield Nuclear Power Plant; Smithers, his devoted assistant (and one of the few gay characters regularly appearing on network television); Apu, the Indian who owns the local Kwik-E-Mart; Ned Flanders, the Simpson's pious next-door neighbor; and Bart's archenemies Sideshow Bob and Principal Skinner are just a few of the recurring characters widely loved by the show's devoted fans.

The Simpsons appeals to Americans because many Americans see themselves in the show. The Simpsons are a family with problems. They do not communicate with each other well, and they trample on each other's feelings. They inadvertently betray each other's trust. They struggle to make ends meet financially, and television plays far too big a role in their lives. But through all their wacky adventures, they truly love one another and try their best to do the right thing. *The Simpsons* is a cartoon full of the entertaining and the fantastical that every week still manages to reveal a little bit of truth about American family life.

In 2007 a movie adaptation, *The Simpsons Movie*, which featured the TV show's actors voicing the characters, was released and fared very well at the box office. As of September 2011 *The Simpsons* was entering its twenty-third season, making it the longest-running sitcom in American history. The well-loved Simpson family even has its own star on the Hollywood Walk of Fame.

Robert C. Sickels

For More Information

Groening, Matt. *Matt Groening's Cartooning with the Simpsons.* New York: HarperPerennial, 1993.

Groening, Matt, Ray Richmond, and Antonia Coffman, eds. *The Simpsons: A Complete Guide to Our Favorite Family.* New York: Harper Perennial, 1997.

Irwin, William, Mark T. Conrad, and Aeon J. Skoble, eds. *The Simpsons and Philosophy: The D'oh! of Homer.* Chicago: Open Court, 2001.

The Simpsons. http://www.thesimpsons.com (accessed July 27, 2011).

The Simpsons Archive. http://www.snpp.com/ (accessed July 27, 2011).

The Simpsons Channel. http://www.simpsonschannel.com/ (accessed July 27, 2011).

Talk Radio

Talk Radio is a lively **radio** (see entry under 1920s—TV and Radio in volume 2) format that features a host who takes calls on the air from listeners. Usually, the shows are politically oriented. The shows may include news and commentary from the host. Many—although not all—talk radio hosts are politically conservative. Their influence has helped empower many of their listeners, who have traditionally felt left out of the political process and believe the national media are liberally slanted. Talk radio has made a substantial impact in national and local politics. Hosts such as Rush Limbaugh (c. 1951–) can urge his fifteen million listeners (per week) to vote for certain politicians and support (or condemn) various causes.

Talk radio provides an audience for "shock jocks" such as Howard Stern (1954–), as well as relationship advice from people such as Dr. Joy Browne (1944–) and Dr. Laura Schlessinger (1947–) in the 1990s. "Loveline" with Dr. Drew Pinsky (1958–) and Adam Corolla (1964–) was so popular among teens and spoke to their lives so directly that it became a television show on **MTV** (see entry under 1980s—Music in volume 5).

Although there had been talk-radio stations as early as the 1930s, the popularity of talk radio exploded in the late 1980s and 1990s. The watershed event was the end of the Fairness Doctrine, a rule enacted by Congress in 1947 that forced radio stations to air a balanced spectrum of views in their programming. Once the Fairness Doctrine was dropped by the White House in 1987, there was a huge leap in the number of talk-radio programs. In 1980, there were a mere 75 radio stations with a talk format in the United States. By 1998, for example, the number had grown to 1,350 stations.

Controversy is the very lifeblood of talk radio, and the hosts themselves often generate it. Schlessinger, for instance, sparked a firestorm of protest after she said in 2000 that homosexuality was "deviant" behavior. Liberal talk radio, however, received a boost in 2004 with the founding of Air America, which featured such progressive hosts as former ***Saturday Night Live*** personality Al Franken (1951–) and Rachel Maddow (1973–). (Franken later became a U.S. senator from Minnesota and Maddow hosted a successful television show on MSNBC.) The enormous increase in Internet use throughout the first decade of the twenty-first century also enabled broadcasters from both sides of the political spectrum to reach a much wider audience. Talk radio will doubtless continue to thrive as long as people feel passionately about political and social issues.

Karl Rahder

For More Information

Fineman, Howard. "The Power of Talk." *Newsweek* (February 8, 1993): pp. 24–28.

Gini, Graham Scott. *Can We Talk? The Power and Influence of Talk Shows.* Cambridge, MA: Perseus Publishing, 1996.

Jennings, Brian. *Censorship: The Threat to Silence Talk Radio.* New York: Threshold Editions, 2009.

Laufer, Peter. *Inside Talk Radio: America's Voice or Just Hot Air?* Secaucus, NJ: Carol Publishing, 1995.

Munson, Wayne. *All Talk: The Talkshow in Media Culture.* Philadelphia: Temple University Press, 1993.

Sterling, Christopher H., and John M. Kittross. *Stay Tuned: A Concise History of American Broadcasting.* 3rd ed. Mahwah, NJ: Lawrence Erlbaum Associates, 2002.

"The Talk Radio Research Project." *Talkers Magazine Online.* http://www.talkers.com/talkaud.html (accessed July 27, 2011).

Teenage Mutant Ninja Turtles

The Teenage Mutant Ninja Turtles were one of the pop-culture rages of the 1980s and early 1990s. With their origins in a little-known comic strip, the Ninja Turtles gained mass popularity as a television **Saturday morning cartoon** (see entry under 1960s—TV and Radio in volume 4) series. The characters then appeared in movies and **video games** (see entry under 1970s— Sports and Games in volume 4) and as popular toys. The key to the Turtles' success was their funky combination of muscle-bound heroism and downright goofiness.

The Teenage Mutant Ninja Turtles first appeared in 1984 as a black-and-white comic strip co-authored by Kevin Eastman (1962–) and Peter Laird (1954–). According to the story the pair devised, the Turtles were born when a load of "mutanagenic" material spilled onto a quartet of pet turtles, giving them super powers. The Turtles—named Leonardo, Michaelangelo, Raphael, and Donatello, after famous artists with the same names—were soon befriended by a mutant rat named Splinter who was a master of the Japanese Ninja **martial arts** (see entry under 1960s—The Way We Lived in volume 4). Splinter taught the Turtles to be Ninjas. The team battled the forces of evil, especially the evil Ninja, Shredder. The comic strip soon became a cult favorite, known for the Turtles' hip, rebellious attitude.

The popular comic was converted to a syndicated **television** (see entry under 1940s—TV and Radio in volume 3) cartoon series

Teenage Mutant Ninja Turtles Leonardo, Michaelangelo, Donatello, and Raphael enjoyed a career from comic strips to television to film. © GROUP W PRODUCTIONS/EVERETT COLLECTION.

(that is, the series was sold to independent TV stations) in 1987. In the cartoon series, the Turtles were made more muscular and were given traits that would make them funny to children: Michaelangelo, for example, frequently said, "Dude," and loved to party. The show was immensely popular and, soon, the Turtles were everywhere. The first Teenage Mutant Ninja Turtle movie came out in 1990. The TV series became a Saturday morning hit on CBS, where it aired until 1997. Two more movies came out in 1991 and 1993. The merchandise followed close behind: toys, lunchboxes, hats, **T-shirts** (see entry under 1910s—Fashion in volume 1), and so on—all bore the Turtles' images, and kids purchased them by the truckload.

In 1997 a live-action series called *Ninja Turtles: The Next Mutation* aired for one season, based more closely on plotlines from the films than on the first series. In 2003 a second animated series debuted that ran for six years. This series hearkened back to the original comic strips with their darker themes. In 2009 a TV movie, *Turtles Forever*, signalled the series' conclusion, uniting the Turtles from the original series with their 2003 colleagues. The Turtles' enduring popularity made these unlikely "heroes" one of the youth-culture sensations of the era.

Tom Pendergast

For More Information

Perez, Michael E. *Teenage Mutant Ninja Turtles.* http://www.mikeystmnt.com (accessed July 27, 2011).

Robie, Joan Hake. *Teenage Mutant Ninja Turtles Exposed!* Lancaster, PA: Starburst, 1991.

Teenage Mutant Ninja Turtles. http://www.ninjaturtles.com (accessed July 27, 2011).

Wiater, Stan. *The Official Teenage Mutant Ninja Turtles Treasury.* New York: Villard Books, 1991.

1980s

The Way We Lived

The stereotypical American in the 1980s was the "yuppie," a nickname for the "young urban professional," a person between twenty-five and thirty-nine years old whose job in management or a profession gave them an income of more than $40,000 a year. The term yuppie described more than an age and an income level; it described a lifestyle as well. Yuppies spent money freely. They sought out material goods as a way of demonstrating to their world that they had "made it." Yuppies drove BMW cars or the newly popular sport utility vehicles (SUVs). They wore Ralph Lauren clothes and Rolex watches, and they drank Perrier water. If they lived in the city and thought that laws did not apply to them, they may have snorted cocaine, the drug of choice among the well-to-do.

Yuppies were the product of an expanding economy, and of a generation of Americans, known as "baby boomers," who were settling into middle age. Although yuppies attracted a great deal of attention in the press as symbols of the rising economy promoted by the Reagan administration (1981–89), they were not a majority. At most, there were only twenty million yuppies in America.

Politicians explained that the rising prosperity enjoyed by the wealthy would benefit all Americans. The expanding economy, they said, was a "rising tide" that would "lift all boats." The tax cuts going to the rich would "trickle down" to less wealthy Americans. However, many Americans were excluded from the decade's prosperity. Incomes among African Americans did not rise in step with those of white Americans. In America's inner cities, poverty remained a real problem. In many cities, youths joined gangs, which offered protection and a sense of belonging. Especially around Los Angeles, California, these gangs became increasingly violent. Their activities were portrayed in a number of movies late in the decade, including *Colors* (1988). Homelessness also became a serious social issue in many American cities.

Many white Americans also felt distanced from the yuppie lifestyles. Conservative Christians became increasingly organized during the decade, thanks to the political support of the Reagan administration. Jerry Falwell (1933–2007) formed a group he called the Moral Majority to present fundamentalist Christian issues, and televangelists preached over the television to millions. A much smaller group of young white Americans organized into groups that protested against the gains made by blacks, Hispanics, and other minority groups. These "skinheads," as they were known, sometimes violently attacked minorities.

The 1980s was a decade of social extremes. Yuppies, Christians, and skinheads all laid claim to media attention, and all had a great influence on American popular culture.

AIDS

The medical condition known as AIDS—the acronym for Acquired Immunodeficiency Syndrome—has been called the modern equivalent of the plague. In the United States, the dreaded condition has had its greatest impact on gay men and on intravenous drug users (those who shoot drugs into their veins with a hypodermic needle). AIDS suppresses the individual's immune system, leaving them open to an array of diseases. First identified in 1981, the disease spread quickly. By 1996, AIDS was the eighth leading cause of death in the United States. By 2001, there had been 793,026 AIDS cases reported, according to the Centers for Disease Control and Prevention (CDC). By 2008, the agency reported the total U.S. death toll at 617,025. In Africa, where AIDS is primarily spread by heterosexuals, AIDS has decimated the populations of several poor countries; in 2009 the estimated number of AIDS-related deaths in sub-Saharan Africa was 22.5 million. Although the death rate from

The AIDS Memorial Quilt on display on the Mall in Washington, D.C. © CORBIS PREMIUM RF/ALAMY.

AIDS-related diseases in the United States has reduced considerably thanks to prevention and breakthroughs in treatment, AIDS remains a major health concern.

AIDS first appeared amid the gay male populations of San Francisco, New York, and Los Angeles in 1981. It has long been characterized as a "gay" disease. From the beginning, fighting AIDS has been a rallying cause for gay activists, who have helped make prevention (especially the battle against "unprotected" sex), medical care for victims, and research into a cure major health issues—despite the difficulty of obtaining funding from the conservative administrations of Ronald Reagan (1911–2004; in office 1981–89) and George H. W. Bush (1924–; in office 1989–93).

One of the unlikely side effects of the AIDS epidemic was a heightened profile for gays and lesbians in all areas of American life. Gay and lesbian groups banded together to combat AIDS, and their outspoken efforts drew attention and respect to their cause. Artists, writers, and filmmakers soon used AIDS as a source of inspiration. *Angels in America* (1992) by Tony Kushner (c. 1957–) was a highly successful **Broadway** (see entry under 1900s—Film and Theater in volume 1) play that dealt with AIDS. *Philadelphia* (1993) was the most high profile of several AIDS-themed movies in the 1980s and 1990s; its star, Tom Hanks (1956–), won an Oscar for his portrayal of an attorney suffering from the effects of AIDS.

The most high profile of all the AIDS-related cultural events, however, was the creation of the AIDS Memorial Quilt. The quilt began in 1987 as a memorial to loved ones who had died as a result of AIDS. Each quilt section measured 3 feet by 6 feet—the size of a human grave. By 1998, the forty-two thousand quilt panels commemorated the deaths of more than eighty thousand people. The quilt stands as a memorial to the deaths of hundreds of thousands of people and to the immense impact that AIDS has had on the gay community and their families in the United States.

Tom Pendergast

For More Information

The AIDS Memorial Quilt. http://www.aidsquilt.org (accessed July 28, 2011).

Centers for Disease Control and Prevention. *Division of HIV/AIDS Prevention.* http://www.cdc.gov/hiv/dhap.htm (accessed July 28, 2011).

Currie-McGhee, L. K. *AIDS.* Detroit: Lucent, 2008.

Giblin, James Cross. *When Plague Strikes: The Black Death, Smallpox, AIDS.* New York: HarperCollins, 1995.

McPhee, Andrew T. *AIDS.* New York: Franklin Watts, 2000.

Ruskin, Cindy. *The Quilt: Stories from the NAMES Project.* New York: Pocket Books, 1988.

Silverstein, Alvin, Virginia Silverstein, and Laura Silverstein Nunn. *AIDS: An All-About Guide for Young Adults.* Springfield, NJ: Enslow, 1999.

White, Katherine. *Everything You Need to Know about AIDS and HIV.* New York: Rosen, 2001.

Cabbage Patch Kids

During the mid-1980s, Cabbage Patch mania swept across America. Cabbage Patch Kids are homely but cuddly sixteen-inch-long baby and toddler dolls, yarn-haired and made of soft material. Unlike most toys produced in that decade, each one is "humanized" and "individualized."

Each Kid has its very own first and middle name, as well as a unique combination of hairstyle, hair coloring, clothing, skin tone, and facial characteristics, all the way down to the placement of freckles. Some have pacifiers, and each comes complete with birth certificate and adoption papers. The uniqueness of the dolls resulted in children treating them as real family members. At the height of their popularity, Cabbage Patch Kids were the toys of choice for millions of children, whose parents went to extreme lengths to obtain them. During the 1983 Christmas season, the toys, whose actual retail price was $25, were selling for up to $2,000!

A crowd of Cabbage Patch Kids. © AGGIE TRUNGLEBUCKETS IMAGE EMPORIUM/ALAMY.

Cabbage Patch Kids came into being as Little People dolls, custom-made toys that were "born" in a cabbage patch. They were created by Xavier Roberts (1955–), a Georgia art student who first designed them in 1976 and sold them at arts-and-crafts fairs. The Little People were so popular that, two years later, Roberts formed his own company, Original Appalachian Artworks, to produce the dolls. He purchased an old house, which he christened BabyLand General Hospital, in which his dolls were "born." They were hand-stitched and hand-signed on their rear ends. Roberts soon began calling them Cabbage Patch Kids because the original name sounded too general. In the early 1980s, he signed a licensing deal with Coleco Industries, a toy manufacturer. One major difference between Roberts's dolls and those produced by Coleco: The heads of the originals were made of cloth, while the toy manufacturer produced them using vinyl. Hasbro bought the rights to produce the dolls in 1988, and it in turn sold the rights to Mattel in 1994. In 2003 retail giant Toys "R" Us purchased the franchise.

During their first nine months on the mass market, Coleco took in over $6 million in Cabbage Patch Kid sales. By New Year's 1984, over three million had been sold; by 1990, the total number sold was $65 million. Additionally, there have been Cabbage Patch Doll variations, or "Specialty Kids." Among them: Toddlers, Preemies, Sippin' Kids, Splashin' Kids, Snacktime Kids, and Pretty Crimp 'n' Curl Kids. In 1999, a Cabbage

Patch Kids stamp was produced by the U.S. Postal Service as part of a series commemorating the 1980s. Throughout the early 2000s, new theme dolls continued to be produced, including dolls representing celebrities such as presidential contenders George W. Bush (1946–) and John Kerry (1943–), comedienne Ellen DeGeneres (1958–), and NBC ***Today*** (see entry under 1950s—TV and Radio in volume 3) co-anchors Matt Lauer (1957–) and Katie Couric (1957–). In 2008, each of the major presidential candidates had his or her own Cabbage Patch Kid.

Rob Edelman

For More Information

Cabbage Patch Kids Home. http://www.cabbagepatchkids.com (accessed July 28, 2011).

Hoffman, William. *Fantasy: The Incredible Cabbage Patch Phenomenon.* Dallas: Taylor, 1984.

Lindenberger, Jan, and Judy Morris. *The Encyclopedia of Cabbage Patch Kids: The 1980s.* Atglen, PA: Schiffer, 1999.

Lindenberger, Jan, and Judy Morris. *The Encyclopedia of Cabbage Patch Kids: The 1990s.* Atglen, PA: Schiffer, 2000.

Roberts, Xavier. *Legend of the Cabbage Patch Kids.* Dallas: Taylor, 1988.

Cocaine

Cocaine is one of the best known and most dangerous of the many illegal drugs that have been popular in the United States since the twentieth century. It is derived from the coca plant, which grows in some areas of Latin America. When ingested by humans, it usually produces feelings of great well-being, confidence, and mental clarity. The effect is short-lived, however, and the aftermath of cocaine use is often characterized by irritability, anxiety, paranoia—and the intense desire for more cocaine. The drug is habit-forming to many and addictive to some. The effects of its long-term abuse include nasal and sinus deterioration, brain damage, increased likelihood of strokes, and, in some cases, death. Some susceptible persons, like college basketball star Len Bias (1963–1986), can die as a result of their first experience with cocaine.

Concentrated cocaine was first extracted from coca leaves around 1860. It soon appeared as an ingredient in a variety of foods, beverages, medicines, and personal-care products. A cocaine-laced wine called Vin Mariani was introduced in 1863 and proved very popular. Its consumers are believed to have included Queen Victoria (1819–1901), Thomas Edison (1847–1931), and at least one pope. **Coca-Cola** (see entry under 1900s—Food and Drink in volume 1) gets its name from the cocaine that was part of its original formula (which has long since been changed).

Eventually, cocaine's addictive properties and adverse health effects started to be noticed, and various states passed laws against it, beginning in 1887. At the same time, the drug began to develop a negative public image, often being associated in the press and in popular fiction with pimps, prostitutes, thieves, and racial minorities. In 1914, the federal government designated the drug a Class I Narcotic, which meant it was illegal except by prescription.

Cocaine use began to decline in the 1920s, partly due to its illegality but also because of the ready supply of another stimulant—amphetamines. These were legal, cheap, and produced a "high" that some said was superior to cocaine. Cocaine's decline continued until the 1960s, when amphetamines were also outlawed. The ban sent both drug abusers and drug dealers back to cocaine, which formed the basis for the cocaine problem that continues to plague the United States.

That problem was made worse around 1980 when "crack" cocaine—known on the street as "rock"—was developed. Made by mixing cocaine with baby powder or a similar substance, crack is a paste that hardens easily. It can then be broken into small bits that are usually smoked in small glass pipes. Crack is substantially more powerful than powdered cocaine, producing a faster high and consequently a deeper comedown. It is thus ferociously addictive. Crack use became a particularly serious concern in many of America's inner cities during the 1980s and 1990s. Its related social problems included domestic abuse and neglect, robbery and prostitution committed for drug money, and warfare between rival **gangs** (see entry under 1980s—The Way We Lived in volume 5) over the immense profits to be made from the crack trade.

Popular-culture depictions of cocaine use have largely reflected the drug's status in society. When cocaine was legal, many publications regularly carried advertisements for products that featured the drug as a major ingredient. But by the start of the twentieth century, shocking stories began to appear in magazines and novels about the horrible crimes committed by cocaine addicts. These accounts were often tainted with the racism common at the time, suggesting that blacks, in particular, were being turned into violent degenerates by cocaine use.

New entertainment media quickly began to ring the anti-cocaine alarm. A 1928 **silent movie** (see entry under 1900s—Film and Theater in volume 1), *The Pace That Kills,* shows farm boy Eddie moving to the big city and being introduced to cocaine by his new girlfriend. They both become addicts and end up committing suicide. The exact same film was remade in 1935 as a "talkie."

This trend in negative depictions of cocaine use continued in the following decades, reaching a peak in the 1980s when cocaine became a popular recreational drug among some young urban professionals, known as **yuppies** (see entry under 1980s—The Way We Lived in volume 5). A series of popular novels depicted cocaine-related anxiety among the yuppie set, including *Bright Lights, Big City* (1984; filmed in 1988) by Jay McInerney (1955–), *Less than Zero* (1985; filmed in 1987) by Bret Easton Ellis (1964–), and *The Mysteries of Pittsburgh* (1988) by Michael Chabon (1963–). Cocaine dealers were convenient villains in fiction and film. None was more depraved or evil than Tony Montana, the Cuban immigrant played by Al Pacino (1940–) in 1983's *Scarface,* directed by Brian DePalma (1940–).

In the 1990s, a conspiracy theory surfaced that the CIA had helped introduce crack into America's ghettos to distract black Americans from revolting against racism and social injustice. Although endorsed by the Nation of Islam's Louis Farrakhan (1933–), the theory remains unsubstantiated. It is true that penalties for the use of crack are harsher than those involving powdered cocaine, which is more likely to be abused by whites. By 1997, an estimated 1.5 million Americans were regularly using cocaine. The next decade saw several major films about cocaine, including the award-winning *Traffic* (2000) and *Blow* (2001), profiling George Jung (1942–), the modern era's first major cocaine kingpin.

Justin Gustainis

For More Information

Erickson, Patricia G. *The Steel Drug: Cocaine in Perspective.* Lexington, MA: Lexington Books, 1994.

Feiling, Tom. *Cocaine Nation: How the White Trade Took Over the World.* Pegasus, 2010.

Flynn, John C. *Cocaine: An In-Depth Look at the Facts, Science, History, and Future of the World's Most Addictive Drug.* Secaucus, NJ: Carol Publishing Group, 1991.

Inciardi, James A., and Karen McElrath. *The American Drug Scene: An Anthology.* 6th ed. New York: Oxford University Press, 2011.

McFarland, Rhoda. *Cocaine.* New York: Rosen Group, 1997.
Narcanon. *Cocaine Facts.* http://www.cocaineaddiction.com/cocaine.html (accessed July 28, 2011).
Starks, Michael. *Cocaine Fiends and Reefer Madness: An Illustrated History of Drugs in the Movies.* New York: Cornwall Books, 1982.
Streatfeild, Dominic. *Cocaine: An Unauthorized Biography.* London: Virgin, 2002.
Wagner, Heather Lehr. *Cocaine.* Philadelphia: Chelsea House, 2003.
Washton, Arnold M., and Donna Boundy. *Cocaine and Crack: What You Need to Know.* Hillside, NJ: Enslow, 1989.

Gangs

First brought to the forefront of American popular culture by the fictional Jets and Sharks in the 1961 film *West Side Story,* gangs have long been a part of illegal activity around the world. From the Sicilian **Mafia** (see entry under 1960s—The Way We Lived in volume 4) to the Chinese Tongs to the outlaws of the American frontier, gangs have brought together criminals who joined in brotherhood for strength and protection.

During the late 1940s and early 1950s, urban street gangs began to appear in the poor neighborhoods of many U.S. cities. These gangs were mostly made up of young men and women from harsh, underprivileged backgrounds who looked to fellow members for social support and physical protection. Gangs were often divided along ethnic lines. They formed to claim and protect territory from other ethnic groups and newly arriving immigrants. Gang membership in the 1950s did not always involve crime but almost always involved fighting and violence. Films like *The Wild One* (1954) and romantic actors like **James Dean** (1931–1955; see entry under 1950s—Film and Theater in volume 3) and Marlon Brando (1924–2004) gave these gangs a glamorous image, at least to middle-class American youth who were not involved in them.

Although gangs never entirely disappeared, they were overshadowed by the counterculture youth movement and radical politics of the late 1960s and 1970s. Gangs re-emerged in the public awareness in the 1980s, with news reports about the Bloods and the Crips of Los Angeles, California. Early gangs had fought with chains, brass knuckles, and switchblades. These new gangs not only had much more advanced weaponry, they also developed strict organizations and very profitable businesses selling drugs. This frightening new force received abundant attention from the press. This attention resulted in both fear of the gangs and imitation of them.

Meanwhile, gang activity kept increasing. Rising school dropout rates and the lack of jobs both contributed to the rise of gang membership during the 1980s. In Los Angeles alone, the number of gangs increased from four hundred in 1985 to eight hundred in 1990. Films about gang activity like *Colors* (1988) and *New Jack City* (1991), along with popular "gangsta" **rap** (see entry under 1980s—Music in volume 5) music glamorized gang life. Suburban middle-class teens who had little connection with gangs began to wear colors and styles identified with gang members. Although parents and school officials have tried to discourage gangs by outlawing these gang colors and styles in schools, gang activity continued to increase through the first decade of the twenty-first century. According to the U.S. Justice Department, in 2009 criminal gangs had one million members and were the "primary retail distributors of most illicit drugs." Gangs will continue to exist until replaced by something more positive that fulfills their members' needs for self-esteem, protection, and a place to belong.

Tina Gianoulis

For More Information

Alonso, A. A. *Streetgangs.com.* http://www.streetgangs.com/ (accessed July 28, 2011).

Haskins, James. *Street Gangs, Yesterday and Today.* New York: Hastings House, 1977.

Johnson, Julie. *Why Do People Join Gangs?* Austin, TX: Raintree Steck-Vaughn, 2001.

Solis, Adela. *Gangs.* Detroit: Greenhaven Press, 2009.

Venkatesh, Sudhir. *Gang Leader for a Day: A Rogue Sociologist Takes to the Streets.* New York: Penguin, 2008.

Walker, Robert. *Robert Walker's Gangs OR Us.* http://www.gangsorus.com/ (accessed July 28, 2002).

Yablonsky, Lewis. *Gangsters: Fifty Years of Madness, Drugs, and Death on the Streets of America.* New York: New York University Press, 1997.

Generation X

Douglas Coupland (1961–) coined the phrase "Generation X" in his 1991 novel, *Generation X: Tales for an Accelerated Culture.* Born between 1961 and 1981, "X-ers" are the thirteenth generation since U.S.

independence. They have been criticized as "slackers" and "latch-key kids" and described as the "MTV generation." These terms of abuse have usually come from the prior generation, known as the **"baby boomers"** (see entry under 1940s—The Way We Lived in volume 3). Many in the baby-boomer generation see themselves as responsible for advances in civil rights and sexual liberation. In addition, the early baby boomers both fought in and protested against the war in Vietnam (1954–75), an era that defined their values.

The negative view of X-ers is far from accurate. Disgusted with traditional politics, in the early part of the 2000s "Thirteeners" stood at the forefront of campaigns to protect the environment and stop globalization. Generally better educated than their parents, they have also shown themselves to have a strong entrepreneurial streak and were largely the masterminds behind the enormous dot-com boom of the late 1990s that transformed the U.S. economy. They cannot afford to be lazy, because most of them earn less in real terms than their parents did at the same age. Where both members of baby-boomer couples worked for a sense of personal fulfillment as much as for money, X-ers work because they have to. They have inherited huge national debts and crumbling welfare, education, and medical systems.

Growing up with civil unrest, high unemployment, and **divorce** (see entry under 1970s—The Way We Lived in volume 4), Generation X became disillusioned with traditional politics, work, and family life. In Gen-X **television** (see entry under 1940s—TV and Radio in volume 3) shows such as ***Friends*** (1994–2004), ***ER*** (1994–2009), and ***Seinfeld*** (1990–98; see these entries under 1990s—TV and Radio in volume 5), friends often take the place of family. Like many of his generation, *The X-Files* (1993–2002) character Fox Mulder wants to know what happened to his childhood. In music, Generation X enjoys a "decade-blending" mix of the mainstream and the alternative. **MTV** (see entry under 1980s—Music in volume 5) formed Generation X-ers' tastes in the 1980s. In the 1990s, the anxiety-ridden sounds of **Nirvana** (see entry under 1990s—Music in volume 5), R.E.M., and rappers like Puff Daddy (1970–) and Dr. Dre (1965–) became the Thirteeners' voice. With their characteristic ironic response, many typical X-ers might publicly scorn ABBA, Duran Duran, and the Eagles while secretly enjoying them. By the early 2000s, Generation X was clearly making its mark in government, the media, business, and education. In 2008, they were largely responsible for electing the first Generation X president, **Barack Obama** (1961–; see entry under 2000s—The Way We Lived in volume 6).

Chris Routledge

For More Information

Coupland, Douglas. *Generation X: Tales for an Accelerated Culture.* New York: St. Martin's Press, 1991.

Gaslin, Glenn, and Rick Porter. *The Complete, Cross-Referenced Guide to the Baby Buster Generation's Collective Unconscious.* New York: Boulevard, 1998.

Gordinier, Jeff. *X Saves the World.* New York: Viking, 2008.

Howe, Neil, and Bill Strauss. *13th Gen: Abort, Retry, Ignore, Fail?* New York: Vintage Books, 1993.

Minivans

Minivans offer the cargo capacity of a small van or truck with the comfort, luxury, and driving ease of a car. Since their introduction in 1983, minivans have become a symbol of suburbia. The vehicles are identified with the responsibilities of parenthood—especially with the chauffeuring duties of the "soccer mom" who transports kids to after-school activities. The creation of the minivan goes back to the late 1970s, when Chrysler engineer Harold Sperlich (1929–) proposed a vehicle that had large interior space, a sliding side door, a flat floor, and removable seats. The vehicle had to be easy to drive and comfortable, like the family car, but with the utility of a van. The idea was to persuade station-wagon customers to buy an entirely new kind of vehicle.

When the new "minivan" made its debut in 1983, it was an immediate hit. Chrysler had the new market all to itself and sold half a million Dodge and Plymouth minivans in the first year. The success of the minivan rescued the Chrysler Corporation, which was teetering on the brink of bankruptcy at the time. The company's turnaround and the exploits of Lee Iacocca (1924–), Chrysler's colorful chairman, who oversaw the minivan's development, have become legendary business stories. Since 1983, millions of minivans have been sold. Other manufacturers followed Chrysler's lead with their own versions. By the mid-1990s, every major car company offered minivans, such as the Toyota Sienna, the Pontiac Montana, and the Honda Odyssey.

By the late-1990s, sales of **sport utility vehicles** (SUVs; see entry under 1980s—The Way We Lived in volume 5) began to chip away at minivan

A minivan has plenty of storage capacity both inside and outside. © FOTOSEARCH/JUPITERIMAGES/GETTY IMAGES.

sales. More people bought vehicles that looked like they belonged in the wilderness instead of at the **mall** (see entry under 1950s—Commerce in volume 3) or the grocery store. By the new century, "crossover utility vehicles," or CUVs, were also gaining popularity as affluent consumers wanted more fun and style. The smaller CUVs, such as the Ford Escape and the Chrysler PT Cruiser, stressed comfort and better gas mileage. By 2008, soaring prices at the pump had further decimated the minivan market, although families with multiple children continued to buy them.

Karl Rahder

For More Information

Bradsher, Keith. "Was Freud a Minivan or S.U.V. Kind of Guy?" *New York Times.* http://www.nytimes.com/library/financial/071700psych-auto.html (accessed July 30, 2011).

"A Brief History of the Minivan." *Allpar.com.* http://www.allpar.com/model/m/history.html (accessed July 30, 2011).

Political Correctness

The idea of "political correctness" has its roots in the 1960s and 1970s, an era of political activism during which many people became aware of the political forces that shaped their lives. This awareness was expressed through social-change movements. The **civil rights movement** (see entry under 1960s—The Way We Lived in volume 4) fought against racial discrimination. The antiwar movement fought to end the Vietnam War (1954–75). The women's liberation movement fought to improve the status of women in American society. The **gay liberation movement** (see entry under 1960s—The Way We Lived in volume 4) fought to end discrimination against gay people. The purpose of these liberal movements was to change the structure of society so that it would be more fair to all people.

One goal of these movements was to keep people from using words and making assumptions that hurt or belittled people of minority groups. Society had been biased in favor of heterosexual (straight) white men, the movements' supporters argued, and those who wished to make things more fair had to be careful about the language they used and the assumptions they made about people who were not part of the white, middle-class mainstream. Suspect words and assumptions, it soon became clear, were everywhere, from the common use of the word "man" to mean everyone, to the "flesh" colored crayon that was pinkish, not brown or tan, to the books most students were assigned to read in school that were largely written by white, European men—believed to be nothing more than "dead white guys" by critics.

By the 1980s, the term "politically correct," or "PC," was being used to describe the use of replacement terms, such as calling the original inhabitants of North America "Native Americans" rather than "Indians," or using the word "disabled" rather than "crippled." Such changes often reflect what the people within a group wish to be called, although sometimes knowing what that is can be quite difficult. The "correct" term for African Americans, for example, has varied over the decades from colored, to Negro, to Afro-American, to black or African American. There have always been some who have disliked each term. The overall aim of political correctness, however, is to avoid causing offense.

Concerned liberals, especially on college campuses, made a crusade of political correctness from the mid-1980s onward, alarming some conservative people who viewed political correctness as censorship or as a challenge to their values. They portrayed those who practiced political correctness as ridiculous, uptight prudes who could not take a joke. Even among liberals, the practice of carefully examining language and assumptions had largely gone out of style by the mid-1990s. Soon, it was political *in*correctness that was seen as cool and rebellious, while political correctness was ridiculed, as on **television** (see entry under 1940s—TV and Radio in volume 3) programs like ABC's popular *Politically Incorrect* (1993–2002), hosted by Bill Maher (1956–). Each show set up a panel of an unlikely combination of guests who, while talking about legitimate, serious subjects, would, hopefully, offend each other in amusing ways. No matter how political correctness is ridiculed, however, there can be no doubt that it helped eliminate the widespread use of negative racial, sexist, and other slurs directed against minorities or subcultures.

Tina Gianoulis

For More Information

Beard, Henry, and Christopher Cerf. *The Official Politically Correct Dictionary and Handbook.* Rev. ed. New York: Villard, 1995.

Hughes, Geoffrey. *Political Correctness: A History of Semantics and Culture.* Maldon, MA: Wiley-Blackwell, 2010.

Miller, Casey, Kate Swift, and Rosalie Maggio. "Liberating Language." *Ms.* (September-October 1997): pp. 50–55.

Pollitt, Katha. "I'm O.K., You're P.C." *Nation* (Vol. 266, no. 3, January 26, 1998): pp. 10–11.

Weissberg, Robert. *Political Tolerance: Balancing Community and Diversity.* Thousand Oaks, CA: Sage Publications, 1998.

Wilson, John K. *The Myth of Political Correctness: The Conservative Attack on Higher Education.* Durham, NC: Duke University Press, 1995.

Prozac

The drug Prozac was introduced in 1987. By 1990, psychiatrists in the United States prescribed Prozac more often than any other drug. Five years later, its maker, Eli Lilly and Co., reported sales of over $2 billion. Originally designed as an antidepressant, Prozac has since been used to combat obesity, shyness, obsessive-compulsive behavior, and even back pain. It improves mood, energy levels, optimism, and feelings of inadequacy. Not only has Prozac helped millions of people deal with their emotional and psychological problems, but it has changed their understanding of moods and personality.

Prozac is one of a group of "designer" drugs known as Selective Serotonin Reuptake Inhibitors (SSRIs). These drugs work by increasing levels of the chemical serotonin (seh-reh-TOE-nin) in the brain. Older antidepressants are less specific. They change the balance of a number of brain chemicals in the hope that one of them will have the desired effect. In theory, this makes Prozac much safer and easier to monitor. In the early 1990s, however, Prozac was linked with a number of disturbing events. There were reports of people becoming violent or suicidal for the first time while taking Prozac. Several lawsuits tried and failed to link SSRIs with gun massacres and other violent acts.

Throughout the early part of the twenty-first century, however, Prozac continued to be considered a safe and useful drug therapy and remained one of the most popular antidepressants, with Americans filing twenty-two million prescriptions in 2007. The safety of the drug has allowed some people who are not clinically depressed to indulge in "cosmetic pharmacology." In other words, they take Prozac simply to "improve" their personalities. As the initial fears of possible violence to self and others associated with Prozac diminished, the major side effect discussed in the media was the drug's tendency to cause lack of interest in sex.

Aside from its impact on psychiatry, during the 1990s Prozac became a symbol of the "stressed-out" nature of American life. More than any other medicine, it has come to be seen as a cure for the stresses and strains of modern life. Perhaps the most significant side effect of Prozac has been on society itself. Critics fear that the use of Prozac as cosmetic pharmacology devalues the suffering involved in real mental illness. More positively, the widespread use of Prozac may also have made society more tolerant and open about mental-health problems.

Chris Routledge

For More Information

Appleton, William S. *Prozac and the New Antidepressants.* New York: Plume, 2000.

Breggin, Peter Roger. *The Antidepressant Fact Book.* Cambridge, MA: Perseus, 2001.

Glenmullen, Joseph. *Prozac Backlash.* New York: Simon & Schuster, 2000.
Prozac.com. http://www.prozac.com/ (accessed July 29, 2011).
Kramer, Peter. *Listening to Prozac.* New York: Viking, 1993.
National Alliance for the Mentally Ill. "Prozac." *NAMI: The Nation's Voice on Mental Illness.* http://www.nami.org/helpline/prozac.htm (accessed July 29, 2011).
Wurtzel, Elizabeth. *Prozac Nation.* Boston: Houghton Mifflin, 1994.

Road Rage

"Road rage" is a term that was coined by journalists in the late 1980s to describe the angry and aggressive behavior that seemed to be occurring more and more among automobile drivers in the nation's cities. By the mid-1990s, the term "road rage" appeared frequently in magazine articles, in newspaper headlines, and on **television** (see entry under 1940s—TV and Radio in volume 3) talk shows. Some sources stated

A driver loudly expressing his opinion could be road rage. © B.A.E. INC./ALAMY.

confidently that road rage was on the rise and had become a major problem of modern life. Others claimed that the concept of road rage is largely an invention of the media.

Few people would argue that traffic became noticeably worse in the last two decades of the twentieth century. **Highway systems** (see entry under 1950s—The Way We Lived in volume 3) that were designed in the 1950s and 1960s and constructed in the 1970s and 1980s were carrying far more traffic than civil engineers ever imagined. Many Americans lived in **suburbs** (see entry under 1950s—The Way We Lived in volume 3) in which public transportation is scarce, and few would be parted from their cars even in cities that do have public transport systems. By the end of the 1990s, approximately 168 million licensed drivers owned 200 million motor vehicles in the United States. As these cars flooded the freeways, traffic in many cities during rush hours frequently came to a standstill.

At the same time, improvements in computers and other technology have increased the speed and urgency of modern life. This sense of urgency, coupled with the stress of standing still in a traffic jam, often increases drivers' frustration. Many react with anger toward those who seem to be in their way. Road rage can range from screaming at other drivers, to making obscene or threatening gestures, to actual physical violence or even murder. Highway shootings are very uncommon, however, and the fear of being shot does not seem to prevent aggressive driving.

There were various responses to the problem of road rage. Some businesses tried to profit from drivers' fears by offering "road-rage protection," special armoring of cars to protect them from the baseball bats and bullets of angry drivers. Psychologists specializing in road rage developed Web sites and radio talk shows. Police in twenty-four states set up special programs to stop aggressive driving behavior. Some newer cars have advanced computer systems that guide their drivers out of traffic jams onto more open roadways.

However, some challenged the idea that road rage is a growing national phenomenon. These critics claimed that aggressive driving has always been present on American highways, and that the media's use of the catchy term "road rage" has invented an epidemic where none exists. They also claimed that there have been no truly scientific studies about the increase in road rage, and that most of the public's knowledge about it came from exaggerated stories in the media. Although the media's interest in this phenomenon had died down by the turn of the century, road rage was still a factor in U.S. drivers' collective consciousness, with 18 percent of three thousand motorists surveyed in 2009 citing road rage as their main distraction while driving.

Tina Gianoulis

For More Information

Allan, David. *Why We Feel "Road Rage" … And Why It's Your Fault.* Webster, MA: FNA Publishers, 2008.
Eberle, Paul. *Terror on the Highway: Rage on America's Roads.* Amherst, NY: Prometheus Books, 2006.
Ferguson, Andrew. "Road Rage." *Time* (January 12, 1998).
Fumento, Michael. "'Road Rage' Versus Reality." *Atlantic Monthly* (August 1, 1998): pp. 12–15.
James, Leon, and Diane Nahl. *Road Rage and Aggressive Driving.* Amherst, NY: Prometheus Books, 2000.
"Road Wars: Government Programs to Control Road Rage." *Current Events* (Vol. 98, no. 17, February 5, 1999): pp. 1–5.
Stewart, Doug. "We're in a Jam: Easing the Nation's Growing Traffic Congestion Has Experts All Backed Up." *Smithsonian* (April 2001) pp. 36–40.
Twitchell, James B. *Preposterous Violence: Fables of Aggression in Modern Culture.* New York: Oxford University Press, 1989.

Skinheads

Skinheads are loosely organized groups of young people who identify themselves by shaving their heads, tattooing their bodies with symbols, and wearing militaristic black leather jackets and boots. Like punks, skinheads dress and adorn their bodies in outlandish ways to rebel against society. Within this rebellious uniform, skinheads have differing political opinions. While there are anti-racist skinheads and gay skinheads, most skinheads are identified with neo-Nazi politics.

The Nazi party first began in Germany in the late 1920s. It was the party of German leader Adolf Hitler (1889–1945). Its policies included the belief that white Christians were superior to other people and that the white race should improve itself by eliminating people unlike them, such as Jews, homosexuals, people of color, and people with disabilities. Many skinheads are modern Nazis, who believe in the racist policies of the Nazi party and act violently against those they think represent a threat to white superiority. Although they look and act tough and claim to identify with working-class people, they are often the children of middle-class families.

Nazi skinheads demonstrate in Germany. © CARO/ALAMY.

The skinhead movement began in Great Britain, when poor, angry young men shaved their heads and launched violent attacks on the immigrants they claimed were taking their jobs. By the 1980s, there were skinheads in Western and Central Europe, in Russia, in Australia, and across the United States. Their number has continued to grow, especially in difficult economic times, when people often look for someone to blame for their financial hardship. During the economic recession of the 1980s, the number of U.S. skinheads grew from fewer than one hundred in 1985 to over five thousand by 1990. There are skinhead groups in Dallas, Texas; New Orleans, Louisiana; Denver, Colorado; Portland, Oregon; and other major U.S. cities. There are even a number of skinheads within the American armed forces, where their beliefs are tolerated unless they commit a crime.

Skinheads have been convicted of many hate crimes, including the 1998 murder of a caretaker at a Sikh temple in Surrey, British Columbia, Canada; the 1998 death of a black U.S. Marine in Russia; and the 2000 bombing of a Jewish synagogue in Reno, Nevada. Many anti-Nazi groups have arisen in countries with active skinhead populations to try to combat their racist Nazi doctrine with education and protests. On the opposite end of the political spectrum, skinheads in the United States also started groups in the 1990s such as Skinheads Against Racial Prejudice (SHARP) and Red and Anarchist Skinheads (RASH), which stands against fascism, although these groups remained in the minority.

Tina Gianoulis

For More Information

Coplon, Jeff. "Skinhead Nation." *Rolling Stone* (No. 540, December 1, 1988): pp. 54–63.

David, Rod. "'I'm a Nazi Until Death': To the Ugly Question of Why Life Is Unfair, the Skinheads of Dallas Have an Uglier Answer." *Texas Monthly* (Vol. 17, no. 2, February 1989): pp. 84–95.

Kovaleski, Serge F. "American Skinheads: Fighting Minorities and Each Other; Non-Racist Factions Try to Counter Supremacists." *Washington Post* (Vol. 119, January 16, 1996): p. A1.

Moore, Jack. *Skinheads Shaved for Battle: A Cultural History of American Skinheads.* Bowling Green, OH: Bowling Green State University Popular Press, 1993.

Relin, David Oliver, Peter M. Jones, and Steven Manning. "Harvesting Young People's Hate." *Scholastic Update* (Vol. 121, no. 15, April 7, 1989): pp. 4–8.

Travis, Tiffini A., and Perry Hardy. *Skinheads: A Guide to an American Subculture.* Santa Barbara, CA: Greenwood Press, 2012.

Van Biema, David, and David S. Jackson. "When White Makes Right." *Time* (Vol. 142, no. 6, August 9, 1993): pp. 40–43.

Voll, Daniel. "A Few Good Nazis." *Esquire* (Vol. 125, no. 4, April 1996): pp. 102–12.

Sport Utility Vehicles (SUVs)

Sport utility vehicles (SUVs) are seen as safe, strong, and large enough to handle just about anything, from shopping trips to crossing the desert. SUVs have been an important part of the American car market since the end of World War II (1939–45), but the boom in SUV ownership really began in the 1980s, when **baby boomers** (see entry under 1940s—The Way We Lived in volume 3) with growing families chose the sportier look of these large vehicles over traditional family-carting **minivans** (see entry under 1980s—The Way We Lived in volume 5) and station wagons.

The first SUVs were military-surplus Willys-Overland **Jeeps** (see entry under 1940s—Commerce in volume 3). These crude

A Land Rover sport utility vehicle (SUV). © DAVID NOLON PHOTOGRAPHY/ALAMY.

four-wheel-drive vehicles were bought by farmers and outdoor types to carry everything from supplies to camping gear. Although the Jeep and International Harvester utility vehicles were popular with civilians since the 1940s, the first true SUV was the Ford Bronco, introduced in 1966. The success of the Bronco inspired other manufacturers to make big four-by-fours as well. Four-wheel-drive and large engines combine to make SUVs gas guzzlers, so it took the end of the 1970s oil crisis for SUV ownership to truly take hold. Because SUVs are classified as light trucks rather than passenger cars, they do not need to meet tough emissions standards. Consequently, they are not popular with environmentalists.

SUVs are valued for their towing capacity and power, but their safety is also important to buyers. The sheer size of vehicles makes them much safer than smaller passenger cars in collisions. In fact, they inflict so much damage on smaller vehicles that insurers have raised liability rates on SUVs. Although first marketed to farmers and outdoor adventurers, by 2001 most SUV drivers were suburban women who hauled children to and from sporting events and other activities.

Despite their off-road and towing abilities, in 2001 most SUVs were sold as luxury cars. Soft leather upholstery had replaced wipe-clean vinyl, and thick carpeting covered the floors. Yet the names of these monster off-roaders still evoked images of rugged cross-country travel. Imports such as Toyota's Landcruiser and the British Range Rover offered luxury in the wilderness. American-made SUVs included the Ford Bronco and Explorer, the Jeep Grand Cherokee, and the Chevy Blazer. Although SUVs accounted for almost one in four cars sold in the United States at the end of the twentieth century, sales of the oversized vehicles plummeted in the mid-2000s as gas prices rose and the economy tanked.

Chris Routledge

For More Information

Chapman, Giles. *SUV: The World's Greatest Sport Utility Vehicles.* London: Merrell, 2005.

Jacobs, David H. *Sport Utility Vehicles: The Off-Road Revolution.* New York: Todtri, 1998.

Urban Legends

An urban legend is a story, passed from person to person, about an event that is said to have really occurred. The story is phrased in believable terms, but the ending is usually horrifying, shocking, or humorous. By definition, urban legends are false—either completely made up or based on actual events but greatly exaggerated or distorted.

The term "urban legend" has been in use only since the 1930s, but the phenomenon has probably existed as long as human society has. People tend to believe and to pass on stories that are reasonable, interesting, and make a point. Folklore experts who study urban legends say that the accounts usually come from a credible source (a friend, relative, or coworker), have a narrative form (a story with characters and a plot), and contain elements of humor, caution, or horror.

One of the most common types of urban legend is the cautionary tale, such as the account of a man who has a drink in a bar with a strange woman and wakes up in a hotel room, alone, missing one of his kidneys. Similar to this is the contamination story, such as the widely known myth about someone who bites into a piece of fast-food fried chicken, only to find a rat carcass underneath the breading. These kinds of stories are thinly disguised warnings. They tend to reflect the anxieties common in a society—fear of strangers, distrust of **fast food** (see entry under 1920s—Food and Drink in volume 2), concern about gang violence, and so on.

Development of the **Internet** (see entry under 1990s—The Way We Lived in volume 5) has made the problem of urban legends worse, but it also offers a cure. Internet access allows anyone to pass an urban legend on very quickly to a large number of people, whether through a newsgroup, chat room, bulletin board, Web site, or via **e-mail** (see entry under 1990s—The Way We Lived in volume 5). Thus, a misleading story or a malicious rumor can spread widely and rapidly. However, the Internet also allows the development of Web sites that collect current urban legends and identify them as such. Several such sites exist, allowing anyone to check whether the latest "weird story" is fact or another urban legend.

Justin Gustainis

For More Information

Brunvand, Jan Harold. *Encyclopedia of Urban Legends.* Santa Barbara, CA: ABC-CLIO, 2001.

Brunvand, Jan Harold. *Too Good to Be True: The Colossal Book of Urban Legends.* New York: W. W. Norton, 2001.

Craughwell, Thomas J. *The Baby on the Car Roof and 222 More Urban Legends.* New York: Black Dog & Leventhal, 2000.

Mikkelson, Barbara, and David P. Mikkelson. *Snopes.com: Urban Legends Reference Pages.* http://www.snopes.com/ (accessed July 30, 2011).

Toropov, Brandon. *The Complete Idiot's Guide to Urban Legends.* Indianapolis: Alpha Books, 2001.

Urban Legends Research Centre. http://www.ulrc.com.au/ (accessed July 30, 2011).

Williams, John. *The Cost of Deception: The Seduction of Modern Myths and Urban Legends.* Nashville: Broadman & Holman, 2001.

Yuppies

If the 1960s were the decade of protest and civil rights, in the 1970s the counterculture generation entered the mainstream. Much of fashion and design reflected wholesome, back-to-nature values. Educated on radical campuses, young office workers wore their hair long. The stuffed-shirt image of the professional classes was lightened with brightly colored ties, wide lapels, and flared trousers. But in the 1980s came a backlash. Many of the middle-class young who came out of college in the late 1970s and early 1980s went into well-paid jobs in finance, the media, law, and property development. In the economic climate of the early Reagan presidency (1981–89), anyone who was young and ambitious could make a lot of money and make it fast. They became known as yuppies, which stood for young urban professionals. Their motto for life was "Whoever dies with the most toys wins."

Obsessed with their careers and their collections of gadgets, yuppies delayed marriage and children. Unlike their conservative parents, they borrowed heavily in order to buy the latest fashion accessory or status symbol. They lived in newly converted city loft apartments and drove expensive German cars. They wore watches from high-priced Swiss companies like Rolex and bought the latest in electronic wizardry, from **compact disc** (see entry under 1980s—Music in volume 5) players to portable computers. Trading on snob value, yuppies began the trend for designer fashion labels that had become the norm by the 1990s. To the media, these wealthy young professionals were self-indulgent and self-centered. They were dubbed the "me" generation.

The 1980s were compared with the 1920s as a decade of excess. Whereas *The Great Gatsby* by F. Scott Fitzgerald (1896–1940) described the earlier era, the 1980s also had its literature. *Bright Lights, Big City* by Jay McInerney (1955–) and ***The Bonfire of the Vanities*** (see entry under 1980s—Print Culture in volume 5) by Tom Wolfe (1931–) are the key yuppie novels and guides to the "greed decade." For most people, however, the yuppie lifestyle was not really a choice, although middle-class America as a whole benefited from the economic boom of the early Reagan era. Yuppies simply took full advantage of their privileged position.

As more and more women went into well-paid jobs, yuppie couples found themselves with a lot of money and plenty of ways to spend it. Childless yuppie couples became known as "dinks" or "dinkys," because they had "dual incomes and no kids (yet)." Those with children hired nannies, housekeepers, and other servants so they could keep up with their careers and partying lifestyle. Putting a child through the "right" school became as important as taking holidays in the "right" resorts. To get ahead in many companies, it was necessary to drive the "right" car, wear the "right" clothes, and go to the "right" parties. Many yuppies took drugs, but not the low-brow **marijuana** (see entry under 1960s—The

Way We Lived in volume 4) of the counterculture. They used **cocaine** (see entry under 1980s—The Way We Lived in volume 5) and bought it from well-connected dealers who lived the yuppie lifestyle themselves. Cheap credit was useful for those who aspired to the yuppie lifestyle but did not have the income to match. The pressure to keep up appearances was intense, and many yuppies had breakdowns or suffered "burnout" at young ages.

As the boom of the early 1980s ended, yuppies found themselves heavily in debt. Companies began to "downsize" and many white-collar workers were unemployed. Yuppies had to sell their expensive gadgets and toys in order to pay the bills. With the collapse of the stock and housing markets in 1987, many found the value of their assets was far less than the amount of their debts. Others were suffering, too, and yuppies got little sympathy from the rest of the population. "Yuppie" came to mean "young unhappy professional." Rather unfairly, yuppies took the blame for the excess that led to the crash. By the early 1990s, many yuppies were fed up with their materialistic lifestyle. Some could afford to drop out of their well-paid jobs and move to the country to look for a simpler life. Others went to work for charities and environmental agencies. This became known as "downshifting." Those who did it were known as "domos" or "downwardly mobile professionals."

The term "yuppie" was never exactly meant as a compliment, but in the twenty-first century it has no meaning *except* as an insult. Criticized for their lax morals and blamed for the stock market crash of 1987, yuppies were snobbish, self-important, and slightly ridiculous. The yuppie moment has come and gone. The real reason for the death of the yuppie, however, is that in the early twenty-first century, conspicuous consumption—buying expensive items to show off wealth—has spread through most sectors of society. Designer labels, electronic toys, and consumer credit are widespread among all but the very poor. The rich still enjoy a lifestyle that old-time yuppies would recognize, but perhaps the truth is that in everyone's aspirations resides a little bit of yuppie.

Chris Routledge

For More Information

Gaslin, Glenn, and Rick Porter. *The Complete Cross-Referenced Guide to the Baby Buster Generation's Collective Unconscious.* New York: Boulevard Books, 1998.

Piesman, Marissa, and Marilee Hartley. *Yuppie Handbook: The State-of-the-Art Handbook for Young Urban Professionals.* New York: Pocket Books, 1984.

1990s

The Decade America Went Digital

The United States faced several serious challenges as it entered the 1990s. On the one hand, the continued collapse of the Soviet Union meant that the United States was now the lone superpower in the world. America soon found out what that meant when Iraq invaded Kuwait. President George H. W. Bush (1924–) sent in American troops to restore Kuwait and to challenge the armies of Iraqi leader Saddam Hussein (1937–2006). Bush's victory in the Gulf War (1991) brought him high approval ratings at home, but not high enough to override the mounting economic problems the country was facing.

The American economy, which had seemed so healthy for much of the 1980s, had come under increasing strain late in the decade. This strain was due in part to the huge budget deficits created by the Reagan administration (1981–89). As the economy slipped into recession, President Bush was forced to take back a campaign pledge and raise taxes. In the presidential election of 1992, Democratic candidate Bill Clinton (1946–) hammered Bush on the economy. He had help from third-party candidate H. Ross Perot (1930–), a quirky millionaire who bought hours of television time to get out his message. When the election returns came in, Clinton won with just 43 percent of the vote.

Clinton's presidency was troubled from the outset. Republicans hated Clinton, and they used his slim margin of victory and the slight

1990s At a Glance

WHAT WE SAID:

"As if!": An expression of disdain for an idea, as in "Britney Spears is cool? As if!"

"Been there, done that": This phrase, made popular by *The Simpsons* character Bart, implies that a person already has experience with something and does not want to do it again.

Chill: To hang out and be casual.

Crib: One's home or apartment.

Emoticons: :-) : Symbols used to show emotion in an e-mail message; popular emoticons include :-) (happiness) and :-((sadness).

Generation X: The generation of Americans born to baby boomers and yuppies. Critics of the generation said that Gen Xers (or Xers) denounced the values of their parents but offered nothing in their place. Gen Xers countered that they were against mindless materialism and for an expanded environmental consciousness.

"Just Do It": The slogan for Nike's famous advertising campaign was widely used to express toughness and determination in the face of adversity.

"Not!": An interjection tacked on at the end of a phrase to indicate total disagreement, as in "That guy is so cool—not!" Popularized in the *Saturday Night Live* skit and 1992 film *Wayne's World.*

Parental units: Parents.

Phat: Something good or cool, this word was used by rappers but originated in the 1960s.

Trash talk: Nasty barbs exchanged by athletes to try to get each other angry. The term originated in the National Basketball Association but had been around since the 1960s.

24/7: Always, as in 24 hours a day and 7 days a week.

"Whatever": A dismissal of whatever another person has said, this term indicates that the speaker will not even waste his or her time thinking about what someone has said.

WHAT WE READ:

***Dilbert* (1989–):** Scott Adams' comic strip captured the spirit of work life in the 1990s and created a *Dilbert* merchandise industry of coffee mugs, mouse pads, and T-shirts.

***Jurassic Park* (1990):** Science thriller writer Michael Crichton created a minor industry in 1990 with the publication of this book about dinosaurs brought back to life on a distant tropical island. Popular as a book, it was even more popular as a movie with dazzling special effects (1993).

Democratic majority in Congress to challenge every program Clinton created. When the Republicans gained a majority in the House of Representatives in the 1994 elections, they brought the government to a near-standstill. To make matters worse, the Clinton administration and Clinton himself had a knack for getting in trouble. There were small scandals over political nominees and White House travel

***The Bridges of Madison County* (1992):** This romantic story by Robert James Waller told of a woman's passion rekindled late in life by her romance with a traveling photographer. A major movie starred Clint Eastwood and Meryl Streep.

***Men Are from Mars, Women Are from Venus* (1992):** Self-help hero John Gray dissected relationships from the perspective that women and men needed to learn to understand each other's distinctive communicating styles. The book struck a nerve, and remained a best-seller for several years.

***Harry Potter and the Sorcerer's Stone* (1998):** The first in a series of books for young adults about youthful wizard Harry Potter and his adventures at Hogwarts, a school for wizards. J. K. Rowling's books were the publishing sensation of the late 1990s and early 2000s.

Anything from Danielle Steel or Stephen King: The two best-selling authors of the 1980s repeated that performance in the 1990s, though they switched positions. Romance novelist Steel topped the list, with 19 novels appearing in the top 10 list for best-selling novels each year. Horror master King was close behind with 10 titles.

WHAT WE WATCHED:

***COPS* (1989–):** The Fox Network established a new genre of TV show when it introduced *COPS* in 1989. Every week the show followed real police in a different city as they chased down criminals and talked about their jobs. This show influenced the many reality TV shows that became popular in 2000.

***Beverly Hills 90210* (1990–2000):** This teen drama helped establish the new Fox Network; made major stars of actors Jason Priestley, Shannen Doherty, Tori Spelling, and several others; and paved the way for later teen dramas, all while dealing with major issues facing teens like divorce, eating disorders, sexuality, drug use, and date rape.

***Seinfeld* (1990–98):** This sitcom, which boasted that it was about nothing, provided a digest of the trivial topics that absorbed Americans in the decade. The show starred Jerry Seinfeld, Michael Richards, Jason Alexander, and Julia Louis-Dreyfus.

***The Simpsons* (1990–):** This animated sitcom about a typical dysfunctional American family is widely hailed as the most creative and intelligent TV show of the decade.

***ER* (1994–2009):** The top-rated drama of the decade, this fast-paced drama followed the professional and personal lives of a group of emergency room doctors and nurses in a busy Chicago hospital.

expenditures—the "Nannygate" and "Travelgate" controversies, named after the famous Watergate scandal of the administration of President Richard Nixon (1913–1994).

Then the scandals got bigger and uglier. A special counsel was appointed to look into investments that the president and his wife, Hillary Rodham Clinton (1947–), had made in Arkansas. This investigation,

1990s At a Glance (continued)

***Friends* (1994–2004):** This sitcom focused on the lives of six Generation X friends living in New York City and made a major star of actress Jennifer Aniston.

***The Lion King* (1994):** This animated film about a young lion in Africa charmed children, re-established Disney as the leading animated filmmaker, and helped revive the animated children's film market.

***Titanic* (1997):** The most expensive film ever made at the time ($200 million), this love story set during the sinking of the passenger liner *Titanic* made a teen idol of star Leonardo DiCaprio.

***Dawson's Creek* (1998–2003):** One of several teen-oriented shows airing on the WB network (which was founded in 1995), this drama presented coming-of-age stories of four high school friends.

WHAT WE LISTENED TO:

Rush Limbaugh (1951–): This arch-conservative hosted the leading political talk radio show of the decade and, thanks to the support of his many dedicated listeners, exercised a great deal of political influence.

Celine Dion (1968–): This Canadian star became one of the top-selling recording artists of the decade with her soaring romantic ballads. She scored big with songs from *Beauty and the Beast* (1990) and *Titanic* (1997).

***Ropin' the Wind* (1991):** Garth Brooks sang his way into the record books with this album, which debuted at the top of both the country and the pop charts at the same time.

"Smells Like Teen Spirit" (1991): This song, from Nirvana's album *Nevermind,* helped define grunge music, the punk rock of a new generation.

"Macarena" (1994): This song by Spanish group Los Del Rio became an international dance sensation that hit the United States in 1996 and soon had thousands of Americans twisting and shaking in the decade's biggest dance craze.

***Jagged Little Pill* (1995):** Alanis Morissette's angry and emotionally honest third album was the best-selling album of the decade, and won Morissette Grammy Awards for Album of the Year and Song of the Year.

***The Miseducation of Lauryn Hill* (1998):** This combination of hip-hop, gospel, soul, and other musical influences helped Lauryn Hill win a Grammy Award and sell four hundred thousand copies of the album in its first week.

Ricky Martin (1971–): The leading teen idol of the 1990s led a craze for Latin music when he released his first English album in 1999. The

called the Whitewater investigation, was soon followed by charges that Clinton, when he was a governor, had sexually harassed a state employee named Paula Jones (1967–). Finally, in 1997, investigators led by Kenneth Starr (1946–) revealed that Clinton had had a sexual relationship with a White House intern, Monica Lewinsky (1973–), and may have lied about it under oath. These charges led the House to pass

single "Livin' la Vida Loca" quickly became a smash single.

WHO WE KNEW:

Bill Gates (1955–): The founder of Microsoft became the richest man in the world thanks to the performance of his company. But some in the computer industry saw Microsoft as a threatening monopoly, spurring the U.S. Justice Department to bring charges against the company.

Anita Hill (1956–): This African American professor and lawyer came to national attention when she testified before the U.S. Senate that Supreme Court nominee (and later justice) Clarence Thomas sexually harassed her in the 1980s.

Michael Jordan (1963–): Hailed as the greatest basketball player of all time, Jordan led the Chicago Bulls to six NBA championships in the decade. He also appeared in a blizzard of advertisements for Nike, Gatorade, and other products.

Ted Kaczynski (1942–): This alienated academic terrorized the nation for seventeen years with a string of mail bomb attacks that earned him the name "The Unabomber." Kaczynski was finally caught after his anti-technology manifesto was published in the *Washington Post* and caught the eye of his brother, who recognized Kaczynski's style and turned him in to prevent further loss of life.

Jack Kevorkian (1928–2011): Better known as "Dr. Death," this Michigan doctor helped a number of his patients end their lives and championed the rights of those who wished to choose "death with dignity" through assisted suicide.

Rodney King (c. 1965–): This part-time laborer became a symbol of police brutality and violence against African Americans when a nearby resident happened to film his brutal beating at the hands of several Los Angeles police officers and released the tape to the world. When the police were acquitted of police brutality, Los Angeles erupted in riots. King appeared on television and asked, "Can't we all just get along?"

Timothy McVeigh (1968–2001): This former army soldier blew up the Alfred P. Murrah federal building in Oklahoma City, Oklahoma, on April 19, 1995, killing 168 people. He was executed in 2001.

Colin Powell (1937–): U.S. army general and chairman of the Joint Chiefs of Staff Colin Powell became an American hero thanks to his leadership during the Gulf War of 1991. In 2001, he became secretary of state under President George W. Bush.

articles of impeachment against the president (to charge the president with misconduct in office) late in 1998. The Senate, however, declined to try the president, and the impeachment scandal died. These endless scandals, however, had taken their toll on Clinton's approval ratings.

Despite the taint of scandal, America thrived under the Clinton administration. The economy picked up dramatically by the mid-1990s

1990s At a Glance (continued)

O. J. Simpson (1947–): This former college and pro football star was accused of the brutal murder of his ex-wife Nicole Brown and her friend Ronald Goldman in 1994 and was involved in a trial that aired live on TV for months. Though Simpson was acquitted of the murders, he later lost a civil case against the families of the victims.

Martha Stewart (1941–): America's leading lifestyle expert created a media empire that included magazines and books, television and radio programs, and a line of homemaking products.

and stayed strong through the end of the decade. Driving the economy was the strong performance of high-technology firms, led by companies known as "dot-coms." The dotcom companies took their name from the domain names that many companies adopted for use on the recently invented World Wide Web. Dot-coms such as Amazon.com, E-Bay, America Online, and Pets.com reinvented the way that many businesses worked. Buying and selling goods over the Internet, and allowing workers more freedom and creativity than they had ever enjoyed before, these companies led the way in what was known as the "New Economy." Biotechnology also boomed, as companies used advanced scientific techniques to improve crop yields, make genetically engineered foods, invent new drugs, and introduce a variety of other innovations.

The strong performance of the "New Economy" fueled an expansion in all the major stock markets. Millions of Americans who had never invested before now invested money in the stock market, either directly or through mutual funds. Overnight, many Americans got wealthy from small companies that hit it big. A new kind of stock trader called a "day trader" became a symbolic figure of how to benefit from the overheated stock market.

Along with the economy, popular culture flourished. Movie-makers poured millions of dollars into making films that were filled with dramatic special effects. *Jurassic Park* (1993) and *Titanic* (1997) are two examples of such films. Network television produced a good number of worthwhile shows, including one of the most loved situation comedies (sitcoms) in TV history in *Seinfeld* and one of the most creative sitcoms in *The Simpsons.* Cable TV offered a growing number of Americans more variety than ever before in home entertainment. Musically, Americans also had many styles from which to choose, from a revived country music scene to alternative rock to rap.

In sports, America watched some of the greatest athletic performances of all time from the likes of basketball's Michael Jordan (1963–), golf's Tiger Woods (1975–), and baseball's Mark McGwire (1963–). McGwire and fellow National League slugger Sammy Sosa (1968–) battled each other in 1998 for the home run race as they chased the record of Roger Maris (1934–1985) for most home runs in a season; McGwire won out with 70 home runs (a record that was eclipsed only three years later by Barry Bonds [1964–]). Americans also enjoyed the accomplishments of a range of female athletes from soccer star Mia Hamm (1972–) to tennis sisters Venus Williams (1980–) and Serena Williams (1981–).

1990s

Commerce

In the 1990s, commerce became e-commerce and the nation was gripped by dot-com fever. The nation's economy had started off the decade in a slump. By the mid-1990s, however, the energizing force of what became known as the dot-com revolution helped fuel the longest sustained period of economic growth in the nation's history. Dot-coms are companies that do business over the World Wide Web. The Web is a system that connects computers in a giant network and allows people to easily buy and sell goods and services electronically (thus the term e-commerce). They are named dot-coms because their World Wide Web URL addresses typically end with ".com."

All over the country—but especially in the Internet boom areas of Silicon Valley, California; Seattle, Washington; and New York City's Silicon Alley—small dot-com companies launched themselves. The small companies had ambitious plans to use the World Wide Web to sell things like books, pet supplies, and groceries. These dot-coms attracted vast amounts of investors' dollars and helped fuel a rapidly rising stock market that made many Americans a good sum of money. The World Wide Web also allowed for the emergence of "day traders," individuals who bought and sold stocks from the comfort of their computer terminals. Some day traders made millions; many others went bankrupt.

If one company benefited most from the growing popularity of computer-based businesses, it was the Redmond, Washington–based Microsoft. Microsoft sold the operating systems that helped run the vast majority of computers in the world. Its competitors said that it used its operating-system dominance to unfair advantage. The U.S. Justice Department filed suit against the company, but the two parties eventually settled out of court.

Outside the world of computers, Americans consumed as they had for decades: excessively. In 1992, America built a giant shrine to the joys of consumerism in Bloomington, Minnesota. The Mall of America, with 4.2 million square feet of floor space, became the largest shopping mall in the country.

Mall of America

The Mall of America—located just outside Minneapolis, Minnesota—is not only the largest indoor shopping **mall** (see entry under 1950s—Commerce in volume 3) but is the most-visited tourist destination in the United States. The Mall of America opened in 1992 at a cost of $650 million. This dazzling home of 520 stores and 11,000 employees is more than a place to shop—it is an experience. The Mall of America has been described by its fans as a shopper's paradise and by its critics as an oppressive monument to American consumerism that numbs its visitors with sensory overload.

Everything about the Mall of America is big: six hundred thousand to nine hundred thousand people visit the mall in a week. The total area is 4.2 million square feet, just about the same floor space as the Sears Tower, a large **skyscraper** (see entry under 1930s—The Way We Lived in volume 2) in Chicago, Illinois. Some 258 Statues of Liberty could be laid inside the mall. There are 4.3 miles of storefront and 125 security cameras. The mall attracts more visitors annually than Disney World; Graceland, the Memphis, Tennessee, home of **Elvis Presley** (1935–1977; see entry under 1950s—Music in volume 3); and the Grand Canyon combined.

The Mall of America is designed to seduce nearly anyone who walks in. Aside from the usual restaurants and other services that can be found at a typical mall, the Mall of America has eight nightclubs, an aquarium with real sharks, and even a "Chapel of Love," where thirty couples a month tie the knot. The mall's seven-acre amusement park has a **roller coaster** and a seventy-four-foot **Ferris wheel** (see these entries under 1900s—The Way We Lived in volume 1).

The mall—like many in the United States—has its own youth subculture. On a typical day, nearly two thousand local teens come to the mall to hang out with their friends. They, and the mall, made news in 1996 when a weekend curfew was imposed because of concerns that some teens were being overly rowdy.

The Mall of America was still going strong in the first decade of the twenty-first century. Even during the tough economy of that period, the Mall continued to boast forty million annual visitors (more than the combined populations of North Dakota, South Dakota, Iowa, and Canada), five thousand weddings per year, and thirty-two thousand tons of annually recycled garbage.

Karl Rahder

For More Information

Gershman, Suzy. "Mall of the Gods." *Travel-Holiday* (October 1996): pp. 82–88.

Guterson, David. "Enclosed. Encyclopedic. Endured. One Week in the Mall of America." *Harper's* (August 1993): pp. 49–56.

Mall of America.com. http://www.mallofamerica.com/ (accessed December 20, 2011).

Meredith, Robyn. "Big Mall's Curfew Raises Questions of Rights and Bias." *New York Times* (September 4, 1996): p. A1.

Microsoft

The Microsoft Corporation, located near Seattle, Washington, is a large, powerful, and profitable company that creates computer software. The tremendous success of Microsoft, which grew in the 1990s to become one of the world's most powerful corporations, is viewed by the public with a wide variety of opinions. Since its formation in 1975, the company has contributed in a major way to the popularization of the PC—the **personal computer** (see entry under 1970s—The Way We Lived in volume 4)—and to growth and improvement in the software that makes computers useful. It has become a major power in the world economy and had an important role in the quickly rising stock market of the 1990s. Many, therefore, see Microsoft as a positive force, creating progress and

Billionaire Microsoft founder Bill Gates in the packaging facility on his company's corporate campus in Redmond, Washington, in 1986. © JOE MCNALLY/GETTY IMAGES.

prosperity for all. Others see the company as a ruthless and unethical giant, crushing competition in order to gain enormous profits for itself. The strong emotions that the company arouses in the public demonstrate the enormous effect that Microsoft has had on modern life.

Part of the mystique of the Microsoft Corporation is that it came from such small beginnings. Bill Gates (1955–) and Paul Allen (1953–) were in eighth grade when they began studying the brand-new science of computers in the late 1960s. They were fascinated by the new technology and began experimenting together. In 1972, they worked out a practical use for a new microprocessor chip, a very tiny computer part, in a device to count traffic on highways. Traf-o-data, the company they formed to sell their invention, was not very successful, but Gates and Allen continued to experiment with designing software for the tiny microprocessor. They combined these two interests in the name of the next company they formed: Micro-Soft (later changed to Microsoft).

Gates dropped out of Harvard University. In 1974, he and Allen set up shop in Albuquerque, New Mexico, continuing to develop computer software. One of their strongest advantages in business was their ability to envision new uses for computer technology. They soon created a computer language for a new, small personal computer that used the new micro-technology, the MITS Altair. Working together during the mid-1970s, Allen and Gates created the first important computer programming languages: BASIC, FORTRAN-80, and COBOL 80. These were codes that programmers entered into the computer to tell it what to do.

Gates and Allen brought their little company back home to Seattle. In 1980, **IBM** (see entry under 1980s—Commerce in volume 5) approached them about designing a disk operating system, or DOS, for a new personal computer IBM was developing. Again, Gates and Allen's foresight helped them realize that this was an important opportunity. At a time when few people really knew what computers were, they began to foresee a future when every home would have its own computer. They wanted to make sure that Microsoft was designing the software for those computers. Since IBM was in a hurry to get the disk operating system, Gates and Allen bought a disk operating system from another small Seattle company without telling them about IBM's interest. Some believe this move was sneaky and dishonest; others think it was brilliant business planning. Gates and Allen made a huge profit selling the renamed MS-DOS to IBM. They also managed to get the other companies who began making copies or "clones" of the IBM computer to use the Microsoft operating system as well.

Suddenly Microsoft was the biggest software company in the world. Allen became ill and retired in 1983 with $6 billion in profits. Gates continued to run Microsoft, developing software for the growing computer industry. In the mid-1980s, another leap forward in technology occurred when MS-DOS was essentially replaced by the Graphical User Interface (GUI), which Microsoft developed for use in the Macintosh computer made by **Apple Computer** (see entry under 1970s—The Way We Lived in volume 4). The GUI made computers much simpler because users could tell the computer what to do by pointing to pictures on the screen using a device called a mouse. Although Apple introduced the GUI, Microsoft soon designed its own GUI, called Windows, which it sold to IBM for use in their computers.

Apple felt that Microsoft had stolen its idea for the GUI. In 1988, it sued Microsoft for copyright violation, but the suit was dismissed.

Other competitors have accused Microsoft of unfair business practices. In 1997, the federal government filed suit against the company, charging that Microsoft had misused its power in the marketplace to keep crush competition by including its Internet Explorer Web browser as part of its installation package. Microsoft made some concessions and the two parties settled the case in 2001.

Microsoft has continued to dominate the computer software market into the twenty-first century, developing new products to serve the ever-expanding personal computer market, such as Xbox, which became a hugely popular **video game** (see entry under 1970s—Sports and Games in volume 4) console, and improved operating systems for Windows. From its small beginnings in the imaginations of two high-school students, the company has grown into a giant corporation with over fifteen thousand employees and billions of dollars in profits. Its chief executive officer, Bill Gates, was long considered the world's richest man, with a personal fortune of more than $50 billion, until he was outranked in 2010 by Mexican tycoon Carlos Slim Helu (1940–). Although Gates is often criticized for his business practices and his enormous wealth, he is still a man with a vision of the changes that computers will continue to bring to society.

Tina Gianoulis

For More Information

Allen, Paul. *Idea Man: A Memoir by the Cofounder of Microsoft.* New York: Penguin, 2011.

Dickinson, Joan D. *Bill Gates, Billionaire Computer Genius.* Springfield, NJ: Enslow, 1997.

Drummond, Michael. *Renegades of the Empire: How Three Software Warriors Started a Revolution Behind the Walls of Fortress Microsoft.* New York: Crown, 1999.

Ferry, Steven. *The Story of Microsoft.* North Mankato, MN: Smart Apple Media, 1999.

Forman, Michael. *Bill Gates, Software Billionaire.* Parsippany, NJ: Silver Burdett Press, 1998.

Gatlin, Jonathan. *Bill Gates: The Path to the Future.* New York: Avon, 1999.

Microsoft. http://www.microsoft.com (accessed July 31, 2011).

Schlender, Brent. "Bill Gates & Paul Allen Talk: Co-founders of Microsoft." *Fortune* (October 2, 1995): pp. 68–77.

Wallace, James. *Hard Drive: Bill Gates and the Making of the Microsoft Empire.* New York: HarperBusiness, 1993.

1990s

Fashion

In the 1990s, fashion went casual as it never had before. From corporations to classrooms, people wore clothes that were comfortable and expressed their own sense of individuality. The trend probably began in American corporations with a tradition called "casual Fridays." On Fridays, rather than wearing standard business attire, employees at many companies were allowed to dress casually, with khaki pants and a casual shirt the norm for men. By the time the dot-com revolution swept the nation, everyday was a casual Friday. Standard business attire was required only by the most formal companies.

A new generation of Americans known as Generation X increasingly set fashion trends. Twenty-something Generation X-ers insisted on their right to display their individuality through clothes, hairstyles, and body decoration. Some searched thrift shops for odd clothes that they could match with items they bought at stores like Old Navy and Gap; others favored the preppy look offered at popular retailer Abercrombie & Fitch. (All three of these stores followed the trend of displaying their brand names prominently on much of the clothing they sold.) Hairstyles varied widely, with men preferring very short hair and women choosing a shifting array of different looks. Body decoration was one of the most notable fads of the decade. People of all ages (but mostly youngsters) got tattoos or had parts of their body—tongues, eyebrows, nipples—pierced and studded. A notable fashion subculture of the decade were the Goths, who dressed like characters in a gothic novel with a heavy emphasis on black.

Abercrombie & Fitch

Abercrombie & Fitch is one of the most visible and innovative retailers of clothing in the United States. In the 1990s, Abercrombie & Fitch was recognized as a trendsetter for young people, competing with other youth-oriented companies such as **J.Crew** (see entry under 1980s—Commerce in volume 5), American Eagle, and **Gap** (see entry under 1960s—Commerce in volume 4). One of Abercrombie & Fitch's innovations was the "magalog": one-part magazine, one-part retail catalog. The Abercrombie & Fitch magalog sparked national controversy in

A man buys clothes at the Abercrombie & Fitch store at the Center Mall in Las Vegas, Nevada. © KUMAR SRISKANDAN/ALAMY.

2000 when its photo spreads featured scantily clad models. Competitors generally follow Abercrombie & Fitch's lead in using such marketing devices.

Abercrombie & Fitch is perhaps best known for eye-catching clothing such as its famous paratrooper pants. The company racked up a staggering $1.06 billion in sales in 1999. Abercrombie & Fitch started life in 1892 as a supplier of outdoor gear for the wealthy and famous. Since the 1990s, the company has concentrated on defining cool, rugged clothing and accessories for teens. In the 2000s, the company was plagued by a series of lawsuits claiming discrimination against women and minorities, and in 2005 Abercrombie & Fitch was ordered to pay $400 million to plaintiffs as well as to alter its hiring and advertising practices. The company continued to flourish in the early 2000s with over three hundred stores in the United States and plans for major expansion into Europe and Asia by 2012.

Karl Rahder

For More Information

Abercrombie & Fitch. http://www.abercrombie.com/ (accessed July 31, 2011).

Barrett, Amy. "To Reach the Unreachable Teen." *Business Week* (September 18, 2000): pp. 78–80.

"Mail Bonding." *Vogue* (November 1997): pp. 170–72.

Perman, Stacy. "Abercrombie's Beefcake Brigade." *Time* (February 14, 2000): p. 36.

1990s

Film and Theater

In the 1990s, special effects continued to dominate the film world. Special effects were used heavily to create the spectacular action that was demanded of every movie studio's most important film of the year: the summer blockbuster. *Jurassic Park* (1993), based on a novel of the same name by Michael Crichton (1942–), set the standard for the decade with its realistic computer-generated dinosaurs that munched on people. Many other movies offered thrills of their own. Whether those thrills came from space, as in *Independence Day* (1996) or *Star Wars: Episode I—The Phantom Menace* (1999), or from nature, as in *Twister* (1996) with its terrifying tornadoes, filmmakers relied on special effects to give their stories impact. *Star Wars: Episode I—The Phantom Menace* had the distinction of featuring the first digitally generated principal character in a movie: Jar Jar Binks.

Of course, not all films used special effects to win audiences. The horror film *Scream* (1996) combined gore with humor. The independently made sensation *The Blair Witch Project* (1999) used quirky filmmaking techniques and sheer suspense to terrify audiences. Both films helped revive a film genre, horror, which had grown stale and unoriginal, with movies produced as if using a formula. Animated films also experienced a revival in the 1990s. *The Lion King* (1994) proved that Disney could still make heartwarming family entertainment, but the real story of the decade was the use of computer-generated animation. *Toy Story* (1995), *Toy Story 2* (1999), *A Bug's Life* (1998), and *Antz* (1998) were all made exclusively on computers. Each film had warmth and humor. All these films also allowed for the creation of an assortment of toys, games, video games, and cross-promotions with fast-food restaurants.

American theater continued the boom that began in the 1980s, with large-scale productions drawing huge audiences in New York and then touring the nation. The major productions of the decade were *The Lion King* (1997; a stage version of the film), *Ragtime* (1997), *Bring in 'Da Noise, Bring in 'Da Funk* (1996), and *Rent* (1996).

Austin Powers

The three *Austin Powers* films brought to the screen by Mike Myers (1963–) are spoof spy thrillers based on classics such as *Our Man Flint* (1965) and the **James Bond** film series (see entry under 1960s—Film and Theater in volume 4). The movies make clever mockery of 1960s music, speech, and fashion. Austin Powers, played by Myers, is the "shag-edelic" spy from 1960s swinging London. He drives an E-type Jaguar, complete with Union Jack paint job, and has a psychedelic jumbo jet. Based on the culture clash between the 1960s and the 1990s, the films' humor is sometimes subtle, sometimes adult, but always very, very silly.

Canadian comedic actor Mike Myers as British spy Austin Powers. © NEW LINE/THE KOBAL COLLECTION/ART RESOURCE, NY.

The first *Austin Powers* movie premiered in 1997. *Austin Powers: International Man of Mystery* sees Powers awaken after thirty years of cryogenic sleep to the news that his old enemy, Dr. Evil (also played by Myers), has returned. The confused Dr. Evil wants to hold the world hostage and sets his ransom demand at … "one million dollars!" He is advised that in the 1990s, $100 billion would be a better suggestion. Austin Powers, working with the grown-up daughter of his 1960s sidekick, soon finds that the era of free love is long gone. The second film,

Austin Powers: The Spy Who Shagged Me (1999), offers more of the same, plus time travel, an agent called Felicity Shagwell, and a one-eighth-size clone of Dr. Evil, called "Mini Me." A third film, *Goldmember,* released in 2002, parodies the first two movies by opening with a biopic called *Austinpussy* that stars actor Tom Cruise (1962–) as Austin before continuing the hero's adventures involving Dr. Evil and new villain Mr. Roboto.

Canadian-born Myers carries a British passport and is a well-known Anglophile (a fan of British culture). As Austin Powers, he indulged his love of all things British, including the spy's terrible teeth. Besides ridiculing 1960s spy blockbusters, the *Austin Powers* movies are also in the tradition of the British "Carry On" comedy movies of the 1950s and 1960s. Between them, the three movies have combined to give Myers an estimated net worth of $175 million. The films found an enthusiastic audience that was more than willing to use catch-phrases from the movie and even wear the costumes. Because of Austin Powers, in the late 1990s and early 2000s, things became "groovy" and "smashing" again for the first time in thirty years.

Chris Routledge

For More Information

Gould, Lance. *Shagadelically Speaking: The Words and World of Austin Powers.* New York: Warner, 1999.

Lane, Andy. *The World of Austin Powers.* New York: Universe, 2002.

McCullers, Michael, and Mike Myers. *Austin Powers: How to Be an International Man of Mystery.* New York: Boulevard Books, 1997.

Official Austin Powers Website. http://www.austinpowers.com (accessed July 31, 2011).

Forrest Gump

Winner of six Academy Awards in 1994, including Best Picture and Best Director, *Forrest Gump* is a good-natured spin through late twentieth-century America. In an Oscar-winning role, Tom Hanks (1956–) plays Forrest Gump, a simple-minded hero with talents for running and catching shrimp. Released after a period of economic gloom at the start of the first term of the Clinton presidency (1993–97), *Forrest Gump* carried the uplifting message to "put the past behind you and move on." It must have been what audiences wanted to hear, because the film grossed over $636 million at the box office.

Tom Hanks stars as the title character in the 1993 Oscar-winning film Forrest Gump. © PHILLIP CARUSO/PARAMOUNT/THE KOBAL COLLECTION/ART RESOURCE, NY.

Gump begins his life in Alabama. A sickly child in leg braces with a low intelligence quotient (IQ) of 75, his future seems bleak. He lives his life by a series of sayings from his mother, and the words "My Mama always said" make up a large part of the script. Gump's down-home wisdom leads him to make a fortune as a shrimp fisherman and to give a half million dollars away. He becomes a hero fighting in the Vietnam War (1954–75) and campaigning for civil rights. It even turns out that **Elvis Presley** (1935–1977; see entry under 1950s—Music in volume 3) learned his hip-swiveling dance from watching Forrest Gump walk with his crippled legs.

Despite its sentimental side, the picture is not all filmed like a piece of Americana in soft focus. Gump's experiences in Vietnam are realistically nasty. His best friend dies and he is unable to save his commanding officer "Lieutenant Dan" from losing his legs. Hanks's performance as the innocent Gump is the film's most impressive feature. He is bullied, cheated, and misused, yet he manages to maintain his dignity.

Gump's view that "Life is like a box of chocolates—you never know what you're going to get" is borne out by his meetings with John Lennon (1940–1980) of the **Beatles** (see entry under 1960s—Music in volume 4), Chairman Mao of China (1893–1976), President Richard Nixon (1913–1994), and others. These meetings appear on screen thanks to some clever special effects. Gump even shakes hands with President John F. Kennedy (1917–1963). The film teaches that in America everyone has the chance to be part of history. If a boy in leg braces can be a college football star and win a Congressional Medal for bravery, the film suggests, then anyone can.

A restaurant chain called Bubba Gump Shrimp Company, the name of the lead character's company in the film, opened in 1996 in California, later adding franchises across the United States and in other countries. As of 2010, there were thirty-two Bubba Gump restaurants around the globe. A screenplay for a sequel to *Forrest Gump,* based on the sequel to the original novel and entitled *Gump and Co.,* was written by Eric Roth (1945–), but a film was never produced.

Chris Routledge

For More Information

Groom, Winston. *Forrest Gump.* Garden City, NY: Doubleday, 1986.
Groom, Winston. *Gump & Co.* New York: Pocket Books, 1995.

JFK

The film *JFK* (1991), a fascinating cinematic theory about the assassination of President John F. Kennedy (1917–1963), was one of the most controversial films of its time. Directed and co-scripted by Oliver Stone (1946–), *JFK* fired up the decades-long debate over who actually murdered the fallen president. Was it lone gunman Lee Harvey Oswald (1939–1963), as was indicated by the "official" Warren Commission, which was entrusted to investigate the crime back in the 1960s? Or was it the end result of an elaborate plot, masterminded by the **Mafia** (see entry under 1960s—The Way We Lived in volume 4), the U.S. government and military, Cuban nationalists, and any number of additional Kennedy-haters?

JFK is based on the obsession of real-life New Orleans district attorney Jim Garrison (1921–1995), played by Kevin Costner (1955–), with uncovering the truth of the assassination. In the course of his investigation, Garrison tries a businessman named Clay Shaw (1913–1974) with plotting to murder Kennedy. Meanwhile, as Garrison's scenario unfolds, Stone offers a parade of characters, some real, some made up, and some composites.

Many Kennedy-assassination conspiracy buffs have chosen to view the content of *JFK* as essentially factual. Their skepticism over the "lone gunman" theory was fueled by the film's explosive script, fast-paced editing, dazzlingly realistic visuals, and riveting performances. Stone seamlessly edited footage from the Abraham Zapruder (1905–1970) film (an amateur home movie that is the only record of the actual shooting of Kennedy) with his own, made-up images. This blending of fact and fiction caused great controversy. Stone seems to present certain aspects of the Kennedy assassination as fact. His film is not a documentary, however, but a cinematic invention offering a single theory.

Much of the content of *JFK* is, at best, clever speculation. Stone's intentions and the subsequent controversy aside, the filmmaker did succeed in returning the issues surrounding one of the saddest and most disturbing moments in American history to the forefront of public awareness. The investigation into the murder of President Kennedy conducted by the U.S. Assassination Records Review Board (ARRB) went on until 1998. The ARRB has stated that all records relating to Kennedy's assassination will eventually be made available to the public.

Rob Edelman

For More Information

Garrison, Jim. *On the Trail of the Assassins.* New York: Warner Books, 1988.

Mackey-Kallis, Susan. *Oliver Stone's America: "Dreaming the Myth Outward."* Boulder, CO: Westview Press, 1996.

Marrs, Jim. *Crossfire: The Plot That Killed Kennedy.* New York: Carroll & Graf, 1989.

Stone, Oliver, producer. *JFK* (film). Warner Bros., 1991.

Stone, Oliver, and Zachary Sklar. *JFK: The Book of the Film, a Documented Screenplay.* New York: Applause Books, 1992.

Trask, Richard B. *National Nightmare on Six Feet of Film: Mr. Zapruder's Home Movie and the Murder of President Kennedy.* Danvers, MA: Yeoman Press, 2000.

The Lion King

The Lion King (1994) is one of the all-time classic animated features produced by the **Disney** Studios (see entry under 1920s—Film and Theater in volume 2)—no small distinction for a movie studio that across the decades has made dozens of highly acclaimed children's films. At once provocative, beautifully made, and highly entertaining, it rates among the most popular and profitable films of its decade.

The Lion King spotlights the life and times of Simba, a princely lion cub in Africa who is heir to the throne of Mufasa, his father. The kingdom is desired by Scar, Mufasa's evil brother, and herein lies the story's conflict. While billed as an original conception, the *Lion King* scenario clearly is rooted in other writings and films, including any number of works by William Shakespeare (1564–1616); *Huckleberry Finn* (1884) by Mark Twain (1835–1910); and *Bambi* (1942), the beloved Disney animated feature. The character of Scar, in all his lying, scheming, and evildoing—he is directly responsible for the death of Mufasa—is classically Shakespearean in nature. The combination of loyalty and deceit within Simba's family may be directly linked to Shakespeare's *Hamlet* (1603). Like Huck Finn, Simba comes to realize that he must face up to his obligations and responsibilities. In *Bambi,* a deer (rather than lion) is king of the animal realm. Both Bambi and Simba suffer the loss of a parent: in a famous sequence, Bambi's mother is killed; in a far more explicit scene, which serves as a textbook example of how movies have changed across the decades, Simba's father loses his life. In fact, the graphically violent death of Mufasa sparked a debate among parents, educators, and the media regarding the depiction of violence and death in children's films.

As with most Disney animated features that center on the lives of animals who are invested with human traits, *The Lion King* serves as a morality play. Through the animals, young viewers are taught invaluable lessons about the importance of responsibility to one's family and community and about the manner in which living beings are interconnected. Yet *The Lion King* is not all about instructing its audience. It is richly entertaining and features magnificent animation. The supporting characters, especially the merry jungle misfits with whom Simba comes in contact upon going into self-exile after his father's death, are funny and colorful. The songs, by Elton John (1947–) and Tim Rice (1944–), are seamlessly woven into the story. Disney released a sequel, *The Lion King II: Simba's Pride*, in 1998 and a prequel, *The Lion King 1½*, in 2004.

In 1998, *The Lion King* became a smash-hit, Tony Award–winning **Broadway** (see entry under 1900s—Film and Theater in volume 1) musical. It featured over one hundred puppets, representing twenty-five different types of animals. Julie Taymor (1953–) directed, designed the costumes, co-designed the masks and puppets, and wrote additional music. As of 2011, the show was still running, making it one of the longest-running Broadway musicals in history.

Rob Edelman

For More Information

Disney Presents The Lion King. New York: Disney Press, 1998.
Finch, Christopher. *The Art of the Lion King.* New York: Hyperion, 1994.
The Lion King (film). Walt Disney Pictures, 1994.

Pulp Fiction

Director-screenwriter Quentin Tarantino (1963–) became the talk of the movie industry with the release of *Reservoir Dogs* (1992), the occasionally brilliant but equally violent saga of some crude, foul-mouthed criminals

John Travolta (left) and Samuel L. Jackson take aim in a scene from the 1994 crime film Pulp Fiction. © MIRAMAX/BUENA VISTA/THE KOBAL COLLECTION/ART RESOURCE, NY.

who come together to pull off a robbery. He solidified his stardom with *Pulp Fiction* (1994), a brazenly hip film, starring John Travolta (1954–) and Samuel L. Jackson (1948–), that became one of the most praised and popular movies of the 1990s. *Pulp Fiction* is named for the sensationalistic crime novels and **pulp magazines** (see entry under 1930s—Print Culture in volume 2) whose prime years came between the 1920s and 1950s. While regarded as popular-culture throwaways at the time of their publication, they were inspiring a new type of American literature: dark, shocking depictions of crime in the shadowy city, often featuring cynical, determined detective heroes. The most famous practitioners of pulp fiction—among them Dashiell Hammett (1894–1961), Raymond Chandler (1888–1959), and Jim Thompson (1906–1977)—became legendary twentieth-century American writers.

In *Pulp Fiction,* Tarantino interweaves three stories concerning various thugs, lowlifes, and desperate characters: a professional killer and his philosophically inclined colleague; their crime-lord boss and his wife; a drug dealer and his wife; a boxer and his lover; a Vietnam veteran; and a no-nonsense "problem solver" who can quickly and efficiently remove all evidence from the grisliest crime scene. While each story focuses on specific characters, characters from the other episodes may suddenly appear to play key roles. The film is book-ended by a robbery in a diner committed by a pair of young, amoral lovers who call each other Pumpkin and Honey Bunny. They might be the same characters Tarantino created for the controversial, blood-soaked movie *Natural Born Killers* (1994) directed by Oliver Stone (1946–).

The characters in *Pulp Fiction* are primarily variations of those in other, earlier movies, many of the pulp-fiction variety. Vincent Vega, the professional killer, played by Travolta, might be one of the "wise guys" played by **James Cagney** (1899–1986) and **Humphrey Bogart** (1899–1957; see entries under 1930s—Film and Theater in volume 2) in 1930s gangster films—with the addition of R-rated dialogue and graphic violence. Mia, the crime boss's wife, played by Uma Thurman (1970–), is a femme fatale (pronounced FEM fah-TAHL), the classic seductive, dangerous woman who would have been played by alluring actresses Lauren Bacall (1924–) or Lizabeth Scott (1922–) in the 1940s. Butch the boxer, played by Bruce Willis (1955–), could be the grandson of John Garfield (1913–1952) in *Body and Soul* (1947), Kirk Douglas (1916–) in *Champion* (1949), or Robert Ryan (1909–1973) in *The Set-Up* (1949), all classic 1940s boxing films. Koons, the Vietnam veteran, played by Christopher Walken (1943–), is an ex-POW who seems to be in a time warp from *The Deer Hunter* (1978), the celebrated Vietnam drama (which just so happened to have featured Walken). Koons offers a monologue (a short speech) in which he refers to a GI named Winocki, which is the name of the character played by Garfield in the World War II film *Air Force* (1943). Meanwhile, the *Pulp Fiction* script is steeped in nostalgia. One of its liveliest sequences is set in Jack Rabbit Slim's, an outrageous 1950s-themed combination nightclub-restaurant.

In the wake of the astounding success of *Pulp Fiction* came a host of catchy-titled imitators, from *Love and a .45* (1994) to *Things to Do in Denver When You're Dead* (1995) to *The Last Days of Frankie the Fly* (1997), all featuring quirky characters and stylish violence. None, however, could match *Pulp Fiction* for its cleverness, brilliance, and knowing pop-cultural references. Tarantino went on to make many other movies, including *Inglourious Basterds,* which was nominated for eight Oscars in 2009.

Rob Edelman

For More Information

Barlow, Aaron. *Quentin Tarantino: Life at the Extremes.* Santa Barbara, CA: Praeger, 2010.

Bernard, Jami. *Quentin Tarantino: The Man and His Movies.* New York: HarperPerennial, 1995.

Charyn, Jerome. *Raised by Wolves: The Turbulent Art and Times of Quentin Tarantino.* New York: Thunder's Mouth Press, 2006.

Clarkson, Wensley. *Quentin Tarantino: Shooting from the Hip.* Woodstock, NY: Overlook Press, 1995.

Dawson, Jeff. *Quentin Tarantino: The Cinema of Cool.* New York: Applause, 1997.

Pulp Fiction (film). Miramax Films, 1994.

Woods, Paul. *King Pulp: The Wild World of Quentin Tarantino.* Rev. ed. New York: Plexus, 1998.

Scream

In 1996, Wes Craven (1939–), director of such modern horror masterpieces as *The Hills Have Eyes* (1978) and *A Nightmare on Elm Street* (1984), shocked everybody who thought his career was over by releasing one of the most popular **horror films** (see entry under 1960s—Film and Theater in volume 4) of all time. *Scream,* starring a host of talented young actors, including Drew Barrymore (1975–), Neve Campbell (1973–), Courteney Cox (1964–), David Arquette (1971–), Rose McGowan (1974–), and Jamie Kennedy (1970–), took America by storm, bringing in over $103 million at the box office, and setting off a new wave of youth-targeted "stalker" films. *I Know What You Did Last Summer* (1997), *Urban Legend* (1998), *Valentine* (2001), and of course *Scream 2* (1997), *Scream 3* (2000), and the stalker spoof *Scary Movie* (2000) (and its respective sequels and spinoffs) all owe much of their success to Craven's original.

A scream-inducing scene from the 1996 horror film Scream.

The intense ten-minute opening of *Scream* became one of the most talked-about scenes in recent movie history. An anonymous caller threatens the lives of high-school cutie Casey Becker (Barrymore) and her boyfriend unless she can answer such questions as "Who was the killer in Friday the 13th?" Like everyone else in *Scream,* Casey has seen such classic slasher movies as *Halloween* (1978), *Prom Night* (1980), and ***Friday the 13th*** (1980; see entry under 1980s—Film and Theater in volume 5). But only true horror fans have a chance to live in this setting ... and even that is not always enough. The main story concerns the efforts of virginal heroine Sidney Prescott (Campbell) to survive the attacks of a slasher-film fanatic with a ghost-face mask and a very sharp knife. Dirt-seeking news reporter Gail Weathers (Cox) also is a key character.

Among the elements that made *Scream* such a winner is the film's clever script, the numerous references to other horror movies, and Craven's expert direction, which manages to frighten audiences even while they are laughing. The script was written by Kevin Williamson (1965–), who would go on to create the hit teen **television** (see entry under 1940s—TV and Radio in volume 3) show *Dawson's Creek.* In the early 2000s, *Scream* had three highly successful sequels. The first two sequels, released in the four years after the first film opened, continued the horrific adventures of characters who had survived the first film, although the first sequel did better at the box office. A fourth sequel,

Scream 4, was released in 2011, eleven years after the first film. Again, Craven directed, Williamson wrote the script, and many of the major actors reprised their roles.

Steven Schneider

For More Information

Emery, Robert J., writer, producer, and director. *The Films of Wes Craven* (video). New York: Fox Lorber CentreStage, 2000.

Muir, John Kenneth. *Wes Craven: The Art of Horror.* Jefferson, NC: McFarland, 1998.

The Ultimate Scream Collection (video). Burbank, CA: Dimension Home Video, 2000.

Wooley, John. *Wes Craven: The Man and His Nightmares.* Hoboken, NJ: Wiley, 2011.

Toy Story

Toy Story (1995) was the first-ever animated feature film whose imagery was computer-generated. Previously, animated films were made up of a series of drawings that were photographed, frame by frame, creating the illusion of motion. The revolutionary computer animation in *Toy Story* was the result of years of experimentation by the technical wizards at the Pixar studio. With the release of *Toy Story,* animated films took on an entirely fresh look, a three-dimensional reality in which characters were endowed with a previously unseen freedom of movement and facial expression. But *Toy Story* was not just a new type of animated film, it was also a clever, funny, and entertaining story.

Toy Story is the tale of a group of toys that are the playthings of a boy named Andy. The toys come to life when humans are not around. The two central toys are rivals: Woody, an old-fashioned doll, a Western sheriff made of cloth; and Buzz Lightyear, a more modern space ranger and action figure. Woody's position as Andy's favorite toy is threatened by the arrival of Buzz. The villain of the piece is neither Woody nor Buzz nor any of Andy's other playthings. He is Sid, a nasty neighbor child who relishes taking toys apart and reassembling them as nightmarish creatures.

Toy Story was the brainchild of John Lasseter (1957–), a computer-animation genius who formerly worked at the **Disney** (see entry under 1920s—Film and Theater in volume 2) studio but left in the mid-1980s

Actors Tim Allen and Tom Hanks are the voices of Buzz Lightyear (left) and Woody in Toy Story. © PHOTOFEST, INC.

to work at Pixar, a Marin County, California–based computer laboratory. At Pixar, he created several short films, including *Luxo Jr.* (1986), *Red's Dream* (1987), *Tin Toy* (1988), and *Knickknack* (1989), all of which are forerunners of *Toy Story.* In those films, objects such as drummer-boy toys, unicycles, and lamps come to life. The objects are endowed with personalities all their own—just like the toys in *Toy Story.*

It took Lasseter and his team eight hundred thousand hours of computer time to create *Toy Story.* In 1995, he earned a Special Academy Award for his work. Lasseter also co-directed *Toy Story 2*, released in 1999, which features many of the same characters from the first film, voiced by the same actors. Eleven years later, *Toy Story 3* was released. Also produced by Pixar, the film was the only one in the series to be released in 3D. *Toy Story 3* broke box-office records for animated films worldwide and was nominated for five Academy Awards.

Rob Edelman

For More Information

Lasseter, John. *Toy Story: The Art and Making of the Animated Film.* New York: Hyperion, 1995.
Toy Story (film). Pixar Animation Studios/Walt Disney Pictures, 1995.
"Toy Story: Official Home Page." *Disney Online.* http://disney.go.com/disneyvideos/animatedfilms/toystory (accessed August 1, 2011).
Toy Story 2 (film). Pixar Animation Studios/Walt Disney Pictures, 1999.

Wayne's World

"You'll laugh. You'll cry. You'll hurl." Using this as a tag line, *Wayne's World* was the surprise hit movie of 1992. Starring Mike Myers (1963–) and Dana Carvey (1955–), *Wayne's World* was a feature-length version of the comic pair's cult *Saturday Night Live* skit on youth culture. Full of digs at big business and advertisers' quests for profit, *Wayne's World* was nevertheless a marketing success. Ironically, its young audience readily bought into the film's cynicism about the world of big business and spent $180 million at the box office to prove how cynical they were. With its clever script and inspired casting, *Wayne's World* is among the best of the many deliberately moronic comedies released during the 1990s.

The simple plot of *Wayne's World* is based around a public-access cable-TV show hosted by Wayne Campbell and Garth Algar. Goaded to "sell out" by an unscrupulous TV executive played by Rob Lowe (1964–), Wayne and Garth embark on a series of adventures. These include meeting their idol Alice Cooper (1948–), who gives them a short lesson on the history of Milwaukee, Wisconsin. Even more entertaining than these strange encounters is the chemistry between Myers and Carvey, which makes the film truly entertaining. Their take on teen language brands everything either "excellent" or "bogus." For a while, even otherwise respectable adults developed the habit of adding an ironic "not" to the end of sentences.

In the early 1990s, *Wayne's World* became something of a cult movie, triggering spin-offs from **T-shirts** (see entry under 1910s—Fashion in volume 1) and action figures to **video games** (see entry under 1970s—Sports and Games in volume 4) and a **roller coaster** (see entry under 1900s—The Way We Lived in volume 1) called "The Hurler." *Wayne's World 2* followed in 1993, but although the audience came back for more, the second film spread the jokes too thinly. Like many popular movies, *Wayne's World* succeeded because it tapped into the mood of a particular time. The real significance of *Wayne's World* is in the way it changed the marketing of teen movies. By aiming directly at its intended audience on its own terms, *Wayne's World* had fans even before it opened. *Wayne's World* is also credited with starting the 1990s trend for "dumb" movies such as *Dumb and Dumber* (1994) and *There's Something About Mary* (1998).

Carvey went on to star in several television series, including *The Larry Sanders Show,* (1992–97) in which he played himself. After making his film debut in *Wayne's World,* Myers went on to write, produce, and star in the enormously successful ***Austin Powers*** movies (see entry under 1990s—Sports and Games in volume 5).

Chris Routledge

Canadian comedic actor Mike Myers (left) as Wayne Campbell and Dana Carvey as Garth Algar took sketch characters from Saturday Night Live *and put them on the big screen in* Wayne's World. © PARAMOUNT/THE KOBAL COLLECTION/ART RESOURCE, NY.

For More Information

Knelman, Martin. *Mike's World: The Life of Mike Myers.* Buffalo, NY: Firefly Books, 2003.

Myers, Mike, and Robin Ruzan. *Wayne's World: Extreme Close Up.* New York: Cader Books, 1992.

1990s

Music

Popular music somehow finds a way to keep growing and changing. If fans got tired of rock and roll, they could turn to alternative rock. Tired of country? Try alternative country. Even rap, a musical style barely a decade old, inspired variations such as gangsta rap. Perhaps the only new thing on the American musical scene was the popularity of Latin or Latin-inspired music. Selena (1971–1995) was a minor sensation with her Tejano hits, but Ricky Martin (1971–) truly hit the big time with his Latin dance tunes late in the decade.

Country music was reborn in the 1990s, thanks to a bevy of young new singers. Garth Brooks (1962–) led the way with his 1991 album *Ropin' the Wind,* which shot to the top of both pop and country charts. Steering away from the hillbilly sounds of country music past, Brooks and such stars as Faith Hill (1967–), Shania Twain (1965–), and the teenaged LeAnn Rimes (1982–) melded pop and country and won millions of listeners.

Alternative rock was a grab-bag term used to refer to a range of bands whose music borrowed from rock and roll but was angrier, edgier, more electronic, or just somehow different. Alternative musical promoters sought to tap the spirit of 1960s music festivals with their traveling shows called Lollapalooza and Lilith Fair, the latter featuring only female performers. Nirvana, led by Kurt Cobain (1967–1994), created a subgenre called grunge that was briefly quite popular.

Several performers hit it big with the teen audience in this decade. *NSYNC, New Kids on the Block, and Backstreet Boys were the most popular of several "boy bands." The undisputed teen sensation of the decade was eighteen-year-old Britney Spears (1981–), whose 1999 album *... Baby One More Time* made the former Mouseketeer a major star.

Alternative Country Music

To a growing number of people, mainstream **country music** (see entry under 1940s—Music in volume 3)—the kind heard on most country radio stations—had grown very stale by the late 1980s. The music industry produced big stars and big hits with this music, but for many people, country music had lost its edge; it was now dull and predictable. Alternative country music emerged in the late 1980s and early 1990s to challenge this mainstream music. It did so by combining older forms of country music—honky tonk, western swing, rockabilly, and even **bluegrass** (see entry under 1940s—Music in volume 3)—with the edge and attitude of **rock and roll** (see entry under 1950s—Music in volume 3), particularly **punk** (see entry under 1970s—Music in volume 4) rock. By doing this, alternative country musicians sought to recapture the spirit and originality of old country music, updated with a touch of rock and roll for the 1990s and beyond.

The origins of alternative country music actually date back to the late 1960s and early 1970s when musician Gram Parsons (1946–1973) helped forge a country-rock sound in such bands as the Byrds and the Flying Burrito Brothers. Parsons's experiments influenced a whole generation of alternative country musicians. The Nitty Gritty Dirt Band bridged the gap between its generation and older stars of country music from the 1940s such as Roy Acuff (1903–1992) in its important album, *Will the Circle Be Unbroken.* Also in the 1970s, more established country artists such as George Jones (1931–), Merle Haggard (1937–), and Willie Nelson (1933–), increasingly forgotten by mainstream country radio, continued to create their unique sounds as part of an "outlaw" country tradition.

In the 1980s and 1990s, alternative country took off in a number of directions. There were harder-edged "cow-punk" bands, such as Jason and the Scorchers and the Mekons, who blended country and punk rock. There were country-rock groups such as Uncle Tupelo and its offshoots Wilco and Son Volt. This period also saw the rise of important artists with unique sounds that did not fit into mainstream country music, artists such as Lyle Lovett (1957–), Steve Earle (1955–), Lucinda Williams (1953–), Gillian Welch (1968–), the Jayhawks, BR5-49, and many others. In 1995, a magazine devoted to this music, *No Depression,* began publication and acted as an important source of information about this developing style.

Alternative country music has served an important role. It keeps one of the United States' most important musical traditions both grounded in its roots and always heading into the future in search of new sounds. Alt-country in the early 2000s is still going strong, featuring newer artists such as Neko Case (1970–) and Richard Buckner (1964–). As of 2011, *No Depression* still exists online and boasts, "we reach more people now than we ever did in print." As a style of music, alt-country has produced some of the most unique voices in modern American music.

Timothy Berg

For More Information

Alden, Grant, and Peter Blackstock, eds. *No Depression: An Introduction to Alternative Country Music, Whatever That Is.* Nashville: Dowling Press, 1998.

Fox, Pamela, and Barbara Ching, eds. *Old Roots, New Routes: The Cultural Politics of Alt.Country Music.* Ann Arbor: University of Michigan Press, 2008.

Goodman, David. *Modern Twang: An Alternative Country Music Guide and Directory.* Nashville: Dowling Press, 1999.

Hinton, Brian. *South by South West: A Road Map to Alternative Country.* London: Sanctuary, 2003.

Kingsbury, Paul, ed. *The Encyclopedia of Country Music: The Ultimate Guide to the Music.* 2nd ed. New York: Oxford University Press, 2012.

No Depression: The Alternative Country (Whatever That Is) Bimonthly. http://www.nodepression.com (accessed August 1, 2011).

Alternative Rock

Alternative rock music, and resultingly its various offshoots such as indie rock and post-punk, grew out of the **punk** (see entry under 1970s—Music in volume 4) and new-wave music movements of the 1970s. In the 1980s, bands like the Replacements, Hüsker Dü, the Smiths, and the Cure came to embody the "alternative" style. In the 1990s, a new generation took up the alternative banner, as artists like

Nirvana (see entry under 1990s—Music in volume 5) and R.E.M. took this independent, or indie, music mainstream and enjoyed enormous success.

It is hard to say where punk ended and "alternative" began, or even to come up with a precise definition for alternative rock. A few of the unique characteristics of the category are its unease with mainstream values and musical styles, its emphasis on its musicians' nonconformity in personal habits and dress, and its adoption of a "do-it-yourself" approach to making, recording, and distributing music. Alternative rockers rarely showed the anger and hostility of their punk rock predecessors. Performers like the Smiths' Morrissey (1959–) and R.E.M.'s Michael Stipe (1960–) preferred to present an attitude of brashness and detached irony rather than to smash guitars and sing politically charged lyrics. Even more raucous artists like the Replacements tended to turn their anger inward, in self-absorbed songs like "Unsatisfied" or the alt-rock standard "I Will Dare."

For most of the 1980s, alternative rock remained safely under the radar of the mainstream record-buying public. A few groups, like Ireland's U2, rose from the college radio underground to enjoy major label success, but the steady cult-like popularity of groups like the Smiths and the Cure was much more typical. That all changed in 1991, when the Seattle, Washington, trio Nirvana scored a massive worldwide hit with its song "Smells Like Teen Spirit" and the album *Nevermind.* Their success ushered in the era of **"grunge"** (see entry under 1990s—Music in volume 5) rock, a form of alternative that also incorporated elements of the classic rock of artists like Neil Young (1945–) and **Led Zeppelin** (see entry under 1970s—Music in volume 4). Other 1990s alternative performers, like Pearl Jam, soon jumped on the bandwagon, and even 1980s veterans like R.E.M. saw their record sales soar. By the middle of the 1990s, alternative had become mainstream. Critics accused the artists of selling out, and many longtime fans grew alienated from the music. Nirvana's lead vocalist Kurt Cobain (1967–1994) seemed to acknowledge these contradictions by committing suicide in 1994—an event that many consider the death knell of alternative rock. An alt-rock revival of sorts emerged in the early 2000s with the popularity of several bands who revived early-'90s post-punk and New Wave styles, including The White Stripes, Arcade Fire, and Modest Mouse.

Robert E. Schnakenberg

For More Information

Azerrad, Michael. *Come As You Are: The Story of Nirvana.* New York: Doubleday, 1993.

McNeil, Legs, and Gillian McCain, eds. *Please Kill Me: The Uncensored Oral History of Punk.* New York: Penguin, 1997.

Reisfeld, Randi. *This Is the Sound: The Best of Alternative Rock.* New York: Aladdin Paperbacks, 1996.

Schinder, Scott. *Rolling Stone's Alt Rock-a-rama.* New York: Delta, 1996.

Skancke, Jennifer. *The History of Indie Rock.* Detroit: Lucent, 2007.

Strong, Martin. *The Great Alternative and Indie Discography.* Edinburgh, Scotland: Canongate, 2000.

Taylor, Steve. *The A to Z of Alternative Music.* 2nd ed. London: Continuum, 2008.

Thompson, Dave. *Alternative Rock.* San Francisco: Miller Freeman Books, 2000.

Grunge

"Grungy" is a slang word that means dirty, old, and beat-up. In the late 1980s and early 1990s, the word became "grunge" and was used to describe a new kind of **rock and roll** (see entry under 1950s—Music in volume 3) music and style of dress that was emerging in Seattle, Washington. The term "grunge" was originally used to describe the loud, jarring **electric guitar** (see entry under 1950s—Music in volume 3) of rock bands such as Mudhoney, Alice in Chains, and Soundgarden, because their guitar was fuzzy and raw, not "clean" and clear. However, the word was soon used to describe the shaggy hair, ragged jeans, thrift-shop flannel shirts, and combat boots worn by the musicians and their fans. It also came to be used to describe a general attitude toward life. Combining some of the features of **heavy-metal** (see entry under 1980s—Music in volume 5) music and **punk** (see entry under 1970s—Music in volume 4) rock, grunge music contrasts a loud, driving rock sound with deeply personal, often sad and protesting, words. Rebellious and indifferent, angry and depressed, harsh and vulnerable, grunge represented many of the contradictions in the lives and attitudes of the young, mostly white, members of **"Generation X"** (see entry under 1980s—The Way We Lived in volume 5), the teenagers of the 1990s.

Like the protest music of the 1960s, the psychedelic rock of the 1970s, and the punk rock of the 1980s, arose from teenage disenchantment with the world of their parents' generation. Both grunge music and grunge style began by rejecting the shallow values associated with

Eddie Vedder of grunge band Pearl Jam performs at Neil Young's Bridge Benefit concert at Shoreline Amphitheater in Mountain View, California, on October 31, 1999. © TIM MOSENFELDER/GETTY IMAGES.

consumerism and commercialism, like buying brand-name clothes. The music is also characterized by anger, loneliness, and drug use. A particularly popular drug among the disenchanted was heroin, the depressive and addictive effects of which seemed to go well with the hopelessness and sadness expressed in much grunge music. Grunge seemed forbidden and dangerous, and its popularity spread quickly.

Because of its anti-commercialism, the success of grunge seemed by definition to bring about its end. National record labels began to produce grunge bands like **Nirvana** (see entry under 1990s—Music in volume 5) and Pearl Jam. Fashion designers began to sell expensive versions of the tattered thrift-shop grunge clothes. Even the spaced-out, wasted look of the heroin addict was imitated by fashion models. In 1994, Kurt Cobain (1967–1994), lead singer for the most nationally successful grunge group, Nirvana, shot himself in his new, expensive Seattle home, in part because he could not cope with becoming one of the successful rich people he had criticized in his songs. Kurt Cobain's suicide made him a legend, and the subsequent rash of books and films about him have further explored grunge and its place in American musical history.

Tina Gianoulis

For More Information

Azerrad, Michael. *Come As You Are: The Story of Nirvana.* New York: Doubleday, 1993.

Azerrad, Michael. "Grunge City." *Rolling Stone* (No. 628, April 16, 1992): pp. 43–46.

Fish, Duane R. "Ripped Jeans and Faded Flannel: Grunge, Youth, and Communities of Alienation." *Popular Music and Society* (Vol. 19, no. 2, Summer 1995): pp. 87–103.

Kennedy, Dana, and Benjamin Svetkey. "Reality Bites: Suicide of Grunge Rock Star Kurt Cobain." *Entertainment Weekly* (No. 219, April 22, 1994): pp. 16–26.

Lowry, Rich. "Our Hero, Heroin." *National Review* (Vol. 48, no. 20, October 28, 1996): p. 75.

Moore, Thurston. *Grunge.* New York: Abrams Image, 2009.

Prato, Greg. *Grunge Is Dead: The Oral History of Seattle Rock Music.* Toronto: ECW Press, 2009.

Strong, Catherine. *Grunge: Music and Memory.* Farnham, UK: Ashgate, 2011.

Lollapalooza and Lilith Fair

The Lollapalooza and Lilith Fair rock-music festivals, which toured the United States in the 1990s, revived the spirit of the most famous rock festival, 1969's **Woodstock** (see entry under 1960s—Music in volume 4) festival, for a new generation of fans. These touring festivals appealed to fans because they offered the opportunity to hear many different music groups perform during one period of time. The festivals brought thousands of fans together for several days in a small community that included food booths, games, rides, displays, and side shows featuring amateur performers.

Lollapalooza was founded in 1991 by Perry Farrell (1959–), a singer in the **alternative rock** (see entry under 1990s—Music in volume 5)

The scene at a Lollapalooza festival at the Winnebago County Fairgrounds in Rockford, Illinois, on June 30, 1996.
© TIM MOSENFELDER/GETTY IMAGES.

bands Porno for Pyros and Jane's Addiction. Farrell wanted to create a forum where a diverse group of alternative bands could reach audiences nationwide. Prompted more by his enthusiasm for music than by desire for profit, Farrell was as surprised as his critics when the first Lollapalooza festival was hugely successful, drawing over six hundred thousand fans in twenty-one cities through the summer. The next years were equally successful, as musicians like Pearl Jam, Ice-T (1959–), Soundgarden, and Sinead O'Connor (1966–) performed on Lollapalooza stages. In 1996, Farrell left the festival, charging that it had become too commercial. That year, the festival headliner was the **heavy metal** (see entry under 1980s—Music in volume 5) group Metallica. The festival lost much of its diversity, booking mostly white male bands, and the 1996 and 1997 festivals were much less successful. In 1998, the festival was canceled but was brought back in 2003 by Farrell in collaboration with the William Morris Agency and Texas-based Capital Sports Entertainment. In its second incarnation, Lollapalooza does not tour, but instead takes place over a single weekend in Chicago. In 2011, the organizers added a second weekend concert, which took place in Santiago, Chile.

When singer Sarah McLachlan (1968–) could not convince her managers to book her on tour with other women's groups, she decided to found an all-women's touring festival. Music-industry heads were sure that Lilith Fair would not succeed, but its first season in the summer of 1997 was very successful. Playing in thirty-seven cities across the country, Lilith Fair was named the top festival tour for 1997, winning over much more established festivals like Lollapalooza. McLachlan booked young female acts with a feminist consciousness, such as Tracy Chapman (1964–), Suzanne Vega (1959–), Jewel (1974–), and the Indigo Girls, along with veterans like Emmylou Harris (1947–) and Bonnie Raitt (1949–). In 1998, the tour expanded to forty–seven cities. In 1999, after three years of festivals, McLachlan married and withdrew from organizing, and Lilith Fair stopped for good.

Tina Gianoulis

For More Information

Ali, Lorraine. "Backstage at Lilith." *Rolling Stone* (September 4, 1997): pp. 28–33.

Childerhose, Buffy. *From Lilith to Lilith Fair.* New York: St. Martin's Press, 1998.

Fricke, David. "Lollapalooza." *Rolling Stone* (September 19, 1991): pp. 9–13.

Neely, Kim. "Lollapalooza '92." *Rolling Stone* (September 17, 1992): pp. 60–65.

Online Diaries: The Lollapalooza '95 Tour Journals of Beck, Courtney Love, Stephen Malkmus, Thurston Moore, Lee Ranaldo, Mike Watt, David Yow. New York: Soft Skull Press, 1996.

Nirvana

Nirvana was one of the most popular and influential **rock and roll** (see entry under 1950s—Music in volume 3) bands of the 1990s. Pioneers of the **"grunge"** (see entry under 1990s—Music in volume 5) style, the Seattle, Washington–based trio helped bring about a mini-revolution in music and fashion, before the tragic suicide of frontman Kurt Cobain (1967–1994) in 1994 brought an abrupt end to the band's career.

Kurt Cobain of Nirvana performs at the Nakano Sun Plaza in Tokyo, on February 19, 1992. © RICHARD A. BROOKS/NEWSCOM.

Formed in 1987, Nirvana consisted of Cobain on lead guitar and vocals, Chris Novoselic (1965–) on bass guitar, and Dave Grohl (1969–) on drums. Their 1989 debut album *Bleach* attracted the attention of rock critics, but it was the 1991 follow-up *Nevermind,* containing the hit single "Smells Like Teen Spirit," that made them into superstars. The group's heavy sound and ragged flannel shirts quickly caught on with teenagers worldwide. Nirvana had a particularly strong impact on **Generation X** (see entry under 1980s—The Way We Lived in volume 5), members of which identified with the group's frustration and angst in the face of a consumerist, mindlessly indulgent society. After a 1993 album, *In Utero,* drug use and depression finally caught up with the sensitive Cobain. He shot himself to death on April 4, 1994, leaving behind his widow, Courtney Love (1964–), a baby daughter, and millions of grieving fans.

Robert E. Schnakenberg

For More Information

Azerrad, Michael. *Come As You Are: The Story of Nirvana.* New York: Doubleday, 1993.

Cross, Charles R. *Heavier than Heaven: A Biography of Kurt Cobain.* New York: Hyperion, 2001.

The Internet Nirvana Fan Club. http://www.nirvanaclub.com/ (accessed August 2, 2011).

True, Everett. *Nirvana: The Biography.* Cambridge, MA: Da Capo Press, 2006.

Wall, Mick. *Nirvana: The Legacy.* London: Omnibus Press, 1996.

Raves

Raves, all-night dance parties often held in secret locations, have come to be identified with youth of the 1990s and early 2000s in much the same way that the love-ins of **hippies** (see entry under 1960s—The Way We Lived in volume 4) were identified with youth of the late 1960s and early 1970s. Although police, parents, and the media tend to focus on the drugs and sex that are often freely available at raves, those who attend the events (known as "ravers") defend their gatherings as safe and loving spaces where they can be accepted for who they are while immersed in the driving beat of electronic music.

The rave scene began in Britain in the late 1980s. The dance parties soon spread among youth around the world, arriving in the United States in 1990. Early raves were traditionally onetime events in garages and warehouses, loosely organized without official permits or media advertising. News of a rave was spread by word of mouth and by handmade flyers. This underground status drew many rebellious young people to the rave scene. By 2000, however, raves had become more legitimate, as nightclubs such as Twylo in New York began to create a rave atmosphere. Those too young to enter the nightclubs, however, continued to find the independent raves the best places to party.

The primary elements of rave culture are sex, drugs, and music. Drugs, from the hallucinogen LSD to the stimulant **Ecstasy** (see entry under 1990s—The Way We Lived in volume 5) to **marijuana** (see entry under 1960s—The Way We Lived in volume 4), are often available for sale at raves. The widespread drug use at raves has led some to nickname ravers "techno-hippies." Ravers defend raves as safe places for experimentation, but there have been deaths and overdoses at raves, fueling parental opposition to the parties. Open sexuality at raves has also drawn media attention. In the strobe-lit dark of raves, sexual experimentation of all types is common. The open and accepting attitude of ravers has drawn many gay and lesbian youth to the rave scene.

Although ravers may appreciate the unlawful atmosphere of their parties, most say that the main attraction of raves is the music, and that the real stars of raves are the DJs, or **disc jockeys** (see entry under 1950s—Music in volume 3). Raves are almost always characterized by the loud, intense beat of electronic music. The many different types of rave music—with names like "house," "jungle," "garage," and "trance"—are generally lumped under the name "electronica." Rave music is played by musicians like Chemical Brothers, Prodigy, and Moby (1965–).

In 1999 and 2000, several movies documenting rave culture were released, including *Groove* (2000), *Better Living Through Circuitry* (2000), *Human Traffic* (1999), and *Rise* (1999). By 2010, rave culture had dwindled and been replaced by the club scene, except in central Europe, where so-called Tecknivals, modeled after the huge U.S. gathering Burning Man, occasionally continued to occur.

Tina Gianoulis

For More Information

Denizet-Lewis, Benoit. "Riding the Rave Scene." *Advocate* (January 18, 2000): pp. 60–63.

Eliscu, Jenny. "The War on Raves." *Rolling Stone* (May 24, 2001): pp. 21–23.

Farley, Christopher John. "Rave New World." *Time* (June 5, 2000): pp. 70–73.

Hoeckel, Summer Forest, Joel T. Jordan, and Jason Jordan. *Searching for the Perfect Beat.* New York: Watson-Guptill, 1999.

Hyperreal. http://www.hyperreal.org (accessed August 2, 2011).

Reynolds, Simon. *Energy Flash: A Journey Through Rave Music and Dance Culture.* Ne w ed. London: Picador, 2008.

Reynolds, Simon. *Generation Ecstasy: Into the World of Techno and Rave Culture.* Boston: Little, Brown, 1998.

Britney Spears (1981–)

Sultry Britney Spears is a singer and dancer—and a teen icon and pop-music princess. Born in Kentwood, Louisiana, Spears began performing at local dances and in church choirs. After auditioning for The Disney Channel's updated version of the old ***Mickey Mouse Club*** (see entry under 1950s—TV and Radio in volume 3) when she was eight and being turned down because of her age, she secured an agent, studied dance and music in New York, and appeared on **television** (see entry under 1940s—TV and Radio in volume 3) commercials and in Off-Broadway plays. Starting at age eleven, she spent two years as a regular on *The Mickey Mouse Club,* and at fifteen began developing her solo singing career. Soon, she was a worldwide phenomenon. Her smash-hit debut album, *Baby One More Time,* came out in 1999. That year, she earned two Grammy Award nominations and MTV Europe Awards for Best Pop Act, Best Female Performer, Best Breakthrough Act, and Best Song.

Pop star and former Mouseketeer Britney Spears performs on Long Island at Jones Beach, New York, on June 27, 2000. © JOHN ROCA/NY DAILY NEWS ARCHIVE/GETTY IMAGES.

Spears's rise has not come without contradictions. On one level, she had a self-proclaimed good-girl image. On another level, her handlers allowed her to be marketed not only as a pop singer but also as a scantily clad sex object. For example, she appeared in a number of provocative Pepsi-Cola advertisements. In the 2000s, Spears frequently made headlines for her series of best-selling albums, including *Blackout* (2007) and *Femme Fatale* (2011), her number-one singles, like "Womanizer" and "Hold It Against Me," and her chaotic personal life, which featured two marriages, two divorces, and numerous hospitalizations for drug abuse. As of 2009, Spears had been nominated for eight Grammy awards and sold one hundred million albums, making her the twenty-first century's top-selling female artist.

Rob Edelman

For More Information

Britney Spears. http://www.britneyspears.com (accessed August 2, 2011).

Dennis, Steve. *Britney: The Life.* London: HarperCollins, 2009.

Heard, Christopher. *Britney Spears: Little Girl Lost.* Montreal, Transit, 2010.

Hurley, Joanna. *Britney.* New York: Scholastic, 2000.

Peters, Beth. *True Brit: The Story of Singing Sensation Britney Spears.* New York: Ballantine Books, 1999.

Spears, Britney, and Lynne Spears. *Britney Spears' Heart to Heart.* New York: Three Rivers Press, 2000.

Tejano Music

Tejano is the Spanish word for "Texan," and Tejano music contains all the flavors of the borderland between the United States and Mexico. Like those who live at the border of two cultures, the music is never quite one thing or the other but is constantly combining elements of both, creating a new and growing culture of its own.

Tejano music has its roots in a music called *conjunto* (Spanish for "together") that evolved in the early 1900s when immigrants from Germany and Czechoslovakia found their way to new homes in south Texas. They brought with them the music of their homelands, energetic polka rhythms played on accordions. This music combined with Spanish lyrics and the complex bass of the *bajo sexto,* a twelve-string Mexican guitar, to create a fusion of styles that appealed to people of many cultures. Famous 1930s conjunto musician Narciso Martinez

Tejano star Emilio Navaira performs in San Antonio, Texas. © ERICH SCHLEGEL/NEWSCOM.

(1911–1992) was popular not only with audiences from his native south Texas but also with French-speaking Mississippi-delta Cajuns, whom he performed for under the name Louisiana Pete. He also drew in audiences of Polish immigrants, performing with the Polski Kwartet.

Conjunto remained largely a regional music until the 1940s, when World War II (1939–45) caused many people to relocate from rural areas to cities. Wherever they went, the Tejanos took their music. When traditional conjunto blended with the big-band music of the 1930s and 1940s, it became a new genre, or type, of music called Tejano. The new Tejano music continued to pick up influences over the decades, adding elements of **country music, rhythm and blues** (R&B; see these entries under 1940s—Music in volume 3), **rock and roll** (see entry under 1950s—Music in volume 3), and **rap** (see entry under 1980s—Music in volume 5) to the original Latin-polka beat. In this way, Tejano reflects the Latino experience in the United States, a constant blending of the traditional with the modern, as well as the joining of many cultures to create something uniquely American.

The popularity of Tejano music got a boost in the 1990s with the huge success of such stars as Emilio Navaira and Selena (1971–1995). Selena was murdered by a fan in 1995, ending her promising career. Rather than only being famous among Tejano fans, both stars successfully "crossed over" into other genres. It reveals a lot about Tejano's many sides that Selena crossed over into **pop music** (see entry under 1940s—Music in volume 3), while Navaira has developed a successful career as a country-music singer. By the start of the twenty-first century, however, interest in Tejano music had declined, although it continued to be practiced in areas with Tejano populations.

Tina Gianoulis

For More Information

Galan, Hector, producer and director. *Songs of the Homeland* (video). Austin, TX: Galan Productions, 1995.

Jones, Veda Boyd. *Selena.* Philadelphia: Chelsea House, 2000.

Leland, John. "Born on the Border: Tejano Music." *Newsweek* (October 23, 1995): pp. 80–85.

q-productions.com: Selena. http://www.q-productions.com (accessed August 2, 2011).

Romero, Maritza. *Selena Perez: Queen of Tejano Music.* New York: PowerKids Press, 1997.

San Miguel, Guadalupe. "The Rise of Recorded Tejano Music in the Post–World War II Years, 1946–1964." *Journal of American Ethnic History* (Vol. 19, Fall 1999): pp. 26–30.

San Miguel, Guadalupe. *Tejano Proud: Tex-Mex Music in the Twentieth Century.* College Station: Texas A&M University Press, 2002.

Selena (film). Burbank, CA: Warner Home Video, 1997.

Wheeler, Jill C. *Selena: The Queen of Tejano.* Edina, MN: Abdo & Daughters, 1996.

1990s

Print Culture

Up until the 1990s, Americans read their newspapers, magazines, and novels the way they always had: on paper. In the 1990s, the growing popularity of books on tape and the Internet revolution brought change to American print culture. Recorded books had been around for some time, but they grew in popularity during the decade. As prices dropped, more and more Americans began to listen to the latest books on tape in their cars or on personal cassette players.

Another major change in print culture was the emergence of the "e-book" and other forms of electronic print media. Book publishers sought to increase their profits by offering some titles electronically. Readers could download the book on to a personal computer or one of several new electronic devices designed just for e-books (if one could stand the less-than-perfect image quality). Magazine and newspaper publishers produced electronic versions of their periodicals online, and users could access the Web sites either free or for a small charge. All the major news outlets offered news via the Web, and Web-only magazines like Salon.com and Slate.com led the way in this new "print" media.

Despite the popularity of these new ways of accessing written information, the majority of Americans stuck with the tried and true popular magazines, newspapers, and best-sellers, that they had always loved. Some familiar names remained at the top of the best-seller lists, including Stephen King (1947–), Danielle Steel (1947–), Tom Clancy (1947–), and John Grisham (1955–). Michael Crichton (1942–2008) was the biggest crossover hit of the decade. Many of his best-selling novels quickly became blockbuster films, including one of the most spectacular of the decade, *Jurassic Park.* Late in the decade, a British novelist named J. K. Rowling (1965–) debuted a book called *Harry Potter and the Sorceror's Stone* that quickly became a sensation in the United States and around the world. While many praised the book for encouraging reading among young people, others tried to ban it for promoting witchcraft. The hubbub over the book made it the publishing sensation of the late 1990s, and Rowling followed her first book with several successful sequels.

Harry Potter Series

Harry Potter novels were the literary phenomenon of the late 1990s. The first in the series, *Harry Potter and the Sorcerer's Stone* (*Harry Potter and the Philosopher's Stone* in the U.K.) appeared in 1997. Fourteen years later, four hundred and fifty million copies of the seven books in the series had been sold. Each of the seven books represents one year the title character, Harry, spends at the wizarding school called Hogwarts.

Harry Potter novels have been credited with starting a boom in children's reading, but adults read them, too. They even come in different dust jackets to appeal to readers of different ages. The *Harry Potter* series is the work of British author J. K. Rowling (1965–), who claims to have invented the boy wizard and Hogwarts school on a train journey between Manchester and London. The success of the *Harry Potter* series has made Rowling one of the best-paid writers in history. In the space of a few years, she was transformed from a low-income single mother into an internationally famous multimillionaire author.

In the world of Harry Potter, people are divided into two groups, muggles and wizards. Muggles are ordinary people. They have no magical powers and include the boring Dursleys, who take in the infant Harry after he becomes an orphan. Far more interesting than muggles are the wizards. Rowling's books celebrate misfits and outsiders, and Harry is special, even among wizards. As a baby, he survived an attack by Lord Voldemort, a wizard so evil other wizards will not utter his name and refer to him only as "He Who Must Not Be Named." Lord Voldemort's magic killed Harry's parents but left the boy with only a lightning-shaped scar on his forehead. For this reason, Harry is a celebrity in the wizarding world, but his fame also means he is the target for Voldemort's wicked plans. The *Harry Potter* stories become significantly darker in theme as Harry ages, covering increasingly mature subjects and themes with the progression of the anthology.

Some of the Harry Potter *books that showed children the magic of reading.* © FRED VICTORIN/NEWSCOM.

From age eleven, Harry attends the Hogwarts School of Witchcraft and Wizardry. There he takes fun-sounding lessons like "Potions," "Care of Magical Creatures," "Defense Against the Dark Arts," and "History of Magic." Like any school, however, what happens outside of lessons is usually much more exciting. Harry and his friends Ron Weasley and Hermione Grainger make secret trips to see Hagrid, the school's good-natured giant groundsman. They visit the wizard town of Hogsmeade and sneak around the corridors of Hogwarts hidden under Harry's invisibility cloak. Hogwarts itself is a magical castle, complete with ghosts such as Nearly Headless Nick and the Bloody Baron. Best of all is the game of Quidditch. The rules of Quidditch are almost as complicated as those of cricket, a sport played at muggle schools in England. Quidditch is exciting and dangerous. It involves flying on broomsticks and two teams who risk life and limb to catch the elusive flying ball, the Snitch. Harry, of course, is an exceptional player. The school is divided into "houses," and each has a Quidditch team. Harry's house is Gryffindor, and he is Gryffindor's ace "seeker" player who pursues the Snitch.

Despite their success, the *Harry Potter* novels have attracted controversy. An American author, Nancy K. Stouffer (1951–), has claimed similarities between Rowling's work and her 1984 book *The Legend of Muggles,* featuring Larry Potter. Meanwhile, some religious groups have argued that Rowling's novels encourage an unhealthy interest in witchcraft and the occult among its readers. *Harry Potter* fans have not always been treated well by the media companies that now control their hero.

Warner Brothers, makers of the eight-part film series based on the *Harry Potter* novels, have e-mailed owners of *Harry Potter* fan Web sites to persuade them to give up their domain names. The *Harry Potter* film series is the highest-grossing film series ever made.

The *Harry Potter* books and movies are at the center of a merchandising industry that includes textbooks on the subjects Harry studies at school and the rules of Quidditch, a game that is now played at over three hundred universities and high schools around the world, according to the International Quidditch Association. It is even possible to buy a "Nimbus 2000" broomstick, though the buyer would have to be a real-life wizard to make it fly. Over Christmas 2000, a major British national radio station devoted its entire Boxing Day (December 26) schedule to a reading of *Harry Potter and the Philosopher's Stone* by actor Stephen Fry (1957–). Whatever their weaknesses, Rowling's novels have managed to hold their own against distractions such as games consoles, teen pop stars, and the **Internet** (see entry under 1990s—The Way We Lived in volume 5). Each new installment in the book series brought with it a media frenzy and a wave of excitement from fans. Like the "Narnia" books and the ***Nancy Drew*** series (see entry under 1930s—Print Culture in volume 2) before it, the adventures of Harry Potter have enriched the lives of a generation of children and their parents.

Chris Routledge

For More Information

Anelli, Melissa. *Harry, a History.* New York: Pocket Books, 2008.

Colbert, David. *The Magical Worlds of Harry Potter.* Updated ed. New York: Berkley Books, 2008.

Kronzek, Allan Zola, and Elizabeth Kronzek. *The Sorcerer's Companion: A Guide to the Magical World of Harry Potter.* 2nd ed. New York: Broadway, 2004.

Routledge, Christopher. "Harry Potter and the Mystery of Ordinary Life." In *Mystery in Children's Literature: From the Rational to the Supernatural.* Edited by Adrienne E. Gavin and Christopher Routledge. London and New York: Palgrave, 2001.

Scamander, Newt (J. K. Rowling). *Fantastic Beasts and Where to Find Them.* New York: Arthur A. Levine, 2001.

Shapiro, Marc. *J. K. Rowling: The Wizard Behind Harry Potter.* Rev. ed. New York: St. Martin's Griffin, 2007.

Whisp, Kennilworthy (J. K. Rowling). *Quidditch Through the Ages.* New York: Arthur A. Levine, 2001.

Zipes, Jack. *Sticks and Stones: The Troublesome Success of Children's Literature, From Slovenly Peter to Harry Potter.* London: Routledge, 2000.

Jurassic Park

In the popular 1990 novel *Jurassic Park* by Michael Crichton (1942–2008), Jurassic Park is the name given to a wondrous attraction constructed on an island off the coast of South America. Using genetic engineering, scientists on the island have cloned dinosaurs from ancient DNA (deoxyribonucleic acid) contained in fossils. Their efforts to control the animals go horribly wrong, however, and the dinosaurs break loose and terrorize visitors to the park. The park contains a *Tyrannosaurus rex,* a huge and dangerous predator, but the real "villains" among the dinosaurs are the much smaller *Velociraptors* (pronounced va-LOSS-ah-RAP-tors), which are quick, intelligent, and hunt in packs. The book fascinated readers with its exploration of what happens when scientists meddle with the creation of life. In this respect, the story echoed the themes of the classic tale of **Frankenstein** (see entry under 1930s—Film and Theater in volume 2).

Steven Spielberg (1946–) directed the 1993 film of the novel, which was a monster hit. The cast included Richard Attenborough (1923–), Laura Dern (1967–), Jeff Goldblum (1952–), and Sam Neill (1947–), but the real stars were the dinosaurs. Animatronic creatures and cutting-edge computer animation combined to make the ancient reptiles look utterly realistic and terribly frightening. The film earned an Oscar for Special Effects.

For the first time in his career, Crichton wrote a sequel to one of his books. *The Lost World* (1995) concerns a scientific expedition that gets into trouble on another South American island. The film version of *The Lost World* was released in 1997, again directed by Spielberg, and again with the special effects proving to be the film's true stars. A third movie, *Jurassic Park III,* was released in 2001 without the involvement of either Crichton or Spielberg. There have long been rumors of a fourth film in the *Jurassic Park* series, but the unexpected death of author Crichton in 2008 put any possible production on indefinite hold. However, it is doubtful that audiences will lose their appetite for imagining what it would be like for dinosaurs to run amok in the modern world.

Justin Gustainis

For More Information

Crichton, Michael. *Jurassic Park.* New York: Alfred A. Knopf, 1990.
Crichton, Michael. *Lost World.* New York: Alfred A. Knopf, 1995.
DeSalle, Rob. *The Science of "Jurassic Park" and "The Lost World," or How To Build a Dinosaur.* New York: Basic Books, 1997.
Jurassic Park. http://www.jurassicpark.com (accessed August 2, 2011).
Larson, Wendy. *The Dinosaurs of Jurassic Park.* New York: Grosset & Dunlap, 1993.
Shay, Don. *The Making of "Jurassic Park."* New York: Ballantine Books, 1993.

1990s

Sports and Games

The 1990s boasted some of the greatest athletes and athletic achievements of the century, and saw a real flowering in women's sports. Leading the way was the man considered by many to be the best athlete of the century: Michael Jordan (1963—). Jordan led the Chicago Bulls to six National Basketball Association (NBA) championships in the decade, dominating the league the way no team had done in thirty years. Tiger Woods (1975—) became golf's most dominant player since Jack Nicklaus (1940–) and an admirable role model for minority athletes who had once been banned from the sport. Two of major league baseball's most hallowed records also fell in the decade. Mark McGwire (1963–) and Sammy Sosa (1968–) engaged in a summer-long home run derby that ended with McGwire setting a new record for home runs in a single season with seventy runs. Cal Ripken Jr. (1960–) broke the fifty-six-year-old record for consecutive games played, previously held by Lou Gehrig (1903–1941), by appearing in his 2,131st game in 1995. Also in baseball, two teams dominated the decade: the Atlanta Braves in the National League, and the New York Yankees in the American League.

Women made a big splash in sports in the 1990s. The U.S. women's soccer team won the first Women's World Cup in 1991 and then won it again in 1999. In the latter game, American player Brandi Chastain (1968–) shot the game-winning penalty kick, ripped off her jersey (revealing a black sports bra), and raised her fists in victory. The image was seen everywhere as a signal that women's sports had arrived. Of course the soccer team had help. American gymnasts won the team gold at the 1996 Summer Olympic Games, and American women hockey players won the gold medal at the 1998 Winter Olympics. A women's professional basketball league, the Women's National Basketball Association (WNBA), was founded in 1997 and continued to flourish in the 2000s. Finally, two African American sisters, Venus Williams (1980–) and Serena Williams (1981–), showed signs of dominating the world of tennis and becoming media stars at the same time.

An interesting sidelight to the major professional sports in the 1990s was the emergence of a new kind of sport called "extreme sports." Pioneered by Generation X thrill seekers, extreme sports were either brand new ideas—like bungee jumping—or variations on old sports—like street luge or sky surfing. Cable-TV sports network ESPN recognized these sports by broadcasting the X Games beginning in 1995 as a kind of alternative Olympics. By 1998, snowboarding had become an Olympic sport, and other sports hoped to gain similar recognition.

Extreme Sports

During the last decades of the twentieth century, extreme sports—also called "adventure" or "action" sports—increased steadily in popularity. Some extreme sports saw a doubling of participants between 1999 and 2000 alone. Especially popular with teens and young adults, extreme sports offer a simple and exhilarating physical challenge to those who have grown up in a technological society filled with complex contradictions. Often dangerous and sometimes even illegal, they are viewed by many as a rebellious challenge to authority.

Americans have always appreciated the skill and bravery of its daredevils and stuntmen. Sam Patch (1807–1829), who thrilled early nineteenth-century audiences by jumping into large waterfalls, died in the Genesee Falls in New York, in 1829. In the 1960s and 1970s, motorcycle stunt-driver **Evel Knievel** (1938–2007; see entry under 1960s—Sports and Games in volume 4) became famous for jumping his bike over rows of buses, trucks, rattlesnakes, and shark tanks. Extreme sports have brought these daredevil stunts off the stage and into the lives of millions of athletes looking for risk, challenge, and the adrenaline rush of success.

Extreme athletes continually seek to increase the level of speed, risk, and thrill of their sport. Many extreme sports were invented or modified by their participants. Surfing, for example, the skill first applied to riding a wooden board on ocean waves, has moved to the streets, the snow, and the air in the extreme sports of skateboarding, snowboarding, and sky surfing. Sky diving was not risky enough for some athletes, so they created paragliding and the highly dangerous BASE jumping (*B*uildings, *A*ntennas, *S*pans, *E*arth jumping), in which participants leap from **skyscrapers** (see entry under 1930s—The Way We Lived in volume 2), cliffs, and bridges, holding their parachute in their hands. Motorcyclists invented freestyle motocross, and young bicyclists who were not old enough to ride motorcycles created BMX stunt riding (BMX stands for bicycle motocross). Cross-country running became extreme marathons, where participants race for a hundred miles or more or run up mountains.

Rock-climbing is one of the most popular extreme sports. © GREG EPPERSON/SHUTTERSTOCK.COM.

Although most extreme athletes play their sports to challenge their own limits and reach their own goals, corporate America has been quick to cash in on the popularity of action sports. Advertisers from sports-equipment manufacturers to Mountain Dew, a soft-drink maker, have used extreme athletes as spokespeople. In 1995, cable network ESPN's vice president of programming, Ron Semiao, created the first national tournament of extreme sports, the X Games, featuring such sports as skateboarding, speed climbing, and street luge (high-speed sledding through city streets). The X Games have become a twice-yearly event, with one series held in summer and one in winter, which are televised on ABC as well as ESPN and ESPN2. By 1998, ESPN had expanded the games internationally, with X Games summer events held simultaneously in the United States and in various cities in Asia. Extreme sports have soared in popularity and some, like snowboarding, have even become events at the **Olympics** (see entry under 1900s—Sports and Games in volume 1).

Tina Gianoulis

For More Information

"Action Sports." *ESPN.* http://espn.go.com/action (accessed December 22, 2011).

Bower, Joe. "Going Over the Top." *Women's Sports and Fitness* (October 1995): pp. 21–24.

Gaines, Ann. *The Composite Guide to Extreme Sports.* Philadelphia: Chelsea House, 2000.

Gutman, Bill. *Being Extreme.* New York: Citadel Press, 2002.

Hamilton, Kendall. "Outer Limits." *Newsweek* (June 19, 1995): pp. 78–82.

"Life on the Edge: Is Everyday Life Too Dull? Why Else Would Americans Seek Risk as Never Before?" *Time* (September 6, 1999).

Pope, S., and Robert E. Rinehart. *Encyclopedia of Extreme Sports.* Santa Barbara, CA: ABC-CLIO, 2002.

Tomlinson, Joe. *Extreme Sports: In Search of the Ultimate Thrill.* Buffalo, NY: Firefly Books, 2004.

Tomlinson, Joe. *The Ultimate Encyclopedia of Extreme Sports.* London: Carlton, 1996.

Michael Jordan (1963–)

Michael Jordan's celebrity has transcended the sport that he became famous for playing and in which he was so magically adept. Not only was he the most important basketball player of his era but he remains the most celebrated hoops star in history and one of the most famous athletes of all time. After attending the University of North Carolina, he starred for the Chicago Bulls from 1984 through 1999, leading them to six **National Basketball Association** (NBA; see entry under 1940s—Sports and Games in volume 3) championships and winning five Most Valuable Player (MVP) awards.

Jordan is fabled as much for his graceful leaping ability, all-around physical dexterity, sharpness and intelligence, and fierce desire to win as for any of his scoring titles or MVP trophies. Additionally, in an era in which athletes were becoming increasingly controversial in the public eye for their greed and uncouth behavior, Jordan has been a model of dignity.

Like **Babe Ruth** (1895–1948; see entry under 1910s—Sports and Games in volume 1) and **Muhammad Ali** (1942–; see entry under 1960s—Sports and Games in volume 4) before him, Jordan's fame has reached beyond the boundaries of athletics. Off the court, he has appeared in countless **television** (see entry under 1940s—TV and Radio in volume 3) ads and starred in a movie, *Space Jam* (1996), in which he cavorted with such beloved animated characters as **Bugs Bunny** (see entry under 1940s—TV and Radio in volume 3), Daffy Duck, and Porky Pig.

Jordan retired twice from the NBA, only to return to the court each time. In 1993, he left basketball to try his hand at professional **baseball** (see entry under 1900s—Sports and Games in volume 1). His baseball career in the Chicago White Sox' minor league system was a flop; he returned to the Bulls in 1995. In 1999, he retired again. A year later, he became part owner of the Washington Wizards, then returned as a Wizards player for the 2001–2002 and 2002–2003 seasons. Following this third retirement, Jordan founded his own company in 2004, Michael Jordan Motorsports, a motorcycle racing team. In 2006 he became a stakeholder in the Charlotte Bobcats, also taking on the job title "Managing Member of Basketball Operations." In 2010, Jordan bought the team outright. Player or not, Jordan remains a world-class figure, just as celebrated abroad as in his native country.

Rob Edelman

The Chicago Bulls' Michael Jordan scores two against the Utah Jazz in Game 6 of the NBA Finals on June 14, 1998. © TOM SMART/GETTY IMAGES.

For More Information

Aaseng, Nathan. *Sports Great Michael Jordan.* Rev. ed. Springfield, NJ: Enslow, 1997.

Christopher, Matt. *On the Court with—Michael Jordan.* Rev. ed. Boston: Little, Brown, 2008.

Halberstam, David. *Playing for Keeps: Michael Jordan and the World He Made.* New York: Random House, 1999.

Jordan, Michael. *For the Love of the Game: My Story.* New York: Crown Publishers, 1998.

Jordan, Michael. *I Can't Accept Not Trying: Michael Jordan on the Pursuit of Excellence.* San Francisco: HarperSanFrancisco, 1994.

Jordan, Michael. *Rare Air: Michael on Michael.* San Francisco: HarperCollins Publishers, 1994.

Leahy, Michael. *When Nothing Else Matters: Michael Jordan's Last Comeback.* New York: Simon & Schuster, 2004.

Lipsyte, Robert. *Michael Jordan: A Life Above the Rim.* New York: HarperCollins, 1994.

Space Jam (film). Warner Bros., 1996.

Tiger Woods (1975–)

Many call Tiger Woods the most celebrated golfer who has ever lived. Remarkably, Woods received this designation while still in his mid-twenties. Woods's multiracial background—his father is African American and his mother is a native of Thailand—has helped to destroy the perception that golf is an elitist, white-men-only sport.

When he was fifteen, Woods became the youngest golfer ever to win the U.S. Junior Amateur title. Then he was the first to earn three consecutive U.S. amateur titles. He turned professional in 1996, and the following year won his initial Masters golf tournament by twelve strokes, the greatest margin for victory in the competition's history. He finished eighteen under par, and at age twenty-one he also was the youngest Masters champ ever. That year, Woods earned over $800,000 on the Professional Golf Association tour, playing in just eight tournaments,

Even rain cannot keep Tiger Woods from playing the Buick Classic at the Westchester Country Club in New York in June 2001.

and ***Sports Illustrated*** (see entry under 1950s—Sports and Games in volume 3) named him its "Sportsman of the Year."

Other victories followed, but all were topped in the 2000–2001 season when Woods achieved the unprecedented by winning all four major golf titles: the U.S. Open, the British Open, the PGA championship, and the Masters. Woods continued his winning streak throughout the first decade of the 2000s, winning fourteen major championships and being ranked the number one player in the world. In 2009 Woods announced that he was leaving competitive golf temporarily to undertake therapy after the media exposed a series of infidelities to his wife. He returned to the game twenty weeks later. Woods is considered the highest-paid athlete in the world, earning $90 million in 2010.

Rob Edelman

For More Information

Londino, Lawrence J. *Tiger Woods: A Biography.* 2nd ed. Santa Barbara, CA: Greenwood Press, 2010.

Lusetich, Robert. *Unplayable: An Inside Account of Tiger's Most Tumultuous Season.* New York: Atra Books, 2010.

Strege, John. *Tiger: A Biography of Tiger Woods.* New York: Broadway Books, 1997.

Tiger Woods: Official Site. http://www.tigerwoods.com (accessed August 3, 2011).

Woods, Earl. *Playing Through: Straight Talk on Hard Work, Big Dreams, and Adventures with Tiger.* New York: HarperCollins, 1998.

Woods, Earl. *Training a Tiger: A Father's Guide to Raising a Winner in Both Golf and Life.* New York: HarperCollins, 1997.

1990s

TV and Radio

Although the number of cable channels and cable subscribers continued to climb in the 1990s, network TV actually made a resurgence. The networks grew in numbers, adding FOX, WB (Warner Bros.), and UPN (United Paramount Network) to the classic "big three" of ABC, CBS, and NBC. The networks also succeeded in offering a number of shows that Americans truly loved. NBC was the dominant network of the decade, and its "Must See TV" lineup included some of the favorite shows on TV.

A comedy named *Seinfeld* (1990–98) was clearly the hit show of the decade. Appearing on Thursday nights on NBC, this show focused on the antics of stand-up comedian Jerry Seinfeld (1954–), playing himself, and his three self-absorbed friends. The joke went that the show was about nothing; in truth, the show captured perfectly the giddy, sometimes silly spirit of the 1990s. Joining *Seinfeld* in the "Must See TV" lineup were the hits shows *Frasier* (1993–2004), *Friends* (1994–2004), and the hospital drama *ER* (1994–2009). Another major network hit was ABC's *NYPD Blue* (1993–2005), perhaps the grittiest police drama ever to air on TV. Several other shows showcased the talents of stand-up comedians: ABC's *Home Improvement* (1991–99), starring Tim Allen (1953–); NBC's *Mad About You* (1992–99), starring Paul Reiser (1957–); and CBS's *Everybody Loves Raymond* (1996–2005), starring Ray Romano (1957–). Perhaps the most striking moment on network television came when Ellen DeGeneres (1958–), the star of the ABC sitcom *Ellen* (1994–98), revealed her homosexuality on the air in 1997. By the end of the decade, it was not at all uncommon to have homosexual characters on major programs, most notably on NBC's hit comedy *Will & Grace* (1998–2006), where two of the three lead characters were gay.

While the major networks generally stuck to the great middle ground of family entertainment, the cable channels and smaller networks pushed the envelope. *The Simpsons* (1989–) on FOX was perhaps the decade's most interesting show, with its bizarre animated version of a dysfunctional American family. Even more twisted were MTV's *The Beavis and Butt-Head Show* (1993–97) and Comedy Central's *South Park* (1997–), whose crude humor and handling of controversial topics won both fans and critics. MTV's *Real World* (1992–) offered a weekly glimpse into the lives of a band of twenty-something strangers thrown together in a house or apartment. *Real World,* along with FOX's *COPS* (1989–), paved the way for the success of a range of "reality TV" shows that were popular late in the decade and into the 2000s; CBS's *Survivor* (2000–) was the most successful example of the genre.

Even kids got something new to watch in the 1990s. Japanese animation, called anime, came to the United States first as *Pokémon* (1997–), a popular TV cartoon as well as a card game and line of toys. Other anime shows such as *Sailor Moon* and *Dragon Ball Z* followed. PBS offered *Barney and Friends* (1992–2009), which showcased a large purple dinosaur, and a British import about Thomas the Tank Engine that appeared in an American version of the show called *Shining Time Station* (1990–93).

Ally McBeal

The FOX television series *Ally McBeal* premiered in 1997 and ran until 2002. During the late 1990s, it garnered a strong audience of mostly young professional female viewers. Starring Calista Flockhart (1964–) in the title role, the show was set in the Boston, Massachusetts, law firm of Cage and Fish. Ally McBeal was one among a team of dynamic young lawyers taking on cases too risky or too controversial for other firms to touch. Nevertheless, the real subject of the show was Ally and her worries about work, men, motherhood, and growing old. Ally McBeal enjoyed

Calista Flockhart as Ally McBeal. © 20TH CENTURY FOX/ THE KOBAL COLLECTION/ART RESOURCE, NY.

money, status, and designer clothes, but she longed for the simplicity of childhood.

Ally McBeal was created by David E. Kelley (1956–), the producer responsible for hospital drama *Chicago Hope* (1994–2000) and the darker legal serial *The Practice* (1997–). *Ally McBeal* quickly became known for its up-to-date take on young working women and the problems they faced. Ally's respectable, well-paid career contrasted with her strange fantasy life. Using computer-generated images, Ally's thoughts and fantasies appeared on screen. Her desire for motherhood took the form of dancing babies. People took on distorted and bizarre shapes according to what Ally thought of them. The show also poked fun at fashionable office life. There was a unisex bathroom where the lawyers and staff exchanged gossip. The firm specialized in fighting bizarre discrimination cases not for ethical reasons but because they paid well. The **yuppie** (see entry under 1980s—The Way We Lived in volume 5) dream of working life being just like college, but with more money, was gently mocked in every episode.

Ally McBeal may have struck a chord with viewers when it first appeared, but many critics were less impressed. The show definitely seemed to strike a blow against professional women everywhere, as the mini-skirted women in the Cage and Fish office often seemed most interested in getting married and having children. Because Ally McBeal was seen as a possible role model for young women, critics worried that Flockhart's stick-thin appearance might encourage eating disorders. As an attempt to represent the lives of professional women at the turn of the twenty-first century, *Ally McBeal* provided at best an incomplete picture. As a popular lightweight comedy of modern manners, the show was a huge success.

Chris Routledge

For More Information

Appelo, Tim. *Ally McBeal: The Official Guide.* New York: HarperPerennial, 1999.

Levine, Josh. *David E. Kelley: The Man Behind Ally McBeal.* Toronto: E. C. W. Press, 1999.

Smith, Greg M. *Beautiful TV: The Art and Argument of Ally McBeal.* Austin: University of Texas Press, 2007.

Anime

The Japanese word for "animation," anime (pronounced ANNee-may) is a general term for any animated image or cartoon. It refers more specifically to the modern animation industry in Japan, with its prolific output of **television** (see entry under 1940s—TV and Radio in volume 3) programs, **video games** (see entry under 1970s—Sports and Games in volume 4), and computer software. These products tend to feature strong fantasy-based story lines that often reflect the escapist dreams of ordinary people. Observers have pointed out that the characters in Japanese anime are more closely related to their real-world fans than are the distant superheroes of American cartoons, who inhabit a universe that is removed from everyday experience. Popular anime series like *Doraemon* (1979–) and *Ranma ½* (1989–) focus on the everyday lives of students and workers who live shadow lives alongside their normal existences.

A still from the 1997 anime film Perfect Blue. © MANGA ENTERTAINMENT/EVERETT COLLECTION.

Anime was relatively unknown in the United States before the 1980s, though a notable exception was the popular ***Speed Racer*** (see entry under 1960s—TV and Radio in volume 4) series of the 1960s. Anime has since become a popular source of entertainment. The **Internet** (see entry under 1990s—The Way We Lived in volume 5) culture of the 1990s allowed fans around the world to play the latest anime games or view new images as soon as they were made available. In the late 1990s, **Pokémon** (1997–; see entry under 1990s—The Way We Lived in volume 5), with its array of card collections, games, and videos, became the most popular anime-derived product among American fans. Several American companies have been releasing English-language anime for the domestic film and video markets, including Miramax's critically acclaimed *Princess Mononoke* (1997). Thousands of anime clubs have sprung up to share information and exchange releases, some of them pirated.

Japan has a centuries-old tradition of cartoonlike images, including caricatures and humorous drawings with sparse lines and stylized features. In the electronic age, anime producers got much of their material from contemporary Japanese comic books, or *manga,* which are written for adults as well as for children. Some of the adult-oriented manga have far more explicit descriptions of sex and violence than are common in the United States. Other manga evoke **Disney** (see entry under 1920s—Film and Theater in volume 2) films with their romantic or picturesque situations. Japanese anime is also noted for its artful use of sound effects and focus on other aspects of its own technology, a style that is uncommon in American cartoons. Easier access via the Internet in the early 2000s allowed anime to balloon in popularity around the world; by 2005 at least five million people subscribed to anime Web sites.

Edward Moran

For More Information

Clements, Jonathan, and Helen McCarthy. *The Anime Encyclopedia: A Guide to Japanese Animation Since 1917.* Rev. ed. Berkeley, CA: Stone Bridge Press, 2007.

Ledoux, Trish, ed. *Anime Interviews: The First Five Years of Animerica, Anime & Manga Monthly (1992–97).* San Francisco: Cadence Books, 1997.

McCarthy, Helen. *The Anime Movie Guide: Movie-by-Movie Guide to Japanese Animation Since 1983.* Woodstock, NY: Overlook Press, 1996.

Poitras, Gilles. *The Anime Companion: What's Japanese in Japanese Animation.* Berkeley, CA: Stone Bridge Press, 1999.

Poitras, Gilles. *Anime Essentials: Every Thing a Fan Needs to Know.* Berkeley, CA: Stone Bridge Press, 2001.

Steiff, Josef, and Tristan D. Tamplin, eds. *Anime and Philosophy: Wide Eyed Wonder.* Chicago: Open Court, 2010.

Barney and Friends

Beginning in the 1990s, a 6-foot, 4-inch talking purple dinosaur named Barney became both one of the most beloved and one of the most hated characters on **television** (see entry under 1940s—TV and Radio in volume 3). Each day, the **Public Broadcasting System** (PBS; see entry under 1960s—TV and Radio in volume 4) presented the half-hour program *Barney and Friends,* in which a stuffed toy dinosaur would come to life and interact with an ethnically diverse cast of young children. Episodes featured Barney and his pals singing, **dancing** (see entry under 1900s—The Way We Lived in volume 1), telling stories, and learning how to get along. Later, two other dinosaurs named Baby Bop and BJ joined them. Barney became a cultural icon for a generation of preschoolers even though many adults found the character to be sickeningly sweet and extremely annoying.

Barney the Dinosaur with some of his colorful friends.

Barney was created in 1988 by Sheryl Leach (1952–) for a home video titled "Barney and the Backyard Gang." Originally, she considered making the title character a bear but transformed him into a dinosaur when she noted the popularity of prehistoric creatures with children. The success of the video was noticed by PBS, which produced a television series featuring Barney beginning in 1992. Barney, who was played by David Joyner (1963–) and voiced by Bob West (1956–), was a cuddly playmate to whom young children could relate. A highlight of every episode occurred when Barney sang his theme song, "I Love You." Soon, millions of preschoolers across the nation were singing Barney's anthem (to the tune of "This Old Man"), which began: "I love you / You love me / We're a happy family."

Although millions of children adored Barney, many adults hated the character and the TV show. They mocked the program's low production values, sappy sentimentality, and extensive merchandising. Some complained that the "children's program" was little more than a cleverly disguised commercial for a multitude of Barney products. In his *Dictionary of Teleliteracy,* David Bianculli conveyed the attitude of many parents when he wrote, "With our children, and our wallets, supporting this magenta monster so indiscriminately, it certainly gives us reason to be fearful of the fuchsia." The animosity toward Barney grew so intense that he became a regular target for crude humor and ridicule on other TV shows and in comedy routines. However, Barney retained his appeal with America's youth and even starred in his own film in 1998. The show ran in the United States until 2009 and was broadcast during many of its seasons in other countries, including Turkey, Israel, and South Korea.

Charles Coletta

For More Information

Barney and Friends. http://www.pbs.org/barney (accessed on August 3, 2011).
Bianculli, David. *Dictionary of Teleliteracy.* New York: Continuum, 1996.
Phillips, Phil. *Dinosaurs: The Bible, Barney, and Beyond.* Lancaster, PA: Starburst, 1994.

Baywatch

During the 1990s, *Baywatch* was one of the most popular and profitable syndicated programs throughout the world (syndicated programs are those sold to independent television stations). With its mix of melodramatic plots, bikini-clad young women, and bare-chested young men, the series presented the California sun-and-surf lifestyle of a team of lifeguards that patrolled the beaches around Los Angeles, California. Although it was criticized as "jiggle TV," audiences in 145 countries embraced *Baywatch* and, at its peak, the program boasted more than a billion viewers.

Actor David Hasselhoff, as lifeguard Mitch Bucannon, runs to save another life in the TV series Baywatch. © EVERETT COLLECTION.

Baywatch focused on the relationships and rescues of a Southern California lifeguard unit led by Mitch Bucannon (David Hasselhoff, 1952–). The lifeguards routinely saved drowning victims, battled drug smugglers, and faced shark attacks—all while engaged in romantic subplots. The young actresses and actors who appeared on the program were better known for their sleek physiques and buff bodies than for their dramatic talents. Many episodes highlighted their physical attributes through music-video sequences featuring the nearly naked lifeguards in various seductive poses. The show changed cast members frequently and made stars out of Yasmine Bleeth (1968–), Carmen Electra (1972–), and Pamela Anderson (1967–). Anderson, the embodiment of the sun-bronzed California blonde, became an international sex symbol because of the series. *Baywatch*'s emphasis on its cast's "wholesome sexuality" is the reason most often cited for its huge international success. In his *Dictionary of Teleliteracy,* David

Bianculli identifies the reason for the program's success: "Basically, to ogle [is] an activity that knows no language barrier."

When *Baywatch* first aired on NBC in 1989, it failed to attract a significant audience and was canceled after one season. However, its producers recognized its potential to garner a large international audience and chose to distribute it to independent stations around the globe. The resulting enormous viewership and profits paved the way for other internationally syndicated programs during the decade.

In 1995, Hasselhoff participated in a short-lived spin-off called *Baywatch Nights.* His character continued to serve as a lifeguard by day and by night he worked in a detective agency. During the final seasons of *Baywatch,* the setting switched to Hawaii, but the focus remained on the beautiful bodies. The series concluded in 2001. *Baywatch* was heralded by the *Guinness Book of World Records* as having had the highest viewership of any show in history, with 1.1 billion in the audience each week at the show's peak. In 2003 a reunion movie was released. *Baywatch: Hawaiian Wedding* starred Hasselhoff, happily revived from a supposedly fatal boating accident that occurred in the show's tenth season, along with several other sexy regulars from the show.

Charles Coletta

For More Information

Baber, Brendan, and Eric Spitznagel. *Planet Baywatch.* New York: St. Martin's Griffin, 1996.

Baywatch. http://www.baywatch.com (accessed August 4, 2011).

Bianculli, David. *Dictionary of Teleliteracy.* New York: Continuum, 1996.

Bonann, Gregory, and Brad A. Lewis. *Baywatch: Rescued from Prime Time.* Beverly Hills: New Millennium Press, 2000.

The Beavis and Butt-Head Show

"Beavis and Butt-Head are not role models. They are not even human, but rather cartoons. Some of the things they do would cause a real person to get hurt, expelled, possibly thrown out of the country. To put it another way: don't try this at home." So read the disclaimer that introduced the controversial cable cartoon show, *The Beavis and Butt-Head Show,* which aired on **MTV** (see entry under 1980s—Music in volume 5) between 1993 and 1997. The show's main characters are two crudely

Beavis and Butt-Head annoy and entertain. © PARAMOUNT/ EVERETT COLLECTION.

animated adolescent boys, complete with acne and braces, who spend much of their time making fun of the music videos they watch on **television** (see entry under 1940s—TV and Radio in volume 3) and fantasizing about being rich, sexy, and cool—states they clearly will never attain.

The Beavis and Butt-Head Show was a harsh satire of the awkwardness, anger, and confusion of adolescence at the end of the twentieth century. The show touched a chord with young, mostly male members of the MTV audience. Created by Texas animator Mike Judge (1962–), *Beavis and Butt-Head* introduced a level of violence and gross-out humor that was new to TV cartoons. Best friends Beavis and Butt-Head are unattractive, dopey, and often mean (just like some teenagers), and audiences around the world tuned in to watch. The show was also later spun off into a film, *Beavis and Butt-Head Do America* (1996), and several **video games** (see entry under 1970s—Sports and Games in volume 4).

Although many teenagers and young adults laughed at Beavis and Butt-Head's misadventures, their parents were less amused. Many blamed the show for a perceived rise in teen violence and disrespect. In late 1993, a five-year-old boy started a fire in his house that caused the death of his younger sister. His mother declared that her son had gotten the idea for the fire from watching Beavis's fascination with fire. During congressional hearings about TV violence, the show was brought up many times as an example of the negative influence of TV on youth, even though most members of Congress had never watched the program.

Following the end of *The Beavis and Butt-Head Show,* Judge went on to create *Daria* (1997–2001) for MTV and *King of the Hill* (1997–) for FOX. In 2010 MTV announced that *The Beavis and Butt-Head Show,* would be revived starting in October 2011. The miscreant duo would still watch and comment on MTV fare while adding contemporary TV shows, movies, and self-made videos from **YouTube** (see entry under 2000s—The Way We Lived in volume 6) to their viewing diet.

Tina Gianoulis

For More Information

Beavis and Butt-Head's Playground. http://www.ccs.neu.edu/home/image/bnb.html (accessed August 4, 2011).

Gardner, James. "*Beavis and Butt-Head.*" *National Review* (May 2, 1994): pp. 60–63.

Matthews, Joe. "Beavis, Butthead & Budding Nihilists: Will Western Civilization Survive?" *Washington Post* (October 3, 1993): p. C1.

McConnell, Frank. "Art Is Dangerous: *Beavis & Butthead,* for Example." *Commonweal* (January 14, 1994): pp. 28–31.

"Mike Judge." *Current Biography* (Vol. 58, no. 5, May 1997): pp. 22–26.

Beverly Hills 90210

In the 1980s, **MTV** (see entry under 1980s—Music in volume 5) appealed to young **television** (see entry under 1940s—TV and Radio in volume 3) viewers with a fast-paced mix of music, fashion, and social concern. In the 1990s, the prime-time TV drama *Beverly Hills 90210* adopted the same formula, added a healthy dose of upper-class teen lifestyles, and became an enormous hit. Its popularity, particularly among younger viewers, helped the FOX network grow into a ratings power-house.

Aaron Spelling (1928–2006), a TV producer whose previous hits had included *Dynasty* (1976) and ***Charlie's Angels*** (1976; see entry under 1970s—TV and Radio in volume 4), created *90210.* The weekly one-hour show, which debuted in October 1990, was set in fashionable Beverly Hills, California (zip code 90210), and followed the lives of a group of high-school classmates. While designed to feature an ensemble cast, including Spelling's daughter, Tori Spelling (1973–), the show quickly propelled a couple of its actors to national stardom. Luke Perry (1966–) played the moody Dylan McKay, a rebellious loner. Shannen Doherty (1971–) appeared as Brenda Walsh, Dylan's girlfriend. Also on hand were Jason Priestley (1969–), Jennie Garth (1972–), Ian Ziering (1964–), Brian Austin Green (1973–), and Gabrielle Carteris (1961–). When adult supervision was needed, burly actor Joe E. Tata (1937–) appeared as Nathaniel "Nat" Bussicio, owner of the local diner hangout, The Peach Pit.

Audiences immediately responded to the glamorous lifestyles of the wealthy characters depicted on the show, copying their dress, musical tastes, and hairstyles. Viewers could also identify with the many real-life

Residing in Beverly Hills 90210*: Ian Ziering (far left), Jennie Garth, Tori Spelling, Brian Austin Green, Gabrielle Carteris, Jason Priestley, Shannen Doherty, and Luke Perry.* © SPELLING/THE KOBAL COLLECTION/ART RESOURCE, NY.

problems dealt with by the fictional teens. Over the course of its ten-year run, *90210* episodes addressed such serious issues as date rape, drug addiction, eating disorders, and premarital sex. Unlike other dramas set in high school, the characters on this show actually aged and changed, just like real people. Later episodes shifted the setting to fictional California University and then out into the working world. A number of the actors, including Doherty and Perry, left the show (Perry later returned), while new ones, including future Academy Award winner Hilary Swank (1974–), signed on. The show maintained good ratings until its cancellation in 2000. By that time, aonly a few of the original actors remained, and the ones who did seemed far too old to play their characters anymore. Spinoffs of the show abounded, including *Melrose Place* and *Models Inc.* In 2008 a show called simply *90210* was premiered, with a plot that focused on a new family, the Wilsons, who had just moved to Beverly Hills. The first two seasons featured many of the characters and actors who appeared in the original show, this time cast in adult roles.

Robert E. Schnakenberg

For More Information

Cohen, Daniel. *Beverly Hills, 90210: An Unauthorized Biography.* New York: Pocket Books, 1991.

McKinley, E. Graham. *Beverly Hills, 90210: Television, Gender, and Identity.* Philadelphia: University of Pennsylvania, 1997.

Mills, Bart, and Nancy Mills. *Beverly Hills, 90210 Exposed!* New York: Harper Paperbacks, 1991.

Wallner, Rosemary. *Beverly Hills, 90210: TV's Hottest Teens.* Edina, MN: Abdo & Daughters, 1992.

ER

One of the most popular and critically acclaimed **television** (see entry under 1940s—TV and Radio in volume 3) dramas of the 1990s was *ER.* The show depicted the medical traumas faced by the doctors and nurses of an inner-city Chicago, Illinois, hospital emergency room. The series, created by author Michael Crichton (1942–2008), debuted in 1994 and was more quickly paced and realistic than previous medical programs. Author Steven Stark, in *Glued to the Set,* discusses *ER*'s mass appeal: "It brilliantly took a number of trends in programming—the push to realism, the focus on dysfunction, and the emphasis on shorter segments—and combined them to create a synthesis of an early-evening 'reality' show, a daytime talk fest, and *Hill Street Blues.*" The program dominated the ratings. In 1998, it became the most highly compensated show in TV history when NBC agreed to pay $13 million per episode.

Before he was the acclaimed author of **best-sellers** (see entry under 1940s—Commerce in volume 3) like ***Jurassic Park*** (see entry under 1990s—Print Culture in volume 5), Crichton was a physician. He based *ER* on his own emergency-room experiences. He believed previous medical dramas like *Marcus Welby* (1969–76), *Medical Center* (1969–76),

The cast of doctors and nurses on NBC's ER*: Alex Kingston (far left), Paul McCrane, Ming-Na, Michael Michele, Anthony Edwards, Goran Visnjic, Noah Wyle, Maura Tierney, Eriq La Salle, Sherry Stringfield, and Laura Innes.* © ROBERT TRACHTENBERG/WARNER BROS. TV/AMBLIN TV/THE KOBAL COLLECTION/ART RESOURCE, NY.

and *The Bold Ones* (1969–72) did not realistically portray the tension and hectic activity of a true hospital environment. Episodes of *ER* were filled with dozens of characters, technical medical jargon, and graphic operating scenes. The *ER* staff seemed to face an unceasing array of gunshot wounds, domestic violence, drug overdoses, and other emergencies that tested both their professional skills and personal emotions. It was not uncommon for episodes to have unhappy endings.

The series frequently examined the personal trials and tribulations of the hospital staff. Among the most prominent characters were: Dr. Mark Greene (Anthony Edwards, 1962–), whose career disrupted his marriage; Dr. Peter Benton (Eriq La Salle, 1962–), an intense surgeon; Nurse Carol Hathaway (Julianna Margulies, 1966–), a compassionate caregiver; and Jeanie Boulet (Gloria Reuben, 1964–), who discovered that she had acquired AIDS from her husband. Actor George Clooney (1961–) became a TV superstar playing Dr. Doug Ross, a womanizing pediatrician. His 1999 departure from the series to embark on a film career marked one of the show's most watched episodes.

Crichton, along with fellow executive producer Steven Spielberg (1946–) and many of television's top writers and producers, crafted an intensely satisfying drama that depicted the hardships faced by medical professionals in the 1990s while continuing to reinforce TV's traditionally positive image of heroic doctors and nurses. The show remained on the air until 2009 and was nominated for 124 Emmy awards, a record in television history

Charles Coletta

For More Information

"ER." *Warner Bros.* http://www2.warnerbros.com/web/ertv/index.jsp (accessed August 4, 2011).

Jones, Mark. *ER: The Unofficial Guide.* London: Contender, 2003.

Pourroy, Janine. *Behind the Scenes at ER.* New York: Ballantine Books, 1995.

Spignesi, Stephen. *The ER Companion: An Unauthorized Guide.* New York: Carol Publishing Group, 1996.

Stark, Steven. *Glued to the Set: The 60 Television Shows and Events That Made Us Who We Are Today.* New York: Free Press, 1997.

Frasier

The situation comedy *Frasier,* which debuted on NBC in 1993 and remained on the air until 2004, depicted the neurotic misadventures of Dr. Frasier Crane, a conceited psychologist living in Seattle, Washington. The series, a spin-off of the popular sitcom (situation comedy; see entry under 1950s—TV and Radio in volume 3) *Cheers,* was widely recognized as one of television's most sophisticated programs. In 1998, the show became the first program to win five consecutive Emmy Awards for Outstanding Comedy Series. *Frasier* offered viewers witty, literate dialogue and often-absurd humor not evident in other sitcoms.

Frasier Crane (Kelsey Grammar, 1955–) first appeared on ***Cheers*** (see entry under 1980s—TV and Radio in volume 5) in 1984 as a

Kelsey Grammer (left) as Dr. Frasier Crane and David Hyde Pierce as his brother Dr. Niles Crane, with Moose the dog as Eddie, analyze the situation in Frasier. © PARAMOUNT TELEVISION/EVERETT COLLECTION.

rival suitor to Sam Malone (Ted Danson, 1947–) for the affections of barmaid Diane Chambers (Shelley Long, 1949–). Frasier was highly educated, somewhat effeminate, snobbish, and a perfect contrast to the jock bar-owner Malone. When *Cheers* left the air in early 1993, NBC announced the character Frasier would be spun-off into his own show.

The premise of *Frasier* was that Dr. Crane had moved to Seattle following his divorce from his wife. He landed a job as host of a radio call-in show. Surrounding Grammer on the series was one of television's best ensemble casts. David Hyde Pierce (1959–) portrayed Dr. Niles Crane, Frasier's arrogant younger brother. Peri Gilpin (1961–) appeared as Roz

Doyle, a radio producer weary of trying to find the right man but always on the lookout. Frasier lived with his father, Martin (John Mahoney, 1940–), a gruff, blue-collar former policeman who was often frustrated by his sons' highbrow mannerisms. Daphne Moon (Jane Leeves, 1961–) was Martin's British physical therapist and the object of Niles' lust (Niles and Daphne eventually married on the show). Rounding out the cast was Eddie, Martin's dog who constantly annoyed Frasier. Many celebrities made guest voice "appearances" on the series as the irritating callers to Frasier's radio program. Most episodes revolved around the sibling rivalry of the Crane brothers, who constantly tried to top each other.

Crane became one of TV's longest-running comedic characters and a true icon of popular culture. The show was one of the longest-lived spinoffs in TV history.

Charles Coletta

For More Information

Angell, David, Peter Casey, and David Lee. *The "Frasier" Scripts.* New York: Newmarket Press, 1999.

Bailey, David, and Warren Martyn. *Goodnight, Seattle: The Unauthorised Guide to the World of "Frasier."* London: Virgin, 1988.

Bly, Robert. *What's Your Frasier I.Q.?: 501 Questions and Answers for Fans.* Secaucus, NJ: Carol Publishing, 1996.

Graham, Jefferson. *Frasier: The Official Companion Book to the Award-Winning Paramount Television Comedy!* New York: Pocket Books, 1996.

Grammer, Kelsey. *So Far.* New York: Dutton, 1995.

Moose, also known as Eddie, with Brian Hargrove. *My Life as a Dog.* New York: HarperEntertainment, 2000.

Friends

The NBC **sitcom** (situation comedy; see entry under 1950s—TV and Radio in volume 3) *Friends* (1994–), which depicted the humorous struggles and romances of a group of "twentysomethings" living in New York City, was one of the highest-rated and most acclaimed television programs of the 1990s. The series boasted fine writing, maintained a strong ensemble cast (a group of regulars who act well together), and was a vital component to NBC's powerhouse "Must See TV" Thursday night lineup. Created by producers Marta Kauffman (1956–) and David Crane (1957–), the series featured attractive actors portraying the pivotal years of early adulthood.

Best Friends *forever: (front) David Schwimmer, Lisa Kudrow, and Jennifer Aniston; (back) Matt LeBlanc, Courteney Cox, and Matthew Perry.* © EVERETT COLLECTION.

Friends revolved around the lives of six friends: Rachel Green (Jennifer Aniston, 1969–), a spoiled rich girl new to the city; Monica Geller (Courteney Cox, 1964–), a neurotic chef; Phoebe Buffay (Lisa Kudrow, 1963–), a flighty massage therapist and singer; Joey Tribbiani (Matt LeBlanc, 1967–), a struggling actor; Chandler Bing (Matthew Perry, 1969–), a management executive; and Ross Geller (David Schwimmer, 1966–), Monica's paleontologist (fossil scientist) brother. Many of the episodes were set in the gang's favorite hangout—Central Perk, a trendy coffeehouse. The romantic relationships of the characters were the main source of a majority of the plotlines. Early seasons focused on the on-again-off-again romance between Ross and Rachel. Several seasons ended with a cliffhanger ending where the couple's relationship was in jeopardy. In later seasons, the Monica-Chandler romance took center stage. The obsessive Monica and skittish Chandler wed in a highly rated 2001 episode.

Friends became a national phenomenon soon after its debut and transformed its previously little-known cast into superstars. Its theme song "I'll Be There for You" by the Rembrandts became a huge hit. The series inspired a host of programs featuring **Generation X**-ers (see entry under 1980s—The Way We Lived in volume 5) living in large cities. The series is also known for popularizing the "Rachel hairstyle"—or hairstyles, as millions of young women adopted Aniston's changing hairdos. Despite its many fans, the series was often knocked for promoting an unrealistic portrait of contemporary urban life. Critics complained that the characters could never afford the luxury apartments they inhabited, and they condemned the lack of minority characters. Others said the show's emphasis on sex was unwholesome for its many young fans. Still, *Friends* remained an intensely popular and profitable program for NBC—as well as the cast, who got rich off their per-episode fees—until it went off the air in 2004. The show's finale was seen by 51 million Americans, which made it the single most-watched television episode of the 1990s.

Charles Coletta

For More Information

Friends. http://www2.warnerbros.com/web/friendstv/index.jsp (accessed August 4, 2011).

Johnson, Lauren. *"Friends": The Official Trivia Quiz Book.* London: Headline, 2004.

Johnson, Lauren. *"Friends": The One About the #1 Sitcom.* New York: New American Library, 2003.

Paulsen, Amy. *True Friends: The Official TV Guide Book.* New York: HarperPaperbacks, 1996.

Spignesi, Stephen. *What's Your Friends I.Q.?: 501 Questions & Answers for Fans.* Secaucus, NJ: Carol Publishing, 1996.

Wild, David. *Friends: The Official Companion.* New York: Doubleday, 1995.

Wild, David. *Friends ... Til the End: The One with All Ten Years.* New York: TimeInc. Home Entertainment, 2004.

The Real World

At the millennium, reality-based **television** (see entry under 1940s—TV and Radio in volume 3) series, known as **reality TV** (see entry under 1990s—TV and Radio in volume 5) came to dominate the television airwaves. The pioneer of this genre, at least on American network TV, was *The Real World* (1991–), which aired on **MTV** (see entry under 1980s—Music in volume 5). The format of the series is simple and effective. Seven young people—all in their twenties, all from different social and economic backgrounds—live together for several months and open their lives to the video cameras. The youths are placed in a stylish house in a major city—the first five shows were shot in New York, Los Angeles, San Francisco, London, and Miami—and their every interaction is recorded on film. Additionally, each participant directly addresses the camera individually, in interviews that shed new light on the unfolding events. The three thousand hours of footage are edited and broadcast as the twenty episodes that make up a season.

To some, *The Real World* is a ground-breaking pseudo-documentary experiment that offers insightful glimpses into the manner in which real young people act and interact. To others, the show is nothing more than a peep show into the lives of housemates who fight and flirt, work out their personal relationships, talk about sex and, sometimes, have sex (but not on camera). Critics wondered how much impact the

Playing in The Real World 2: Los Angeles*: (clockwise from upper left) David Edwards, Jon Brennan, Tami Anderson, Aaron Bailey, Dominic Griffin, Irene Berrera-Kearns, and Beth Stolarczyk.* © MTV/EVERETT COLLECTION.

presence of the video camera had on the manner in which cast members acted and reacted. They asked, Are they in fact *being* themselves on the show, or are they *playing* themselves?

Arguably the most famous *Real World* alumnus is Cuban-born Pedro Zamora (1972–1994), who died of **AIDS** (see entry under 1980s—The Way We Lived in volume 5) just as the final San Francisco–based episode aired. His presence on the show helped educate an untold number of MTV viewers about the disease. Another noteworthy cast member was Puck Rainey (1969–), a scab-picking bike messenger who was booted out of his house because of his inability to get along with his roommates. Some *Real World* alumni have turned their fame into careers in the media, while others have disappeared from the spotlight—except when queried for updated reports on their activities.

The success of *The Real World* led to other reality TV programs, including MTV's own *Road Rules* (1995–2007), ***Survivor*** (2000– see entry under 2000s—TV and Radio in volume 6), *Big Brother* (2000–), and *Temptation Island* (2001). *The Real World* taught a generation of TV producers that all they need do to cash in on the ratings bonanza was pick a diverse group of individuals, leave them by themselves (with an ever-present camera crew) in a jungle or on an island, and record their interactions. The show premiered its twenty-fifth season in 2011, which placed the young stars in Las Vegas. *The Real World* is one of the longest-running reality shows ever produced.

Rob Edelman

For More Information

Johnson, Hillary, and Nancy Rommelmann. *The Real Real World.* New York: Melcher Media, 1995.

"The Real World" Diaries. New York: Melcher Media, 1996.

Solomon, James, and Alan Carter. *"The Real World": The Ultimate Insider's Guide.* New York: MTV Books, 1997.

Reality TV

In the 1990s and early 2000s, the phenomenon known as reality TV became a part of American popular culture. The concept behind the reality TV genre is elementary: take a group of average individuals, who usually are strangers to each other, place them in an artificial living situation or an unusual locale, and have camera crews record their interaction. Such shows are popular with networks because they are inexpensive to produce, and the most successful of them earn astronomical ratings—and profits. They also are controversial. They present themselves as "reality," yet occasionally the behavior of participants is manipulated or suspiciously formulaic. Furthermore, even when there is no obvious pressure, how are participants affected by the constant presence of the camera? Do they react

A scene from Survivor: The Australian Outback *with contestants Colby Donaldson (left) and Keith Famie.* © MONTY BRINTON/ NEWSCOM.

and interact as they ordinarily would, knowing full well that their every action is being recorded and eventually will be broadcast to millions?

The reality TV phenomenon is rooted in two shows: *An American Family* (1973), a special on the **Public Broadcasting System** (PBS; see entry under 1960s—TV and Radio in volume 4) that recorded events in the lives of members of a suburban family; and ***The Real World*** (1991–; see entry under 1990s—TV and Radio in volume 5), an **MTV** (see entry under 1980s—Music in volume 5) series in which seven young people, all twentysomething strangers from diverse backgrounds, live together for a set period of time under the constant, watchful eye of the camera. The success of *The Real World* resulted in *Road Rules* (1995–2007), a spin-off show featuring five youthful strangers on a road trip.

Reality TV shows became a national obsession beginning with the popularity of ***Survivor*** (see entry under 2000s—TV and Radio in volume 6) in 2000, a CBS-TV summer replacement series. During the spring of 2000, sixteen average Americans went into isolation on the deserted Malaysian island of Pulau Tiga. They competed in games and contests, and every few days team members voted to banish an individual from the island. Eventually, after thirty-nine days, there was a lone survivor—Richard Hatch (1961–), a divorced, openly gay real estate agent—who won $1 million. The show fascinated viewers, who gathered around their TV sets by the millions each week to see who would be eliminated. *Survivor* soon became television's top-rated program, besting its primary competition, the quiz show ***Who Wants to Be a Millionaire*** (1999–; see entry under 1990s—TV and Radio in volume 5). In fact, it earned some of the best ratings ever for a summer replacement show, with its two-hour finale drawing over forty million viewers.

The "reality" of reality TV came into question when one *Survivor* contestant, Stacey Stillman (1972–), sued CBS and the show's producers, claiming that fellow competitors had been manipulated into voting her off the island. One of the participants admitted that this was precisely what occurred. Meanwhile, Mark Burnett (1960–), the show's creator, acknowledged that stand-ins occasionally were employed during the filming.

Survivor has since been followed by multiple sequels as well as a mass of imitators. A sampling: *Big Brother* (2000–), in which strangers come to live in a house in Los Angeles, California; *Fear Factor* (2001–2006; 2011–), involving contestants who are required to overcome their worst fears; *Boot Camp* (2001), featuring contestants who enter an eight-week military-style training program; and *Murder in Small Town X* (2001), in which contestants compete to unmask a fictional killer. Low points of the genre have been *Temptation Island* (2001–2003), spotlighting couples who come to a desert island and test their devotion to each other; and *Who Wants to Marry a Multi-Millionaire?* (2000), which featured a bachelor choosing one of fifty women to marry on the show. The "couple," Rick Rockwell (1957–) and Darva Conger (1966–), divorced soon thereafter. Musical versions of reality TV became popular in the 2000s with the debut of such wildly popular programs as ***American Idol*** (2002–) and ***Dancing with the Stars*** (2005–; see both entries under 2000s—TV and Radio in volume 6).

Rob Edelman

For More Information

Devolld, Troy. *Reality TV: An Insider's Guide to TV's Hottest Market.* Studio City, CA: Michael Wiese Productions, 2011.

Ouellette, Laurie, and James Hay. *Better Living Through Reality TV: Television and Post-Welfare Citizenship.* Malden, MA: Blackwell, 2008.

Pozner, Jennifer L. *Reality Bites Back: The Troubling Truth About Guilty Pleasure TV.* Berkeley, CA: Seal Press, 2010.

Reality News Online. http://www.realitynewsonline.com/index.html (accessed August 5, 2011).

Seinfeld

The **sitcom** (situation comedy; see entry under 1950s—TV and Radio in volume 3) *Seinfeld,* which aired on NBC from 1990 to 1998, was one of the most successful programs in **television** (see entry under 1940s—TV and Radio in volume 3) history. Created by comedian Jerry Seinfeld (1954–) and writer Larry David (1947–), the series focused on the daily life of a moderately successful New York stand-up comic named Jerry Seinfeld. The main character was self-obsessed, immature, and concentrated on trivial matters and small details. He was surrounded by a core group of three friends: George Costanza (Jason Alexander, 1959–), a stocky, neurotic, balding loser; Elaine Benes (Julia Louis-Dreyfus, 1961–), a temperamental, single working-woman; and Cosmo Kramer (Michael Richards, 1949–), a bumbling "hipster doofus." The creators referred to their program as the "anti-sitcom" because there was none of the hugging or learning endemic to most situation comedies. The series

A scene about nothing from Seinfeld*: Julia Louis-Dreyfus (far left), Jerry Seinfeld, Michael Richards, and Jason Alexander.* © NBC-TV/THE KOBAL COLLECTION/ART RESOURCE, NY.

introduced many colorful characters and memorable catchphrases to the American public and is considered to be one of TV's best works of the 1990s.

More than thirty million viewers tuned in each week to see the *Seinfeld* foursome tangle with the minor annoyances of modern urban life. However, the program almost did not make it to the air. In 1989, NBC aired a pilot titled *The Seinfeld Chronicles* that was deemed "weak" by focus groups. Some executives feared the show was too hip, too urban, and too Jewish to appeal to the American masses. *Seinfeld* returned in 1991 as a mid-season replacement and soon emerged as the most important show of NBC's "Must See TV" Thursday lineup.

Seinfeld was unlike previous sitcoms in that nothing was considered sacred. Humor was mined from such taboo topics as the mentally and physically challenged, ethnic groups, religion, constipation, and masturbation. Every character the foursome encountered was ruled by his or her own weird obsessions and peculiarities. By the mid-1990s, the series was firmly at the center of American popular culture as terms like "Soup Nazi," "master of their domain," "Spongeworthy," and "Yadda, yadda, yadda" became national expressions.

According to A. J. Jacobs in *Entertainment Weekly*, "*Seinfeld* is faster, denser, and more dialogue-heavy than other sitcoms." The series dared to be pitiless, ironic, and emotionally distant in a format that prizes sentimentality. Jerry and his gang were detached from life's larger issues. They displayed a sense of skepticism and ironic detachment largely absent from network TV. When it ceased production in 1998, millions hailed the program, which was billed as "the show about nothing," as something truly special. The series finale was watched by seventy-six million people.

Charles Coletta

For More Information

Delaney, Tim. *Seinology: The Sociology of "Seinfeld."* Amherst, NY: Prometheus, 2006.

Fretts, Bruce. *The Entertainment Weekly Seinfeld Companion: Atomic Wedgies to Zipper Jobs; An Unofficial Guide to TV's Funniest Show.* New York: Warner Books, 1993.

Jacobs, A. J. "You've Been a Great Audience! Good Night!" *Entertainment Weekly* (August 3, 1998): pp. 4–8.

Lavery, David, and Sara Lewis Dunne. *"Seinfeld," Master of Its Own Domain: Revisiting Television's Greatest Sitcom.* New York: Continuum, 2006.

Seinfeld. http://www.spe.sony.com/tv/shows/seinfeld (accessed August 5, 2011).

Seinfeld, Jerry. *SeinLanguage.* New York: Bantam Books, 1993.

Seinfeld, Jerry, et al. *Sein Off: The Final Days of Seinfeld.* New York: Harper Entertainment, 1998.

Tracy, Kathleen. *Jerry Seinfeld: The Entire Domain.* Secaucus, NJ: Carol Publishing, 1998.

South Park

The animated comedy *South Park* premiered on Comedy Central in 1997 and immediately became one of the most controversial programs in **television** (see entry under 1940s—TV and Radio in volume 3) history. Created by Trey Parker (1969–) and Matt Stone (1971–), the series depicts the raunchy and bizarre adventures of a group of third graders living in South Park, Colorado. The main characters (all voiced by Stone

An animated crowd of friendly faces everywhere in South Park. © PHOTOFEST, INC.

and Parker) include Stan Marsh, Kyle Broslovski, Kenny McCormick, and Eric Cartman. The youngsters swear constantly, delight in coarse behavior, and disrespect adult authority. The program's profane humor is contrasted by its simplistic animation style, which imitates paper cut-outs.

South Park was a huge hit with teens, "twentysomethings," and even children. Many parents criticized the series for encouraging profanity and raunchiness in their kids. Despite vocal opposition, the series remained enormously popular and spawned a mountain of merchandise. Its memorable catch-phrase "They killed Kenny! You bastards!" was repeated often when the mumbling Kenny met a grisly end in every episode. In 1999, the characters moved to the silver screen to appear in *South Park: Bigger, Longer, Uncut,* a musical that was even more profanity-filled than the series. Parker and Stone continued the vulgar humor they popularized in *South Park* in a live-action **sitcom** (situation comedy; see entry under 1950s—TV and Radio in volume 3) titled *That's My Bush!* (2001), which featured the wacky antics of President George W. Bush (1946–). In 2011, the show concluded its fifteenth season. Parker and Stone were under contract with Comedy Central to create new shows until 2013.

Charles Coletta

For More Information

Arp, Robert. *"South Park" and Philosophy.* Malden, MA: Blackwell, 2007.
Gegax, T. Trent, et al. "South Park: The Rude Tube." *Newsweek* (March 23, 1998): pp. 56–62.
Parker, Trey, and Matt Stone. *"South Park" Guide to Life.* Philadelphia: Running Press, 2009.
SouthParkStudios.com. http://www.southparkstudios.com (accessed August 5, 2011).

Thomas the Tank Engine

Thomas the Tank Engine began life as a character in stories told by Reverend Wilbert Awdry (1911–1997) for his son, Christopher Awdry (1940–), who had measles. In May 1945, Awdry's first illustrated book, *The Three Railway Engines,* was published. In 1946, *Thomas the Tank Engine* appeared. Based on the adventures of Thomas, a small steam-powered locomotive on a British branch line, Awdry's stories sold well around the world. By 2001, Thomas the Tank Engine had become part of an international media franchise. Spin-offs from the books included a **television** (see entry under 1940s—TV and Radio in volume 3) series first broadcast in England from 1984 to 1998 and then on the **Public Broadcasting System** (PBS; see entry under 1960s—TV and Radio in volume 4) in the United States beginning in the 1990s, a feature film, replica toys, and games.

Thomas's adventures range from dealing with argumentative rail cars to racing against a road-going bus. However foolish he may be, cheeky Thomas always manages to win over Gordon and Henry, two snobbish mainline locomotives, and the company manager, Sir Topham Hatt. Awdry stopped writing books for the Railway Series in 1972. Christopher Awdry has continued his father's work since 1983. The toys based on the

Thomas the Tank Engine on track for another adventure. © PHOTOFEST, INC.

books have gained enormous popularity with parents of the early twenty-first century, mainly because of their low-tech wooden design.

Chris Routledge

For More Information

Sibley, Brian. *The "Thomas the Tank Engine" Man: The Story of the Reverend W. Awdry and His Really Useful Engines.* New York: Random House, 1996.

Thomas and Friends Website. http://www.thomasandfriends.com/usa/Thomas.mvc/Home (accessed August 5, 2011).

Who Wants to Be a Millionaire?

On August 16, 1999, America was introduced to the latest **game-show** (see entry under 1950s—TV and Radio in volume 3) sensation when *Who Wants to Be a Millionaire?* made its debut on the ABC network. The show was already a hit in Great Britain. Now, with new American host Regis Philbin (1933–), it became a blockbuster on the American side of the Atlantic as well. The light-hearted multiple-choice quiz program is widely credited with reviving the game-show genre.

Millionaire's creator was Michael P. Davies (1966–), a veteran British TV producer. The basis of the show was simple: contestants, who were selected by a telephone screening process, had to answer a series of increasingly difficult multiple-choice trivia questions, with an ever-increasing cash prize attached. To help contestants along, a variety of "lifelines" were provided, including the abilities to phone a friend and to

Host Regis Philbin asks Who Wants to Be a Millionaire? © PHOTOFEST, INC.

poll the live audience for answer suggestions. Its eerie space-age set and dramatic music distinguished the show from other game shows.

When *Millionaire* earned big ratings in Britain, Davies decided to try adapting it for American audiences. After an intensive search, morning talk-show host Philbin was selected as host. The friendly Philbin brought a mischievous flavor to the program with his New York accent and strange vocal rhythms, most notably his curious decision to emphasize the wrong word when saying the title question (he pronounced it "Who *wants* to be a millionaire"). A natural showman, Philbin soon developed his own signature lines when interacting with contestants. His oft-repeated question "Is that your final answer?" (later shortened to an abrupt "Final?") quickly began appearing on **T-shirts** (see entry under 1910s—Fashion in volume 1) and other merchandise. The question soon entered the list of classic TV catchphrases.

Who Wants to Be a Millionaire?'s popularity grew by strong word of mouth and the show was soon attracting huge audiences. Even after the initial appeal died down, the show remained a solid ratings winner for ABC. Its success inspired a revival of prime-time game shows. Some, like the British import *The Weakest Link,* proved fruitful, while others, like the imitative *Greed,* did not. Since 2002, *Who Wants to Be a Millionaire?* has been hosted by Meredith Vieira (1953–), former co-host of *The View* and ***Today*** (see entry under 1950s—TV and Radio in volume 3).

Robert E. Schnakenberg

For More Information

Fisher, David. *Who Wants to Be a Millionaire.* New York: Hyperion, 2000.
Philbin, Regis. *Who Wants to Be Me?* New York: Hyperion, 2000.

1990s

The Way We Lived

A strange thing happened in the 1990s, something that had not happened in nearly a hundred years: a technological revolution reoriented the entire economy and revolutionized the way people thought and the way they lived. The last time it had happened was at the turn of the twentieth century. Then, the spread of the automobile and its modern manufacturing processes changed the way people lived, worked, and thought about concepts like distance and time. In the 1990s, it was the Internet that changed everything.

Personal computers (PCs) had been growing in popularity through the 1980s, but it was the invention of the World Wide Web and the widespread use of e-mail (along with a host of other technological advances) that turned PCs from work machines into tools for living. The World Wide Web allowed individuals and businesses to share information with other computer users in a visually engaging way. E-mail allowed people to communicate instantaneously with friends or business contacts anywhere on earth that was connected to the Internet.

Soon people were shopping, chatting, falling in love, learning, and wasting time over the Internet—all at ever-increasing speeds. The number of Internet users in the United States and Canada rose from 18 million (or 6.7 percent of the population) in 1995 to 106.3 million (39.37 percent) in July 1999—and the number of users kept climbing throughout the decade, showing no indication of stopping. Because the Internet allowed people to always be connected, it changed the way they worked. Many Americans could now work at home and easily tap into the files they needed at their workplace. Laptop computers allowed them to take their work on the road. Cellular phones and beepers meant that people were never out of touch. As a result, the boundaries between work and regular life became blurred.

The Internet had its dark side as well. Chat rooms—online forums where people could meet and converse—became popular. Chat rooms allowed people to relate to others anonymously, but they sometimes allowed strangers to prey on the young or the unwary. Computer pirates called hackers took pleasure in their ability to penetrate supposedly secure computer sites, often with costly consequences. Computer viruses threatened to disrupt the increased productivity that computers allowed. The most feared computer glitch of the decade was the so-called Y2K bug, a problem embedded in every computer that analysts feared would wreak havoc when the year 1999 turned to 2000 on New Year's Day. Businesses and government spent billions preparing for Y2K and many feared economic disaster, but as the New Year turned, nothing happened.

The Internet was not the only story of the decade, however. Several dramatic events gripped the nation's attention. In 1993, the Branch Davidians, a religious cult led by a man who called himself David Koresh (1959–1993), engaged in a long standoff with the federal government. The standoff resulted in a massive blaze that killed between seventy and eighty people—and was shown live on TV. Exactly two years later, Timothy McVeigh (1968–2001) ignited a bomb in front of a federal office building in Oklahoma City, Oklahoma, that killed 168 people and destroyed the building.

The top story of the decade, however, was the trial of former football star O. J. Simpson (1947–) for the murder of his ex-wife and her friend. From the moment Simpson led police on a low-speed car chase through the streets of Los Angeles, to the investigation, and on through a trial that lasted for nine months, every moment of the saga was captured by TV cameras and broadcast live, turning the entire event into a spectacle. Simpson was acquitted of murder but became a social exile, and America was forced to grapple once again with its attitudes about race.

On the lighter side, American drug companies came up with a variety of treatments for the ills that beset people, such as Prozac for depression and Viagra for male impotence. Both drugs were eagerly sought even by those who did not experience real symptoms, and their use was widely covered in the media. Young people had their fixations as well. Early in the decade, small stuffed animals called Beanie Babies became such a hit that collectors began to bid the prices of the cute creatures up to unlikely heights. Late in the decade, the Pokémon craze hit. Young kids across the country poured over the latest Pokémon trading cards and watched Pokémon cartoons.

Aromatherapy

Scents have been used to enhance mood, relieve stress, and cure diseases for centuries. Aromatherapy, a version of this ancient practice, was "invented" in the 1930s but became truly popular in the early 1990s. National chains of beauty salons and spas began to provide relaxation services, such as massage, that included aromatic oils and incense.

The inhalation of the scent of various aromatic plants or the application to the skin as essential oils was thought to affect a person's mood. Although no regulations for aromatherapy products were in effect at the end of the twentieth century, many brands of aromatic oils and incense were sold for personal use across the nation. Among the brands are pure aromatic products, some made from chemical derivatives, and others produced by electronic technology and supplied via the **Internet** (see entry under 1990s—The Way We Lived in volume 5).

While aromatherapy is mostly limited to the use of scents for individual purposes, businesses have become interested in using aromas to influence larger numbers of people. At the beginning of the twenty-first century, some factories have vented in the scent of lemon and peppermint to increase worker productivity. Marketers have used "environmental fragrancing," filling stores with the pleasant scents of leather or flowers, to keep customers in shops longer. Lawyers have even tried to influence jurors by squirting scents near them. Although aromatherapy first gained attention as part of the growth of undocumented new-age health practices, studies in the first decade of the twenty-first century have suggested that definite antiviral and antibacterial properties exist in the essential oils used in aromatherapy, especially useful in the production of mouthwash.

Sara Pendergast

The typical aura of aromatherapy. © SHUTTERSTOCK.COM.

For More Information

AromaWeb. http://www.aromaweb.com (accessed August 7, 2011).

"Beyond Scratch and Sniff—Aromatherapy Points to the Healing Powers of Our Sense of Smell—or So Some Say." *Seattle Times* (March 15, 1992): p. 30.

Classen, Constance, David Howes, and Anthony Synnott. *Aroma: The Cultural History of Smell.* New York: Routledge, 1994.

Davis, Patricia. *Aromatherapy: An A–Z.* Rev. ed. London: Vermilion, 2005.

Farrer-Halls, Gill. *The Aromatherapy Bible.* New York: Sterling, 2005.

Holloway, Marguerite. "The Ascent of Scent." *Scientific American* (November 1999).

Keville, Kathi. *Aromatherapy for Dummies.* New York: Wiley, 1999.

Keville, Kathi, and Mindy Green. *Aromatherapy: A Complete Guide to the Healing Art.* 2nd ed. Berkeley, CA: Crossing Press, 2009.

"On the Nose: Scientists Say Aromas Have Major Effect on Emotions." *Los Angeles Times* (May 13, 1991): p. B3.

Beanie Babies

A batch of Beanie Babies, one of the 1990s' hottest-selling toy collectibles. © GINA KELLY/ ALAMY.

First introduced by toy company Ty, Inc., in 1993, Beanie Babies soon became one of the top-selling toys of the 1990s. Small stuffed animals with beanbag bottoms, each Beanie Baby comes with a heart-shaped tag containing the animal's name (such as Legs the frog, Flitter the butterfly, and Chocolate the moose) and a short poem. Popular with children, the toys were soon in demand among adults who often collected them because their value was rising. Stores could not keep Beanie Babies in stock. Customers lined up outside to wait when new shipments of the toys were due.

In 1996, almost a hundred million Beanie Babies were sold. Many collectors own dozens, trying to collect all 264 different animals. Collectors paid up to $13,000 for rare Beanies, though the retail price ranged from $5 to $7.

In what many thought was a clever sales plan, Ty, Inc., announced in 1999 that it would make no more Beanie Babies. After a public outcry and an **Internet** (see entry under 1990s—The Way We Lived in volume 5) vote, however, the company continued to sell Beanies. The popularity of Beanies waned throughout the early 2000s, although digital versions of the toys began to be marketed online starting in 2008 under "Beanie Babies 2.0." Buying Beanies over the Internet also entitled their owners to access a special interactive Web site devoted to the toys.

Tina Gianoulis

For More Information

"Bean There, Done That: Why Did Toy Mogul H. Ty Warner Pull the Plug on His Superpopular Beanie Babies?" *People Weekly* (September 20, 1999): pp. 72–74.

Fox, Les, and Sue Fox. *The Beanie Baby Handbook.* New York: Scholastic Press, 1998.

Samuels, Gary. "Mystique Marketing." *Forbes* (October 21, 1996): pp. 276–78.

Ty. http://www.ty.com (accessed April 2, 2002).

Branch Davidians

The Branch Davidians, a religious offshoot of the Seventh-Day Adventists, was founded by Benjamin Roden (1902–1978) in 1955. Upon his death in 1978, his wife, Lois Scott Roden (1905–1986), succeeded him; along with his son, George, the Rodens were challenged by a rival faction, led by Vernon Howell (1959–1993). Howell took control in 1987 and later changed his name to David Koresh (1959–1993).

Koresh claimed to be the Messiah and exercised absolute authority over his hundred or so followers, based at Mount Carmel Ranch near Waco, Texas. He claimed sexual rights over the women in the group; seven had children by him. Koresh also ordered the stockpiling of guns.

In February 1993, agents of the U.S. Bureau of Alcohol, Tobacco, and Firearms raided the compound to seize illegal weapons. Gunfire was exchanged, killing and wounding people on both sides. A fifty-one-day

The Mount Carmel Branch Davidians compound near Waco, Texas, engulfed in flames on April 19, 1993. © GERALD SCHUMANN/ NEWSCOM.

siege followed, with the FBI trying to negotiate Koresh's surrender. On April 19, tanks were sent in to flood the compound with tear gas. Fire broke out, but few Branch Davidians fled the blaze. Eighty-one of them, including Koresh, died inside. Exactly two years later, angry over the FBI's raid on the Branch Davidian compound, Timothy McVeigh (1968–2001) ignited a bomb in front of a federal office building in Oklahoma City, Oklahoma, that killed 168 people and destroyed the building. McVeigh was executed in 2001.

Justin Gustainis

For More Information

Linedecker, Clifford L. *Massacre at Waco, Texas.* New York: St. Martin's, 1993.

Reavis, Dick J. *The Ashes of Waco: An Investigation.* New York: Simon & Schuster, 1995.

Thibodeau, David. *A Place Called Waco: A Survivor's Story.* New York: PublicAffairs, 1999.

Treanor, Nick. *The Waco Standoff.* San Diego: Greenhaven Press, 2003.

"Waco." *Time.com.* http://www.time.com/time/daily/newsfiles/waco (accessed April 4, 2002).

Wright, Stuart. *Armageddon in Waco.* Chicago: University of Chicago Press, 1995.

Cellular Phones

Easily carried in purse or pocket, cellular **telephones** (see entry under 1900s—The Way We Lived in volume 1) are hand-held, wireless devices that became increasingly common throughout the world in the 1990s. Cellular phones permitted users to make and receive telephone calls from almost any location. Cellular phones are technically two-way **radios** because they rely on signals from antennas that have been installed across the landscape. Antennas are placed on buildings in cities and towns or on freestanding towers in rural areas. Each antenna emits a microwave signal that saturates the area, or cell, surrounding it. Signals are broadcast over a large number of channels, permitting many conversations to take place simultaneously, as with standard telephone service. As a caller travels across the service area, the transmission is relayed from one cell to another, usually without a noticeable break in the connection.

In 1981, the Federal Communications Commission (FCC) adopted the rules for cellular radiotelephone service by setting aside part of the

A woman has a conversation using an early, larger version of the cellular phone. © DAN HALLMAN/GETTY IMAGES.

800-MHz (megahertz) frequency band for two competing systems in each market. By August 2001, according to the FCC, there were more than thirty million cellular telephones in the United States and its possessions and territories, and more than twenty thousand cell sites. By 2010 it was estimated that 4.6 billion people had cell phones worldwide, many of which were **smart phones** (see entry under 2000s—The Way We Lived in volume 6), such as iPhones. Cellular telephones have also become very popular in countries, such as China, that do not have an extensive telephone system.

The widespread use of cellular telephones has created concerns about good manners and safety. Many people become annoyed at cell-phone users who carry on loud, personal conversations in restaurants, trains, parks, or other public places. In the wake of motor-vehicle accidents caused by cellular-phone distractions, some localities have enacted legislation prohibiting drivers from using the devices while their vehicles are in motion. Some consumer activists have raised concerns about the adverse effect of microwave signals on personal health, though sellers of the systems maintain that such concerns are exaggerated.

Edward Moran

For More Information

"Cellular Summary." *Federal Communications Commission.* http://wireless.fcc.gov/cellular/celfctsh.html (accessed August 7, 2011).

Hanson, Janice. *24/7: How Cell Phones and the Internet Change the Way We Live, Work, and Play.* Westport, CT: Praeger, 2007.

Stetz, Penelope. *The Cell Phone Handbook: Everything You Wanted to Know About Wireless Telephony (But Didn't Know Who or What to Ask).* 2nd ed. Newport, RI: Aegis, 2002.

Chat Rooms

Since the mid-1990s, when large numbers of people all over the world began going "online" to explore the **Internet** (see entry under 1990s—The Way We Lived in volume 5), millions of them have been chatting with each other in the many chat rooms that have emerged in cyberspace. Chat rooms can be described as the contemporary equivalent of the old "party line," the early telephone exchanges in which several customers shared the same number and thus could eavesdrop on one another's conversations. Today, anyone with Internet access and a password can enter into a conversation. Choices include any number of general chat rooms for anonymous socializing or special-interest chat rooms to discuss more specialized topics.

A typical chat room can consist of a dozen or more people using their keyboards to enter quick, pithy statements that are displayed in real time on the screen. To a novice, this can seem like a babble of disconnected voices. Regular users quickly get used to the art of following the discussion thread. Because of the condensed nature of the messages, chatters have developed a shorthand language of abbreviations: "sup" for "what's up?," "k" for "okay," "ic" for "I see," "lol" for "laughing out loud," and so on. Symbols called emoticons communicate meaning, too: for example, ":-)" for a smile, ":-(" for a frown, and "{}" for a hug.

Many chat room discussions seem trivial and even unintelligible, but others have become the digital equivalent of the corner bar or coffeeshop where regular customers routinely gather to "shoot the breeze." Some chat rooms have become serious forums for the exchange of information about topics such as medicine, architecture, food, history, and travel; others have become support groups for people dealing with stressful situations; still others have become informal dating services for people seeking romantic situations.

Chat rooms are seen by some experts as places that facilitate human interaction in a society that is itself anonymous. Advocates of global understanding praise chat rooms for creating a "global village" forum in which people from around the world can share information with each other. The relative privacy of chat rooms—in which anonymous participants are known only by their self-invented name or "handle"—has its downside, however. In a relatively few cases, strangers have taken advantage of trusting chatters to extract personal information or to arrange personal meetings that have resulted in criminal activity. The anonymity also allows people to explore other dimensions of their personalities. Some people crave the psychological insights they claim to receive while posing as a person of a different gender, race, or class. In the early 2000s, so-called "social networking" sites such as **Facebook** (see entry under 2000s—The Way We Lived in volume 6) began to take the place of chat rooms in fulfilling the social needs of Internet users.

Edward Moran

For More Information

Henderson, Harry. *The Internet.* San Diego: Lucent Books, 1998.
Komorn, Julie. *Chat Chat Chat.* New York: Scholastic, 1999.
Mutchler, Matthew. "Yes, Virginia, There Are Normal People in Cyberspace." *Zine 375.* http://eserver.org/zine375/cyberspace.html (accessed August 7, 2011).

Coffee

With its complex flavors and varied brewing methods, coffee is more than just a drink. Like lovers of fine wines, dedicated coffee drinkers seek out new blends and roasts. They spend hundreds of dollars on equipment to make the perfect cup of coffee. Paradoxically, coffee is also an everyday drink. In its powdered "instant" form, it can be made quickly or bought from vending machines. Coffee drinking has been traced back to sixth-century Yemen (pronounced YEH-men; a country in the southwestern corner of the Arabian Peninsula), but it became popular in Europe and

America in the seventeenth century. Most coffee contains caffeine, a mildly addictive chemical that increases heart rate, boosts appetite, and decreases or eliminates fatigue. Because of caffeine, coffee is the number-one morning "pick-me-up" in America. As of 2011, 58 percent of the adult population drank coffee, amounting to 110 million daily drinkers. As of 2004, the premium placed on high-quality beans among coffee aficionados made coffee the number-one export for twelve countries.

Most coffee is made from the roasted beans of the Arabica or the cheaper Robusta coffee plant. The two are often blended. The beans are ground up and infused with boiling water. This releases the flavor, the dark color, and the all-important caffeine. Arabica beans come from South America. Robusta is native to Africa, particularly Kenya. Because many Dutch colonies were based in those regions,

A typical coffeehouse menu board. © SHUTTERSTOCK.COM.

the Netherlands forms the center of the world coffee trade. Coffee is a difficult crop to grow and harvest and supply varies from year to year. For this reason, coffee is bought and sold like other precious commodities, such as gold and silver. There is even a coffee "futures" market, where traders gamble on the future price of the beans to secure the best deal.

The medical effects of caffeine are well understood. The drug affects the nervous system and to a lesser extent the digestive system. Coffee can be used to make users hungry on demand at breakfast time. Because it encourages digestion, it is also useful after a large meal. Medical opinion broadly agrees that up to three cups of coffee every day can be taken without ill effect. Many coffee drinkers develop a tolerance that allows them to drink much more than that. Some coffee drinkers experience rapid heartbeat and irritation of the stomach. Like other drug users, regular coffee drinkers experience withdrawal symptoms, such as headaches, if they are deprived of coffee for long periods.

The removal of caffeine from coffee prevents these side effects. Decaffeinated coffee first became popular at the end of the nineteenth century. Decaffeination can be done in several different ways. The most popular methods involve rinsing the beans in various chemicals. In the mid-1990s, there were fears that the process could cause cancer. This later turned out to be untrue. Since the nineteenth century, coffee experts have worked hard to get rid of the caffeine yet keep the drink's taste and aroma. Even so, many coffee drinkers find that "decaf" tastes metallic and thin when compared with the "real" thing.

Coffee's links with the arts, literature, and politics have always been strong. Coffeehouses and specialty cafés provide somewhere for people to meet and talk. Many offer newspapers and books for their customers to read and discuss. In the 1980s, specialty shops began to sell coffee at high prices, packaged to appeal to "discriminating" drinkers. The trend for "gourmet" coffee led to a rapid growth in the number of independent cafés in every American city. The Pacific Northwest became America's coffee capital. The international chain **Starbucks** (see entry under 1980s—Commerce in volume 5) began as a local coffeehouse in Seattle, Washington. In the seventeenth century, coffeehouses were places where poets, writers, and political activists met. Early coffeehouses were thought by many to be dangerous places. In the twenty-first century, coffee is more respectable. It is drunk in business meetings, at restaurants, and on the street.

Percolated coffee, popular in the 1950s, gradually gave way to the "drip" process, in which hot water is dripped through coffee grounds and filtered into a container. By far the biggest growth in coffee in the 1990s was in the popularity of espresso. Invented in Italy, espresso coffee is made by forcing boiling water through densely packed coffee grounds. The best espresso coffee is a thick, oily liquid with a film of light brown froth on the top. Often sold in tiny amounts that cost several dollars per cup, espresso coffee is a popular daytime drink due to its stimulating properties. For many commuters, collecting coffee from an "espresso shack" on their way to work has become part of their daily routine. Specialty shops have improved the quality of coffee around the world. However, some critics argue that the cultural importance of coffee has changed as well. In the seventeenth century, coffeehouses were places where people discussed politics, ideas, and the arts. In the twenty-first century, they are most often places where people talk about coffee.

Chris Routledge

For More Information

Allen, Stewart Lee. *The Devil's Cup: Coffee, the Driving Force in History.* New York: Soho, 1999.

Banks, Mary. *The World Encyclopedia of Coffee.* London: Anness, 1999.

Castle, Timothy James. *The Perfect Cup: A Coffee Lover's Guide to Buying, Brewing, and Tasting.* Reading, MA: Anis Books, 1998.

"Coffee." *National Geographic Society.* http://www.nationalgeographic.com/coffee (accessed December 23, 2011).

Coffee Science Source: The Online Source for Coffee, Caffeine and Health Information. http://www.coffeescience.org (accessed August 7, 2011).

Pendergrast, Mark. *Uncommon Grounds: The History of Coffee and How It Transformed Our World.* New York: Basic Books, 2000.

Weissman, Michaele. *God in a Cup: The Obsessive Quest for the Perfect Coffee.* Hoboken, NJ: Wiley, 2008.

Ecstasy

Ecstasy is the "street" name for MDMA (3, 4-Methylenedioxymethamphetamine), an amphetamine derivative that was made a controlled substance by the U.S. government in 1985. The drug stimulates serotonin (pronounced seh-reh-TOE-nin) production in the brain. The drug causes feelings of euphoria, or extreme well-being, lasting up to twelve hours, as well as the stimulant effects common to amphetamines.

MDMA was patented by a German firm in 1913 but was never marketed widely. It remained largely unknown until the mid-1970s, when some American psychotherapists began giving it to their patients, many of whom reported positive results. It also gained a reputation as a recreational drug, under the name "Ecstasy." Ecstasy became popular among young people attending all-night dance parties called **"raves"** (see entry under 1990s—Music in volume 5). Use of the drug has been increasing since the 1990s.

Medical research on MDMA has been limited in scope and the results inconsistent. Some studies have found long-term brain damage resulting from regular use of the drug. Other studies suggest that nerve damage can occur. In the early 2000s, clinical studies were underway to determine the benefits of MDMA in treating post-traumatic stress disorder (PTSD) and alleviating the stress experienced by people with terminal cancer.

Justin Gustainis

For More Information

Beck, Jerome, and Marsha Rosenbaum. *Pursuit of Ecstasy: The MDMA Experience.* Albany: State University of New York Press, 1994.

Connolly, Sean. *Ecstasy.* Chicago: Heinemann Library, 2001.

Eisner, Bruce. *Ecstasy: The MDMA Story.* 2nd ed. Berkeley, CA: Ronin, 1994.

Holland, Julie, ed. *Ecstasy: The Complete Guide.* Rochester, VT: Park Street Press, 2001.

Pilcher, Tim. *E: The Incredibly Strange History of Ecstasy.* Philadelphia: Running Press, 2008.

E-mail

Although the technology was invented in the 1960s, the popularity of e-mail took off in the 1990s. As the cost of connecting computers to the **Internet** (see entry under 1990s—The Way We Lived in volume 5) fell, e-mail became the easiest way for computer users to send written messages to one another. Its advantages over the regular mail are speed, convenience, and low cost. Word-processed documents, images, sounds, and moving pictures can be e-mailed around the world in a matter of seconds. While "snail mail" (via the postal system or an overnight service) is still important for transporting packages, legal documents, and the like, e-mail has become the key personal and business communication tool of the twenty-first century.

The much-used symbol for e-mail. © VEERACHAI VITEEMAN/ SHUTTERSTOCK.COM.

Since the 1990s, e-mail has revolutionized global communications. Curiously, it was developed during the **Cold War** (1945–91; see entry under 1940s—The Way We Lived in volume 3), a period when global communications were highly restricted. The U.S. Defense Department's Advanced Research Projects Agency (ARPA) came up with e-mail as a way of communicating between computers in distant government facilities. At first, this was limited to computers within ARPA. In the mid-1970s, it was discovered that users from outside were using the network to send messages to one another. In the twenty-first century, Internet service providers use a very similar system to store messages in personal electronic mailboxes that subscribers can access at will.

E-mail is not just a communication tool. It has also changed how language is used. E-mails tend to be less formal than a letter, so "Dear Christopher" might be replaced with a more relaxed "Hi!" E-mails can be written as the sender might speak but, unlike speech, there is no tone of voice, facial expression, or body language to help indicate meaning. Emoticons, symbols "drawn" using the computer keyboard, work around this problem. Some e-mailers add a **smiley face** (see entry in 1990s—The Way We Lived in volume 5) to show they are joking or an unhappy face to express displeasure. The spread of **cellular telephones** (see entry under 1990s—The Way We Lived in volume 5) in the late 1990s took this further. Text messaging, or "texting," between cell phones—especially **smart phones** (see entry under 2000s—The Way

We Lived in volume 6)—is a form of e-mail, but the difficulty of typing text using a ten-digit telephone keypad soon led "2 a nu 4m" of spelling.

As long ago as the early 1970s, e-mail was used by political campaigners to work for the impeachment of President Richard M. Nixon (1913–1994). By the late 1980s, it enabled activists in China and the former Soviet bloc countries to communicate with journalists and supporters in the West. News of the buildup to the Tiananmen Square massacre in Beijing in 1989 emerged by e-mail, as did information about the revolutions in Eastern Europe in the late 1980s and early 1990s. By the late 1990s, most governments had realized the value of e-mail and the Internet in creating an impression of openness. In 2001, Russian president Vladimir Putin (1952–) went one step further, answering questions sent in by e-mail on a live "Webcast."

Although e-mail communication can be informal, friendly, and liberating, it can also be a problem. E-mail allows writers to hide their identities behind invented names, something twenty-first-century criminals are all too ready to exploit. Adult sex offenders can pose as children in online discussion forums called **chat rooms** (see entry under 1990s—The Way We Lived in volume 5) with the aim of luring real children to a dangerous in-person meeting. Not being able to see the person with whom one is interacting makes it easier for some people to be insulting or offensive. Sending offensive, attacking e-mail is known as "flaming." It is most common in online communities like newsgroups or chat rooms, in which people do not know each other well.

The ability to copy one message to huge numbers of addresses makes e-mail ideal for sending bulk advertising messages, or "spam," to many thousands of people. These e-mails are usually unwanted. By 2001, they were becoming less common as legitimate advertisers realized spam was putting off customers and laws were enacted forbidding its use. More popular are "chain" e-mails. These work in the same way as a standard chain letter, but the speed of e-mail means they can circle the globe in a matter of hours. Chain e-mails use up space in mailboxes and waste a great deal of human time and energy. For this reason, chain e-mails can be more costly to business than software-based computer viruses.

In fact, the most serious problems with e-mail are also the problems with older forms of written communication. The speed and simplicity of e-mail simply makes problems more intense. All of the benefits of e-mail, however, are new. Documents can be shared over distances of thousands of miles and senders can receive almost instant responses. E-mailers can communicate with groups of others simultaneously. Travelers can make contact with friends, relatives, or employers without being tied to telephone calls. E-mail has brought major changes to how people regard their work, think about where they live, and who they consider part of their community. In the 1990s, it triggered a revolution in working at home—"telecommuting"—that by the twenty-first century had become quite common, with one 2011 survey reporting that nearly 25 percent of American workers did some of their work from home.

Chris Routledge

For More Information

Freeman, John. *The Tyranny of E-mail: The Four-Thousand-Year Journey to Your Inbox.* New York: Scribner, 2009.

Hafner, Katie, and Matthew Lyon. *Where Wizards Stay Up Late: The Origins of the Internet.* New York: Simon & Schuster, 1996; also available at http://www.olografix.org/gubi/estate/libri/wizards/email.html (accessed August 7, 2011).

Jordan, Shirley. *From Smoke Signals to E-mail: Moments in History.* Logan, IA: Perfection Learning, 2000.

Rothman, Kevin F. *Coping with Dangers on the Internet: Staying Safe Online.* New York: Rosen, 2001.

Shipley, David, and Will Schwalbe. *Send: Why People Email So Badly and How to Do It Better.* New York: Knopf, 2008.

Tunstall, J. *Better, Faster Email: Getting the Most Out of Email.* New York: Allen and Unwin, 1999.

Wolinsky, Art. *The History of the Internet and the World Wide Web.* Springfield, NJ: Enslow, 1999.

Hackers

Even though much of the world's business, political, and social life is conducted electronically, most people who use computers have little understanding of how they actually work. Computer hackers, on the other hand, seem to possess the keys to understanding and controlling computers that many computer users lack. Admired by some, hated by others, and feared by many, hackers are part of an intellectual subculture whose members love computers and also love the challenge of breaking into computer security systems, often simply to prove that it can be done.

Though the term "hacker" has been used for several decades to label those who illegally break into computer systems, it was first used in the mid-1960s at the Massachusetts Institute of Technology (MIT) to mean a highly skilled computer addict. Hacking in its modern sense first became widely known in 1985, when the movie *War Games* introduced a good-hearted teenage hacker whose skill at breaking into computers almost brings about World War III.

In 1988, hackers received more publicity when a group of Cornell University graduate students created a computer virus, nicknamed the Internet Worm, that crashed six thousand computers around the country and shut down the **Internet** (see entry under 1990s—The Way We Lived in volume 5) for two days. Since then, the vulnerability of computer systems to clever hackers has been the source of worry for many. In spite of ever-increasing security measures, corporation and government computers have proved vulnerable to attack over and over. In 1995 alone, hackers attempted to break into U.S. Defense Department computers 258,000 times—and over half of the attempts were successful. By the early 1990s, hackers were organizing groups and meeting across the globe to discuss issues related to their craft. The largest U.S. conference is DEF CON, which has taken place since 1993. In 2010, DEF CON was attended by ten thousand people.

Some hackers use their skills to damage or shut down computer systems. Others have altered computer data in order to steal money. However, many hackers do not break into computers for vandalism or personal gain. These hackers often feel rebellious towards authority and wish to cross computer boundaries simply to prove that they can. Some people respect or romanticize these hackers as defenders of freedom on the Internet. Law enforcement officials view computer hacking as a serious crime, however, and prosecute hackers as criminals.

Some hackers who have been convicted of computer crimes, and others who simply want to keep access to the Internet open and free, work *with* the authorities. They seek out spots where computer systems are vulnerable to hacking and help make them more secure, as well as assisting in the development of Internet security measures.

Tina Gianoulis

For More Information

Brand, Stewart. "We Owe It All to the Hippies: Forget Antiwar Protests, Even Long Hair: The Real Legacy of the Sixties Generation Is the Computer Revolution." *Time* (Vol. 145, no. 12, Spring 1995): pp. 54–57.

"A Brief History of Hackers and the Internet." *Current Events* (Vol. 99, iss. 20, March 10, 2000): p. 2.

Hafner, Katie, and John Markoff. *Cyberpunk: Outlaws and Hackers on the Computer Frontier.* New York: Simon & Schuster, 1991.

Levy, Steven. *Hackers: Heroes of the Computer Revolution.* New York: Penguin Putnam, 1984.

Mitnick, Kevin D. *The Art of Intrusion.* Indianapolis: Wiley, 2005.

Mitnick, Kevin D. *Ghost in the Wires: My Adventures as the World's Most Wanted Hacker.* New York: Little, Brown, 2011.

Roush, Wade. "Hackers: Taking a Byte Out of Computer Crime." *Technology Review* (Vol. 98, no. 3, April 1995): pp. 32–41.

Internet

The Internet was probably the single most important influence on American culture in the final few years of the twentieth century. The Internet provided Americans with an incredibly diverse set of tools—not only did **e-mail** (see entry under 1990s—The Way We Lived in volume 5) revolutionize the way people communicated with one another, but the World Wide Web brought information, entertainment, new ways of shopping, and access to government into American homes. By 2001, the Internet had been available to a mass audience for less than a decade. In that short amount of time, it had sparked debates about censorship, challenged legal systems around the world, and altered the way stock markets operate. It added new words to the English language, including "Web site," "download," and "Internet." It has also revolutionized **advertising** (see entry under 1920s—Commerce in volume 1), triggered a growth in new journals and magazines unseen since the seventeenth century, and caused turmoil in the global economy.

One of the most exciting things about the Internet is that it manages to be old and new at the same time. It has been widely available only since the mid-1990s, yet by then it was already almost thirty years old. With roots going back to the telegraph networks of the nineteenth century, the Internet of 2001 was originally dreamed up by the military in the late 1960s. In 1969, the Advanced Research Projects Agency Network (ARPANET) was created to link computers around the country. At first, it included just twenty computers, or "nodes," that communicated using a special language. The real beauty of the system was that it could find the best and easiest route to send information. If a node was destroyed, the system would keep on working. The Internet of the twenty-first century works in a similar way.

Although universities began to use the system in the 1970s, in its early years the Internet was tightly controlled by the military. In 1979, there were just 188 "host" computers. Twenty years later, there were over fifty-six million. Even in the 1970s, the advantages were obvious. E-mail allowed messages to be sent to hundreds of people at the same time. Discussion areas called news groups allowed users to talk to people around the world about subjects in which they had a common interest. For those using it in the 1970s and 1980s, the Internet was a dream come true. It was free from advertising, free from corporate control, and most importantly, free from censorship.

The invention of the World Wide Web (WWW) in 1990 made the Internet available to a mass audience. Created by Tim Berners-Lee (1955–) at the European Laboratory for Particle Physics (CERN), "World Wide Web" was the name of the very first browser software. Until then, the Internet was difficult to use. There were no graphics, and users had to understand a series of complex computer commands. "Surfing" was impossible because documents had to be downloaded before they could be read. Berners-Lee's browser made "hypertext" links connecting one document to another more effective. It also allowed documents to be accessed directly on screen. The first WWW server (info.cern.ch) was set up at the CERN laboratories in Switzerland in 1991.

Government schemes on both sides of the Atlantic made the Internet available in schools in the early 1990s, while CERN made its Web technology freely available. Soon the spread of **personal computers** (see entry under 1970s—The Way We Lived in volume 4) made the Internet a powerful cultural force. From about 1994, once enough people had access to the Web in their homes, companies sprang up to advertise and trade there. Known as "dotcoms," they were so named because their World Wide Web addresses typically ended with ".com" (for "company"). Companies selling everything from books to gardening tools, and offering services from stock-market trading to online auctions, appeared in a matter of months. In the late 1990s, dotcoms seemed to offer unlimited growth and profits. Billions of dollars poured into companies that had little or no chance of survival. The money was lost just as quickly when high-tech stock markets around the world collapsed in 2000.

By the end of the twentieth century, the Internet was settling in as an important information and entertainment medium. In the twenty-first century, people consult the Internet for medical, legal, gardening, and cooking advice. Using the Internet, they can access the world's libraries and information archives, as well as music, films, and computer software. Court rulings have tried to protect traditional industries such as music publishing from having work copied and shared for free, but the fact is that the Internet was designed to find ways around restrictions. This worries some commentators, who see the Internet as a provider of pornography, hate literature, and damaging "virus" software. They see it as a threat to traditional business, education, and government. The more optimistic believe that it has given people freedom to express themselves. As its short, turbulent history shows, the Internet has always been unpredictable, as was evidenced by the **Y2K scare** (see entry under 2000s—The Way We Lived in volume 5), during which computer security experts predicted (wrongfully, it turned out) that the World Wide Web would cease to function at the exact moment of transition between 1999 and 2000, a prediction that created global panic. Whether or not the Internet's effect on culture and society will be for the better is in the hands of the people who use it.

Chris Routledge

For More Information

Gralla, Preston, and Michael Toller. *How the Internet Works.* 8th ed. Indianapolis: Que, 2007.

Hafner, Katie, and Matthew Lyon. *Where Wizards Stay Up Late: The Origins of the Internet.* New York: Touchstone Books, 1998.

Leiner, Barry, et al. "A Brief History of the Internet." *Internet Society.* http://www.isoc.org/internet/history/brief.shtml (accessed August 7, 2011).

Levine, John R., and Margaret Levine Young. *The Internet for Dummies.* 13th ed. Hoboken, NJ: Wiley, 2011.

Segaller, Stephen. *Nerds 2.0.1: A Brief History of the Internet.* New York: TV Books, 1998.

Sterling, Bruce. "A Short History of the Internet." *ebookbrowse.* http://ebookbrowse.com/bruce-sterling-a-short-history-of-the-internet-pdf-d14603487 (accessed December 24, 2011).

Wolinsky, Art. *The History of the Internet and the World Wide Web.* Berkeley Heights, NJ: Enslow, 1999.

Zakon, Robert H. *Hobbes' Internet Timeline v5.3.* http://www.zakon.org/robert/internet/timeline/ (accessed August 7, 2011).

Pokémon

Created in 1996 as a game for the Nintendo Game Boy hand-held gaming console, Pokémon (pronounced "POH-kay-mon") soon became a worldwide youth phenomenon. Seen in **video games** (see entry under 1970s—Sports and Games in volume 4), **Saturday morning cartoons** (see entry under 1960s—TV and Radio in volume 4), films, books, and thousands of trading cards, Pokémon (short for "pocket monsters") is a unique world, populated by over 150 creatures with magical powers that enable them to transform themselves into stronger and stronger monsters. Children around the globe have been captivated by the world of Pokémon, collecting the pocket monsters and memorizing their names and powers with a skill that often amazes their parents.

It took game designer Satoshi Tajiri (1965–) six years to design his imaginative new game, designed for use on the Nintendo Game Boy. Inspired by the bug collections he made in his youth and the outlandish monsters he had seen in old Japanese **horror movies** (see entry under 1960s—Film and Theater in volume 4), he created "Poketto Monsuta" (Japanese for "Pocket Monsters"). After its release in Japan in 1996, the new game was an instant hit. Soon after, millions of Japanese children were watching Pokémon cartoons on TV and collecting trading cards and other Pokémon products. The game was introduced in the United States in 1998, followed shortly by the TV series in the same year. Within a month, *Pokémon* was the most-watched children's show in the United States. By 2011, fourteen Pokémon movies had been released, and dozens of books of Pokémon adventures, making Pokémon a multibillion-dollar business and the second-most profitable videogame franchise in the world, after the "Mario" series, also produced by Nintendo.

In the game and in the cartoon show, the goal is basically the same: players must capture and befriend small, fantastically shaped creatures with names like Pikachu, Squirtle, and Charmander. Once captured, monster trainers must prepare their Pokémon for battle with the Pokémon of other trainers. Once trained, Pokémon transform themselves into different, but related creatures. For example, Charmander transforms first into Charmeleon, then into Charizard.

Although many adults appreciate the creativity and imagination of the Pokémon world, others worry that the fad encourages children to spend too much time and money collecting the hundreds of different

Pokémon products. Some even fear that Pokémon is dangerous to children. In Turkey, several children were injured jumping from roofs like the flying monsters they saw on **television** (see entry under 1940s—TV and Radio in volume 3). In Japan, in 1997, some doctors claimed that a rapidly blinking light on the *Pokémon* cartoon made some children suffer seizures.

Tina Gianoulis

For More Information

Deacon, James, and Susan McClelland. "The Craze That Ate Your Kids." *Maclean's* (November 8, 1999): pp. 74–79.

Pojo's Unofficial Big Book of Pokémon: The Complete Player and Collector's Guide to Every Card and Character. Chicago: Triumph Books, 2000.

Pokémon.com: The Official Pokémon Web Site. http://www.pokemon.com (accessed August 7, 2011).

Radford, Benjamin. "The Pokémon Panic of 1997." *Skeptical Inquirer* (Vol. 25, iss. 3, May 2001): pp. 26–30.

O. J. Simpson (1947–)

O. J. Simpson—football star, media personality, and murder suspect—has been both revered and reviled by the American public. In the 1960s and 1970s, Simpson won fame as a record-breaking college and professional football player. After his retirement from sports, he enjoyed a career as a movie and **television** (see entry under 1940s—TV and Radio in volume 3) actor, sportscaster, and star of TV commercials. Then, in the mid-1990s, he became the focal point of one of the twentieth-century's most notorious, controversial, and media-hyped murder cases.

Orenthal James Simpson grew up in San Francisco, California, and had a troublesome childhood. At age two, he suffered from rickets, a disease caused by a deficiency of vitamin D. Rickets can cause soft and deformed bones in growing children, and Simpson wore leg braces for the next three years. When he was thirteen, he joined the Persian Warriors, a street **gang** (see entry under 1980s—The Way We Lived in volume 5). Eventually, his life became consumed by athletics. He starred as a football player at the University of Southern California, rushing for 3,187 yards during the 1967 and 1968 seasons while scoring 34 touchdowns. In 1968, he set a National Collegiate Athletic Association (NCAA)

A confident-looking O. J. Simpson (right) and his attorney, Johnnie Cochran, at his murder trial in March 1995. © MYUNG J. CHUN/ NEWSCOM.

record of 334 carries in a season and 1,654 yards gained. He was an All-American during both years and won the Heisman Trophy as the most outstanding college football player in 1968.

The Buffalo Bills of the **National Football League** (NFL; see entry under 1920s—Sports and Games in volume 2) selected Simpson as their number-one draft pick in 1969. During his tenure with the Bills from 1969 through 1977, he scored 70 touchdowns and rushed for 10,183 yards on 2,123 carries. In 1972, he was the American Football Conference (AFC) Player of the Year. The following year, he became the first NFL player to rush for over 2,000 yards in a season, finishing with 2,003 yards, and was named the league's Most Valuable Player. Then in 1975, he rushed for 1,817 yards, scored 23 touchdowns—yet another NFL record—and was again named league MVP. Simpson retired after playing briefly for the San Francisco 49ers, was elected to the Pro Football Hall of Fame, and was named to the NFL's Seventy-fifth Anniversary Team.

After his NFL retirement, Simpson remained in the public eye. He was handsome and had a friendly smile and an amiable public personality, which made him a natural for movies and television. He began acting professionally well before leaving football. While in college, he appeared on episodes of several TV series. He made his screen debut in *The Klansman* (1974) and *The Towering Inferno* (1974) and also appeared in *Killer Force* (1975), *The Cassandra Crossing* (1976), *Capricorn One* (1978), *Firepower* (1979), three *Naked Gun* films (released in 1988, 1991, and 1994), and a number of TV series and made-for-TV movies. He became a football broadcaster, working for ABC and NBC, and starred in a number of commercials for Hertz rental cars. It would be no exaggeration to have described Simpson at the time as one of America's most likable, highest-profile celebrities.

Then in 1994, Simpson was accused of the murders of Nicole Brown Simpson (1959–1994), his ex-wife, and Ronald Goldman (1968–1994), her friend. The killings took place on the night of June 12, on the front steps of Nicole's condominium in Brentwood, a well-to-do Southern California community. The world watched as the slayings first were reported. In subsequent days, Simpson was questioned by the authorities. Then he was notified that he was to be arrested and charged with the killings. Instead of surrendering to the police, Simpson penned a note for the media and fled in a white Ford Bronco. Television cameras followed the car as it traversed the Los Angeles–area freeways with the police on its tail, a real-life drama unfolding before the eyes of millions. The chase ended at Simpson's Rockingham estate, where he was placed under arrest and led off to the L.A. County Jail.

Simpson was arraigned and eventually entered an "absolutely 100 percent not guilty" plea. The six-day preliminary hearing and nine-month trial became an American obsession, consuming hours upon hours of television airtime. The major networks televised them in whole or in part, and the cable news stations boosted their rating with wall-to-wall coverage followed by detailed analysis of the unfolding events and heated pro- and anti-Simpson debate. Additionally, various prosecuting and defense attorneys, homicide detectives, witnesses, journalists, and legal analysts emerged as celebrities, coming away with book deals and, in some cases, their own TV shows.

Just after Simpson's arraignment, the district attorney's office leaked to the media a tape of a 911 telephone call that a frantic and fearful Nicole Brown Simpson had made in October 1993. On the tape, she tearfully pleads for assistance as an angry Simpson yells and swears in the background. This was the first hint that Simpson's easygoing public personality was a sham. Two earlier instances of domestic violence between the Simpsons eventually were revealed. However, audiences wondered, did the fact that the Simpsons' relationship was often volatile mean that O. J. was capable of killing Nicole? Was there any hard evidence proving his guilt?

In the end, the case's notoriety derived as much from the defendant's race as from the nature of the crimes and his celebrity status. As the trial ran its course, many were pro- or anti-Simpson based solely on the fact that he was an African American. After the closing arguments, the jury—which consisted mostly of African Americans—deliberated for only four hours before rendering a not-guilty verdict. The announcement was made on October 3, 1995. Simpson was freed because of his attorneys' ability to convince the jury that a combination of crime-lab ineptitude and police impropriety—including possible evidence planting and tampering—resulted in making an innocent man appear guilty. Simpson's lawyers, who came to be known as the "Dream Team," successfully played what came to be known as the "race card," implying that Mark Fuhrman (c. 1952–), one of the case's original investigating detectives, was a racist. They believed that Fuhrman had both the motive and the opportunity to remove a bloody glove from the crime scene and plant it in Simpson's house. Ultimately, those who were pro-Simpson believed that justice won out with his acquittal, yet many who felt he was guilty were convinced that the jury voted him free in an act of racial solidarity.

Simpson's time in court was not yet over. The family of Ronald Goldman had filed a wrongful death lawsuit against him, which resulted in a civil trial. In this trial, unlike during the murder trial, Simpson was called to the witness stand. On February 4, 1997, a predominantly white jury found him liable for the wrongful deaths of Nicole Brown Simpson and Ronald Goldman and assessed him $33 million in damages, although Simpson did not pay much of this fine. In 2008 Simpson was convicted of armed robbery and kidnapping and was sentenced to thirty-three years in jail. As of 2012, he was serving his sentence at the Lovelock Correctional Center in Nevada. To this day, Simpson's guilt or innocence in the murders of his estranged wife and Goldman remains a favorite topic of debate for many Americans.

Rob Edelman

For More Information

Baker, Jim. *O. J. Simpson's Most Memorable Games.* New York: Putnam, 1978.

Bosco, Joseph. *A Problem of Evidence: How the Prosecution Freed O. J. Simpson.* New York: William Morrow, 1996.

Bugliosi, Vincent. *Outrage.* New York: W. W. Norton., 1996.

Clark, Marcia, and Teresa Carpenter. *Without a Doubt.* New York: Viking, 1997.

Cochran, Johnnie L., and Tim Rutten. *Journey to Justice.* New York: Ballantine, 1996.

Darden, Christopher, with Jess Walter. *In Contempt.* New York: Regan Books, 1996.

Dershowitz, Alan. *Reasonable Doubts.* New York: Simon & Schuster, 1996.

Devaney, John. *O. J. Simpson: Football's Greatest Runner.* New York: Warner Paperback Library, 1974.

Elias, Tom, and Dennis Schatzman. *The Simpson Trial in Black and White.* Los Angeles: General Publishing Group, 1996.

Fox, Larry. *The O. J. Simpson Story: Born to Run.* New York: Dodd, Mead, 1974.

Fuhrman, Mark. *Murder in Brentwood.* Washington: Regnery, 1997.

Gibbs, Jewelle Taylor. *Race and Justice: Rodney King and O. J. Simpson in a House Divided.* San Francisco: Jossey-Bass, 1996.

Gilbert, Mike. *How I Helped O. J. Get Away with Murder.* Washington: Regnery, 2008.

Goldberg, Hank. *The Prosecution Responds.* New York: Birch Lane Press, 1996.

Gutman, Bill. *O. J.* New York: Grosset & Dunlap, 1974.

Kennedy, Tracy, Judith Kennedy, and Alan Abrahamson. *Mistrial of the Century.* Beverly Hills, CA: Dove Books, 1995.

Knox, Michael, with Mike Walker. *The Private Diary of an O.J. Juror.* Beverly Hills, CA: Dove Books, 1995.

Lange, Tom, and Philip Vannatter, as told to Dan E. Moldea. *Evidence Dismissed.* New York: Pocket Books, 1997.

Morrison, Toni, and Claudia Brodsky Lacour, eds. *Birth of a Nation'hood: Gaze, Script, and Spectacle in the O. J. Simpson Case.* New York: Pantheon, 1997.

Petrocelli, Daniel, with Peter Knobler. *Triumph of Justice: The Final Judgment on the Simpson Saga.* New York: Crown, 1998.

Roberts, Peter. *OJ: 101 Theories, Conspiracies, & Alibis.* Diamond Bar, CA: Goldtree Press, 1995.

Schiller, Lawrence, and James Willwerth. *American Tragedy: The Uncensored Story of the Simpson Defense.* New York: Avon, 1995.

Shapiro, Robert, with Larkin Warren. *The Search for Justice.* New York: Warner, 1996.

Simpson, O. J. *I Want to Tell You.* Boston: Little Brown, 1995.

Singular, Stephen. *Legacy of Deception.* Beverly Hills, CA: Dove Books, 1995.

Toobin, Jeffrey. *The Run of His Life: The People vs. O. J. Simpson.* New York: Random House, 1996.

Uelmen, Gerald F. *Lessons from the Trial: The People vs. O. J. Simpson.* Kansas City, MO: Andrews McMeel, 1996.

WWJD? (What Would Jesus Do?)

The simple question "What would Jesus do?"—often abbreviated with the initials "WWJD?"—sparked a youth-based revival of Christian faith in the 1990s and became one of the marketing sensations of the decade. The WWJD? movement started in 1989 when Janie Tinklenberg, a youth leader at an evangelical church in Holland, Michigan, led a book discussion with her youth group. The book under discussion was *In His Steps,* an inspirational story penned in 1896 by minister Charles M. Sheldon (1857–1946). The book told of a congregation who experienced spiritual and moral renewal when they asked themselves "What would Jesus do?" in every situation they encountered.

Sheldon's book had already sold millions of copies and inspired many over the course of the twentieth century. In the 1990s, however, his simple message became the center of renewed spiritual fervor and a merchandising boom. Youth leader Tinklenberg approached a nearby company, the Lesco Corp., and asked if they could make a woven bracelet bearing the initials "WWJD?" that young Christians could wear as a sign of their faith. The bracelets were immediately popular, and not just in Michigan. During the first seven years of marketing, Lesco sold three hundred thousand bracelets. In 1997, radio announcer Paul Harvey (1918–2009) mentioned the bracelets on his program and sales exploded, reaching fifteen million by year's end. Lesco and other companies soon began selling a broad range of WWJD? merchandise,

WWJD? (What Would Jesus Do?) fish logo. © DYNAMIC GRAPHICS GROUP/JUPITERIMAGES/GETTY IMAGES.

including mugs, key chains, jewelry, **T-shirts** (see entry under 1910s—Fashion in volume 1), and other items at Christian book stores and Web sites.

By 1998, the WWJD? phenomenon had gone national. Major retailers like **Wal-Mart, Kmart** (see these entries under 1960s—Commerce in volume 4), and Barnes and Noble offered WWJD? merchandise, and WWJD?-based sermons and youth groups swept through Christian congregations. Fore-Front Records released a WWJD? **compact disc** (see entry under 1980s—Music in volume 5) with music by Christian groups. The Zondervan publishing company issued a WWJD? Interactive Devotional Bible. Beverly Courrege's book *WWJD?: Think About It* became a **best-seller** (see entry under 1940s—Commerce in volume 3). Supporters of the trend praised the new devotion to Jesus's teachings, but critics wondered whether Jesus himself would approve of the vigorous marketing of his teachings and the profits that such marketers were earning. In 2010, a film titled *What Would Jesus Do?,* starring Adam Gregory (1987–), was released straight to the DVD format.

Tom Pendergast

For More Information

Beaudoin, Tom. "A Peculiar Contortion." *America* (September 18, 1999): pp. 16–19.

Courrege, Beverly. *WWJD?: Think About It.* Nashville: Thomas Nelson, 1998.

Nussbaum, Emily. "Status Is … for Evangelical Teen-Agers, Jewelry for Jesus." *New York Times Magazine* (November 15, 1998): pp. 6, 93.

Sheldon, Charles M. *In His Steps: "What Would Jesus Do?"* Chicago: Advance Publishing, 1899; Westwood, NJ: Barbour and Co., 1989.

What Would Jesus Do?: The Official Website. http://www.wwjd.com (accessed August 7, 2011).

Y2K Scare

As the end of the twentieth century and the end of the second millennium approached, governments, corporations, and people around the world worried that their computer systems would stop working. The reason for this concern lay in conditions created in the early days of computing. To save memory and computing power, early programmers used a two-digit date system, which listed the year 2000 (Y2K) as "00."

"Y2K-ready" sticker. © RYAN MCVAY/PHOTODISC/JUPITERIMAGES/GETTY IMAGES.

This meant that when the date clicked over from 1999 to 2000, many of the world's computers would think it was 1900. It was feared that many would stop working altogether because of internal signal conflicts. On planes, at military installations, and in medical life-support systems, the consequences could be disastrous.

In the closing years of the twentieth century, countries spent billions of dollars correcting computer systems to make them "Y2K compliant." Banks, social security systems, and food distribution centers were all thought to be at risk. World leaders tried hard to reassure citizens that the problem was under control. In fact, there was more to the "millennium bug" than just New Year's Eve. Back in the 1970s, programmers used the number 9999 to mark the end of a sequence of commands. This meant that the date 9/9/99 was also potentially a problem. Developing countries were furthest behind. Not only were their computers older, and therefore more at risk, but they could not afford to fix the Y2K bug. In early 1999, the World Bank found that only 21 of 139 developing countries had done anything about it.

The Y2K scare created a global panic, but as midnight came and went on January 1, 2000, no computer glitches were reported. Cynics attributed the hysteria about the bug to computing companies cashing in on a nonexistent problem. In an age uncomfortable with its reliance on technology, the end of the millennium was bound to create superstitious fears. Whether the Y2K problem was solved in the nick of time, or was not really there at all, will probably never be known for sure. Some computer systems actually did experience difficulty as the year turned to 2010, a situation known as the "Y2K+10" problem. This was attributed to discrepancies between computers that operated with a hexadecimal system and those that ran on a binary decimal system. The most serious problem of this nature happened in Germany, where some twenty million ATM cards ceased to function.

Chris Routledge

For More Information

Brallier, Jess M. *Y2Kids: Your Guide to the Millennium.* New York: Grosset & Dunlap, 1999.

Everything 2000: Computer Y2K. http://www.everything2000.com/computer/a_computer.asp (accessed December 27, 2011).
Savage, Jeff. *Y2K.* Austin, TX: Raintree Steck-Vaughn, 1999.
Yourdon, Edward, and Jennifer Yourdon. *Time Bomb 2000: What the Year 2000 Computer Crisis Means to You.* 2nd ed. Upper Saddle River, NJ: Prentice Hall, 1999.

Where to Learn More

The following list of resources focuses on material appropriate for middle school or high school students. Please note that the Web site addresses were verified prior to publication, but are subject to change.

Books

America A to Z: People, Places, Customs and Culture. Pleasantville, NY: Reader's Digest Association, 1997.

Beetz, Kirk H., ed. *Beacham's Encyclopedia of Popular Fiction.* Osprey, FL: Beacham, 1996.

Berke, Sally. *When TV Began: The First TV Shows.* New York: CPI, 1978.

Blum, Daniel; enlarged by John Willis. *A Pictorial History of the American Theatre, 1860–1985.* 6th ed. New York: Crown, 1986.

Brinkley, Douglas. *The Great Deluge: Hurricane Katrina, New Orleans, and the Mississippi Gulf Coast.* New York: Morrow, 2006.

Brooks, Tim, and Earle Marsh. *The Complete Directory to Prime Time Network and Cable TV Shows, 1946–present.* 9th ed. New York: Ballantine, 2007.

Cashmore, Ellis. *Sports Culture: An A to Z Guide.* New York: Routledge, 2000.

Condon, Judith. *The Nineties (Look at Life In).* Austin, TX: Raintree Steck-Vaughn, 2000.

Craddock, Jim. *VideoHound's Golden Movie Retriever.* Rev. ed. Detroit: Gale, 2011.

Daniel, Clifton, ed. *Chronicle of the Twentieth Century.* Liberty, MO: JL International Pub., 1994.

Dunning, John. *On the Air: The Encyclopedia of Old-Time Radio.* New York: Oxford University Press, 1998.

Dunning, John. *Tune in Yesterday: The Ultimate Encyclopedia of Old-Time Radio 1925–1976.* New York: Oxford University Press, 1998.

Ehrenreich, Barbara. *Nickel and Dimed: On (Not) Getting By in America.* New York: Metropolitan Books, 2001.

Epstein, Dan. *20th Century Pop Culture.* Philadelphia: Chelsea House, 2000.

Finkelstein, Norman H. *Sounds of the Air: The Golden Age of Radio.* New York: Charles Scribner's, 1993.

Flowers, Sarah. *Sports in America.* San Diego: Lucent, 1996.

Friedman, Thomas L. *Hot, Flat, and Crowded: Why We Need a Green Revolution—and How It Can Renew America.* New York: Picador, 2009.

Gilbert, Adrian. *The Eighties (Look at Life In).* Austin, TX: Raintree Steck-Vaughn, 2000.

Godin, Seth. *The Encyclopedia of Fictional People: The Most Important Characters of the 20th Century.* New York: Boulevard Books, 1996.

Gore, Al. *An Inconvenient Truth.* Emmaus, PA: Rodale Press, 2006.

Grant, R. G. *The Seventies (Look at Life In).* Austin, TX: Raintree Steck-Vaughn, 2000.

Grant, R. G. *The Sixties (Look at Life In).* Austin, TX: Raintree Steck-Vaughn, 2000.

Green, Joey. *Joey Green's Encyclopedia of Offbeat Uses for Brand-Name Products.* New York: Hyperion, 1998.

Green, Stanley. *Encyclopedia of the Musical Theatre.* New York: Da Capo Press, 1976.

Hischak, Thomas S. *Film It with Music: An Encyclopedic Guide to the American Movie Musical.* Westport, CT: Greenwood Press, 2001.

Katz, Ephraim. *The Film Encyclopedia.* 6th ed. New York: Collins, 2008.

Kirkpatrick, David. *The Facebook Effect: The Inside Story of the Company That Is Connecting the World.* New York: Simon & Schuster, 2011.

Lackmann, Ron. *The Encyclopedia of American Radio: An A–Z Guide to Radio from Jack Benny to Howard Stern.* New York: Facts on File, 2000.

Lebrecht, Norman. *The Companion to 20th-Century Music.* New York: Simon & Schuster, 1992.

Levitt, Steven D., and Stephen Dubner. *Freakonomics: A Rogue Economist Explores the Hidden Side of Everything.* Rev. ed. New York: Harper, 2009.

Lissauer, Robert. *Lissauer's Encyclopedia of Popular Music in America: 1888 to the Present.* New York: Facts on File, 1996.

Lowe, Denise. *Women and American Television: An Encyclopedia.* ABC-CLIO: Santa Barbara, CA, 1999.

Maltin, Leonard, ed. *Leonard Maltin's Movie Encyclopedia.* New York: Dutton, 1994.

Martin, Frank K. *A Decade of Delusions: From Speculative Contagion to the Great Recession.* Hoboken, NJ: Wiley, 2011.

McNeil, Alex. *Total Television: The Comprehensive Guide to Programming from 1948 to the Present.* 4th ed. New York: Penguin, 1996.

National Commission on Terrorist Attacks. *The 9/11 Commission Report: Final Report of the National Commission on Terrorist Attacks Upon the United States.* New York: Norton, 2004.

Newcomb, Horace, ed. *Encyclopedia of Television.* 2nd ed. Chicago: Fitzroy Dearborn, 2004.

Packer, George. *The Assassins' Gate: America in Iraq.* New York: Farrar, Straus, and Giroux, 2005.

Rosen, Roger, and Patra McSharry Sevastiades, eds. *Coca-Cola Culture: Icons of Pop.* New York: Rosen, 1993.

Schlosser, Eric. *Fast Food Nation.* New York: Houghton Mifflin, 2001.

Schwartz, Herman M. *Subprime Nation: American Power, Global Capital, and the Housing Bubble.* Ithaca, NY: Cornell University Press, 2009.

Schwartz, Richard A. *Cold War Culture: Media and the Arts, 1945–1990.* New York: Facts on File, 1997.

Sennett, Richard. *The Culture of the New Capitalism.* New Haven, CT: Yale University Press, 2007.

Sies, Luther F. *Encyclopedia of American Radio, 1920–1960.* 2nd ed. Jefferson, NC: McFarland, 2008.

Slide, Anthony. *Early American Cinema.* Rev. ed. Metuchen, NJ: Scarecrow Press, 1994.

Tibbetts, John C., and James M. Welsh. *The Encyclopedia of Novels into Film.* 2nd ed. New York: Facts on File, 2005.

Tibbetts, John C., and James M. Welsh. *The Encyclopedia of Stage Plays into Film.* New York: Facts on File, 2001.

Vise, David A. *The Google Story.* Updated ed. New York: Delacorte Press, 2008.

Weisman, Alan. *The World Without Us.* New York: St. Martin's Press, 2007.

Wilson, Charles Reagan, James G. Thomas Jr., and Ann J. Abadie, eds. *The New Encyclopedia of Southern Culture.* Chapel Hill: University of North Carolina Press, 2006.

Woodward, Bob. *Bush at War.* New York: Simon & Schuster, 2002.

Web Sites

Bumpus, Jessica. "The Noughties' Fashion Highlights." *Vogue* (December 22, 2010). http://www.vogue.co.uk/spy/celebrity-photos/2010/12/22/the-noughties (accessed September 23, 2011.)

Markowitz, Robin. *Cultural Studies Central.* http://www.culturalstudies.net/ (accessed August 7, 2011).

"The Noughties: Year by Year." *The Sunday Times,* October 20, 2009. http://women.timesonline.co.uk/tol/life_and_style/women/the_way_we_live/article6881549.ece (accessed September 23, 2011).

"100 Songs That Defined the Noughties." The *Telegraph,* September 18, 2009. http://www.telegraph.co.uk/culture/music/rockandpopfeatures/6198897/100-songs-that-defined-the-Noughties.html (accessed September 23, 2011).

"Pictures of the Decade." *Reuters*. http://www.reuters.com/news/pictures/slideshow?articleId=USRTXRYG2#a=1 (accessed September 23, 2011.)

"A Portrait of the Decade." *BBC News,* December 14, 2009. http://news.bbc.co.uk/2/hi/8409040.stm (accessed September 23, 2011).

Washington State University, American Studies. *Popular Culture: Resources for Critical Analysis.* http://www.wsu.edu/%7Eamerstu/pop/tvrguide.html (accessed August 7, 2011).

Yesterdayland. http://www.yesterdayland.com/ (accessed August 7, 2011).

Zupko, Sarah. *Popcultures.com: Sarah Zupko's Cultural Studies Center.* http://www.popcultures.com/ (accessed August 7, 2011).

Index

Italic type indicates volume number; **boldface** indicates main entries; (ill.) indicates illustrations.

A

D

H

K

O

P

Q

R

S

U

W